ALIENS IN
ANCIENT EGYPT

"Our fascination with history, with who we are and where we came from, drives the quest for knowledge that Xaviant Haze displays in this stunning culmination of his own years of intense research and inquiry. Delving in to the ancient Egyptian culture, Haze questions our assumptions of human history with new and innovative ideas of how the advancement of knowledge may have occurred, and who or what was behind it. . . .This book is a guided tour of a civilization that continues to intrigue and define the entire human race. *Aliens in Ancient Egypt* is highly recommended reading for those who want to know how the distant past can shape the present—and the future—of humanity."

MARIE D. JONES, AUTHOR OF *VIRAL MYTHOLOGY:
HOW THE TRUTH OF THE ANCIENTS WAS ENCODED AND
PASSED DOWN THROUGH LEGEND, ART AND ARCHITECTURE*

"Contains powerful evidence that advanced beings (ABs) were the creators of Egypt's highly developed civilization before the worldwide cataclysm of 11,500 BP. This intervention narrative involving a space-traveling species is well documented, written with intelligent and logical reasoning. The reader will never again accept the human story found in conventional textbooks. The author deftly weaves recent discoveries in archaeology with 21st-century theories in energy, genetics, astronomy, reincarnation, and space travel—raising the possibility that the next advanced civilization in our galaxy will be human."

PAUL VON WARD, AUTHOR OF *WE'VE NEVER BEEN ALONE*

"*Aliens in Ancient Egypt* presents an interesting, entertaining, and instructive overview of diverse references that suggest the presence of nonhuman influences on human development in ancient times. Xaviant Haze does a great job of helping us see Egyptian textual passages with fresh eyes, in particular through his comparisons to the writings of ancient India and the first-contact experiences of primitive tribal groups in more recent times."

LAIRD SCRANTON, AUTHOR OF *THE SCIENCE OF THE DOGON*

"This fascinating book shines a spotlight onto arguably the most mysterious period of ancient Egyptian history and asks some profound questions about the origins of this culture's sacred knowledge and the true identity of their gods. Packed with intriguing theories, this book will appeal both to those with an interest in ancient mysteries and to believers in extraterrestrial visitation."

NICK POPE, MINISTRY OF DEFENSE UFO PROJECT, 1991–1994

"This line of research is new thinking and will help us look deeper into our past and true human origins."

JASON MARTELL, FOUNDER OF XFACTS.COM AND
AUTHOR OF *KNOWLEDGE APOCALYPSE*

"In *Aliens in Ancient Egypt*, Xaviant Haze lays out the proof for alien intervention in such a manner the evidence becomes irrefutable. We have been waiting for this book for a long time."

JAY WEIDNER, RENOWNED FILMMAKER, HERMETIC SCHOLAR, AND
AUTHOR OF *THE MYSTERIES OF THE GREAT CROSS OF HENDAYE:
ALCHEMY AND THE END OF TIME*

"*Aliens in Ancient Egypt* is a thought-provoking study that may indeed help many seekers of alternative wisdom and reality fulfill their quest. This latest work by Xaviant Haze is set to light the fuse of even more controversy, and that in itself is a very good thing!"

PAT REGAN, AUTHOR OF
UFO: THE SEARCH FOR TRUTH

"Xaviant Haze writes a fascinating inquiry into mankind's distant past. This book should be in the library of every serious researcher!"

STEVEN MYERS, AUTHOR OF *LOST TECHNOLOGIES
OF THE GREAT PYRAMID*

"A much-needed, new, and fresh exposé regarding the alien mysteries of ancient Egypt."

MIKE BARA, AUTHOR OF *ANCIENT ALIENS ON THE MOON*
AND COAUTHOR OF *DARK MISSION*

"The history of ancient Egypt, though having been studied intensely for more than 100 years, has generally ignored the mysterious representations of elongated skulls, especially those of Akhenaten, the Amarna family, and Osiris. In *Aliens in Ancient Egypt*, Xaviant Haze explores this perplexing phenomenon and the possible connection between the royal bloodlines of Egypt with off-planet visitations in the distant past."

BRIEN FOERSTER, COAUTHOR OF
THE ENIGMA OF CRANIAL DEFORMATION

ALIENS
IN ANCIENT
EGYPT

THE BROTHERHOOD
OF THE SERPENT
AND THE SECRETS OF
THE NILE CIVILIZATION

XAVIANT HAZE

Bear & Company
Rochester, Vermont • Toronto, Canada

Bear & Company
One Park Street
Rochester, Vermont 05767
www.BearandCompanyBooks.com

Bear & Company is a division of Inner Traditions International

Library of Congress Cataloging-in-Publication Data
Haze, Xaviant.
   Aliens in ancient Egypt : the Brotherhood of the Serpent and the secrets of the
Nile civilization / Xaviant Haze.
      pages cm
   Includes bibliographical references and index.
   ISBN 978-1-59143-159-6 (pbk.) — ISBN 978-1-59143-828-1 (e-book)
   1. Egypt—Civilization—To 332 B.C. 2. Civilization, Ancient—Extraterrestrial
influences. 3. Human-alien encounters. 4. Egypt—Antiquities. I. Title.
   DT61.H395 2013
   001.9420932—dc23

                                                            2013016366

Printed and bound in the United States

10   9   8   7   6   5

Text design and layout by Virginia Scott Bowman
This book was typeset in Garamond Premier Pro and Gill Sans with Trajan Pro
and Gill Sans used as display typefaces

To send correspondence to the author of this book, mail a first-class letter to the
author c/o Inner Traditions • Bear & Company, One Park Street, Rochester, VT
05767, and we will forward the communication, or contact the author directly at
xaviantvision@gmail.com.

CONTENTS

PREFACE

There are great ideas, undiscovered breakthroughs available to those who can remove one of truth's protective layers.

NEIL ARMSTRONG, AMERICAN ASTRONAUT
AND THE FIRST PERSON TO WALK ON THE MOON

THIS BOOK HAS BEEN BUILDING inside me for many years. I have always loved the subject of aliens and ancient Egypt. My love of Egypt stems from the very first images I saw of the Sphinx and the Great Pyramid as a child. This fascination continued after reading Norman Mailer's *Ancient Evenings* and became a full-blown obsession when my friend Ben showed up at my house with a printed version of the *Egyptian Book of the Dead*. I remember reading the first fifteen pages and my brain melting as if I were on a literary acid trip. And of course, when you read Erich von Däniken's *Chariots of the Gods?* as a teenager, there is no turning back.

It has taken fifteen years of both personal and professional research to write this book. All I can hope is that I have saved you, the reader, from spending hours upon hours of your life reading and researching material that might end up being only 10 percent usable. When you have finished reading this book, hopefully you will have come up with many more questions and mapped out new paths to drive toward.

INTRODUCTION

SOME OF THE MOST MYSTERIOUS monuments of ancient history are found in Egypt. In full view, yet unnoticed underneath the feet of tourists and visitors, is a road that has tantalized academics and historians for decades. It's a less traveled road that gives way to the alluring landscapes of early Earth's first inhabitants. Along this road can be found thrilling stories, chance discoveries, and evidence of floods, giants, and an alien invasion, all of which, understandably, are not subjects the mainstream academics would profit by bringing out. So they close our eyes to this evidence.

But much like the children's game of peek-a-boo, the Earth wants to reveal its secrets. It wants to show us the beginning of time, our time—the beginning of our story and our history. These revelations may be attacked by mainstream Egyptologists, but the flood of new information cannot be stopped. Modern educators cite the Golden Age of Egypt as the unparalleled height of cultural, architectural, philosophical, and perhaps even spiritual enlightenment. Ancient cultures from all parts of the world share myths that speak of evolved levels of consciousness, heightened awareness, superior science, sublime art, and sacred architecture, dating back tens of thousands of years. In world history classes early in our schooling, we receive the subliminal impression that there was an "advanced" civilization in ancient Egypt.

The ancients' superior agricultural skills, their knowledge of cosmology, and their overall grasp of the formulas of nature all indicate

1

that they not only were advanced, but they were much more so than we are, thousands of years later. This means that humankind has declined from a high point over the passage of eons. Merging the surviving myths and what we have uncovered about ancient history, we come face-to-face with undeniable evidence of not one, but several high points of advancement; in other words, more than one Golden Age. These ages of greatest development have come and gone, but they have left their mark in the mysterious land of Egypt. This mighty empire has produced several Golden Ages, the last of which is marked by the rise of the New Kingdom, and the rule of Pharaoh Akhenaten, whose story has been purposefully kept in obscurity for centuries.

What really happened in Egypt during the Amarna period? This epoch of Egyptian history gave rise to tremendous progress in the arts, and in agriculture, astronomy, and other sciences, which encompassed an understanding of quantum physics. But overnight it was all destroyed. Our modern world rose from the ashes of the aftermath, turning from a peaceful creative society, which worshipped the mother principle, to the patriarchal rule of war, which is at its height today. The amount of disinformation related to Pharaoh Akhenaten and the Amarna period during the beginning of the New Kingdom (1570–1070 BCE) is overwhelming. Unraveling the layers of mysteries associated with this period of history is the only way to learn the truth. What happened during Akhenaten's reign that was so profound that it forced him and his family to be erased from history? And when he accidentally resurfaced in the early nineteenth century, who, again, launched a disinformation campaign against him and his legacy full force?

This book proposes to reveal evidence previously kept hidden that Akhenaten's empire represented such a high degree of knowledge, rooted in the most remote and ancient of times, that even in the nineteenth century this information was considered too threatening to make public. Why? Because it undermined those in power and clearly indicated alien involvement in this high degree of understanding. The remnants of this alien-human interaction are of such immense proportions that, to this day, science, religion, and government in our contemporary world are all influenced by it. The alien connection was not a casual one, not a flyby stopover, but a prolonged period of rule intended to raise humanity from its inherently base and barbaric nature. The aliens' approach was handed down in a time so distant that it has been relegated to the mythology of creation. But since then, something went terribly wrong.

The sophisticated civilization of ancient Egypt arose seemingly overnight, complete with advanced levels of art, agriculture, astronomy, and physics. Then, with the death of Pharaoh Akhenaten, much of this higher knowledge was lost—or suppressed. But evidence of this former Golden Age—the alien visitors behind its rise and those behind its decline—still exists. Some of this evidence lies in plain sight and can be found by examining the deliberately obscured reign of Akhenaten and Nefertiti, the last dynasty to understand the sophistication of stargates, sacred geometry, free energy, and antigravity technologies. This is knowledge handed down to us from an advanced interstellar alien race in the remote past.

During the reign of Akhenaten, the highly controversial ancient reptilian race, known in Egypt as the Shemsu Hor, infiltrated the Egyptian priesthood and banking systems and formed the Brotherhood of the Snake—a secret society intent on destroying Akhenaten's flourishing kingdom and suppressing the sacred knowledge of the pharaohs.

However, the evidence of aliens in ancient Egypt—such as the reptilian beings depicted in the Temple of Hathor, Thutmose III's alien encounter, and the mysterious monuments buried in the vast sands of the Egyptian desert that can only be seen from satellites in space—does survive. So does the connection between ancient aliens in Egypt and Mars, including the Martian materials used in Egyptian monuments, such as the pyramids. The original purposes of the pyramids were to transmit uplifting energy throughout the planet to help expand consciousness. But unfortunately, they were decommissioned after the Great Flood of prehistory. Based on the strange art and a legacy of elongated skulls that Akhenaten's Amarna dynasty left behind, along with discoveries of various other elongated and alien skulls found throughout the world, perhaps we can start to unravel the ancient puzzle connecting Egypt with ancient aliens. Among these discoveries are the jaw-dropping megalithic ruins of the Osirian complex, the famous helicopter hieroglyphs of Abydos, and the mysterious stone blocks that litter the Giza Plateau and contain an abundance of minerals only found on Mars. These new discoveries, together with evidence of ancient Egypt's mystical past and leaked information regarding secret space programs and NASA's fascination with Egyptian symbols and iconography, prove there was some sort of off-world alien influence deep in Egypt's remote past.

1

THE GOLDEN AGE

Believe it. Men have ever been the same, and all the
Golden Age is but a Dream.

WILLIAM CONGREVE (1670–1729),
ENGLISH PLAYWRIGHT AND POET

72 steps in Jacob's Ladder
72 languages confused by the Tower-of-Babel
My slang damages amateurs. Egyptian Priests spoke 72
*   languages*
In the history of Taoism there are 72 Immortals
I'm more than nice with my medible-morsals
Me Make ya meet mortuary with my speak from my
*   molars*
It's oh so serious. Osiris was buried with 72 followers
Confucius had 72 disciples. I diss and confuse ya and
*   spit 72 icicles*
I'm 1 Trinary-Star but that equals 3
3 Jedi Knights couldn't fuck with me
In 72 years the Earth moves 1 degree

JOSH RIZEBERG, SLAM CHAMPION AND
FOUNDER OF THE ZULU NATION CHAPTER OF
TACOMA, WASHINGTON

WHEN SEARCHING FOR THE TRUTH about the origins of human civilization, we come upon some strange anomalies. Mainstream academics and Egyptologists date the beginnings of civilization to around six thousand years ago, even though carbon-14 dating has established that the earliest human remains are from about 2.5 million years ago. Adherents of the six-thousand-year chronology insist that the pyramids were constructed as recently as 2450 BCE, but scholars and alternative historians working outside of academia have unearthed evidence of a much earlier time line for human civilization and construction of the pyramids.

Despite these recent scientific findings, modern scholars almost universally endorse the six-thousand-year time frame. This time frame fits better with the current paradigm of history. According to this paradigm, humans hunted and gathered about five thousand years ago, then groups came together for protection from warring tribes. While grouped together, they invented writing and formed societies and gradually began building large structures, such as pyramids. If this time line is true, then there shouldn't be any evidence contradicting it. Yet evidence abounds of alien visits to our planet during prehistory, alien interactions with humans, and technological transfers from aliens to humans.

A cross-disciplinary approach helps us combine hard evidence and theory to reach a greater understanding of our ancient past. If we consider the data coming from astronomy, geology, astrology, and climatology, we can arrive at strongly supported conclusions about the chronology of ancient Egypt. John Anthony West is an intellectual pioneer responsible for undermining the traditional views of Egyptology. Described as an "alternative Egyptologist," West has immersed himself deep into the exclusive study of ancient Egypt for over forty years.

His books have influenced generations of Egyptian enthusiasts, and his mantelpiece even boasts an Emmy Award for his work on the groundbreaking television documentary *The Mystery of the Sphinx,* hosted by screen legend Charlton Heston.[1] In the early sixties, a young John Anthony West roamed the sun-soaked Mediterranean island of

Figure 1.1. The Giza pyramids and the Giza Necropolis in Egypt, seen from above. Photo taken on December 12, 2008. Courtesy of Robster1983.

Ibiza, meeting with writer Norman Mailer, artist Alan Schemer, poet Jack Beeching, actor Terence Stamp, and like-minded individuals. West was exposed to new ideas and philosophies that propelled him to his own Golden Age.[2] Inquisitiveness led him to search the beginnings of civilization further back than what had been generally accepted. Imagine his astonishment when he was immediately cut off from grants and academic support. West was not deterred, and going forth with determination and passion, he has produced a mountain of material for truth-seeking scholars to explore.

Aiming to disprove the traditional chronology held by established Egyptology, West has pursued and documented an enormous amount of evidence, and then written and published his findings. He pointed out that the ancient Egyptians spoke highly of the "first time," or "Zep Tepi," but modern Egyptology ignores or, for some reason, downplays this significantly. West believes that once the establishment investigates Zep Tepi, a can of worms will be opened, shattering what has been taught for hundreds of years. Evidence of this mysterious time is found on the Palermo stone, one of the earliest Egyptian historical texts, carved on a black basalt stele. Discovered near Memphis in 1866, the Palermo stone's journey to London took a detour through Sicily, where a Sicilian family kept it in their home and actually used it as a doorstop. Finally, in 1895, a French archaeologist noted its importance.

In 1902 renowned art historian Heinrich Schafer published the first information regarding the Palermo stone, the most important feature of which is the listing of rulers that predate Menes, the first "official" ruler of Egypt.[3] This goes back thousands of years into the predynastic period, and into what John Anthony West referred to as the Zep Tepi.

Figure 1.2. The Palermo stone is a list of Egyptian pharaohs and is of great importance to the Egyptian chronology. Regional Archaeological Museum in Palermo (September 28, 2006). Courtesy of Giovanni Dall'Orto.

John Anthony West is not alone in his theory about Zep Tepi. Robert Bauval, a best-selling author who first pointed out the Great Pyramid's alignment with the stars of Orion's belt, also shares West's view.[4] Born and raised in Egypt, Bauval has focused his studies on the fascination the ancient Egyptians had with the stars. Bauval provided the first clues as to where to look concerning the roots of possible alien contact deep in Egypt's past by pointing out the ancient Egyptians' strange obsession with the star Sirius. The ancient Egyptians were fixated on Sirius, which they called Sa-Ptah in hieroglyphs. According to the ancient indigenous teachings of Egypt, this means "The One who comes from the Blue, through the waters, from the stars."[5] Ptah was the predynastic god of creation in Memphite theology. We know the core components of legends and myths; they do not develop spontaneously. They are based on reality, and one thing we know about reality is that it is not supernatural. It is therefore worth considering that Ptah may have been a real being, perhaps an emissary from an interstellar race. Clues to how far back this traveling starseed goes might require dating techniques a little more sophisticated than what we currently have at our disposal.

We use what is called carbon-14 dating to determine the age of artifacts. It is the traditional method accepted by scholars. However, we should point out that carbon-14 dating is extremely limited and

Figure 1.3. The god Ptah at the Louvre Museum. Courtesy of Neithsabes.

susceptible to all types of errors because it works only on organic materials, and simply touching organic materials contaminates a sample. Stone cannot be carbon-dated but can be dated by the use of precessional astronomy. Precession is the motion of the axis of the Earth, which wobbles like a spinning top due to gravitational pull. Spanning a period of 26,000 years, this remarkable cycle is due to a synchronicity between the speed of the Earth's rotation around the Sun and the speed of rotation of our galaxy. In order to move one degree on the horizon it takes seventy-two years. This is a process the dictionary refers to as a "Platonic year," which is described as "a period of about 26,000 years, equal to the time required for a complete revolution of the equinoxes."[6] The word *horizon* stems from the ancient Egyptian, meaning the line in the sky where both the Sun and Moon disappear. The line was guarded by the god Horus, thus evolving etymologically into the word *horizon* that all English speakers are familiar with.

Plato's "year" was understood by ancient cultures across the globe, with more than two hundred mythologies related to this vast cycle of time. At least thirty different cultures from antiquity have since handed down tales and folklore concerning their own interpretation of what we know today as precession.[7] It is amazing to think that only three hundred years ago one of the world's brightest minds had trouble understanding this solar event, when thousands of years in the past it was common knowledge for the ancient Egyptians.

Intrigued by this process, astronomer Sir Isaac Newton tried to include this ancient cycle in his philosophies of the zodiac.[8] One of the ways to measure the 26,000-year cycle is through the ages of the zodiac, which the ancient Egyptians clearly understood. The zodiac itself is a symbolic translation of precession. Over time the number seventy-two has been used to denote this secret knowledge, and the number has been incorporated in ancient, mythical stories that, at best, make for fanciful reading since the implications are lost to us. Upon closer examination and cross-referencing, we find that these astronomical myths are star maps—mathematical observations of the sky, mixed with astrotheology.

The Temple of the Zodiac celebrates precession and its movement into the era of Pisces. The time it takes Earth to precess one degree on its axis is 71.6 years, a number that has been rounded up to 72, and which appears in strange locations and chronicles in the past. Many examples of the number 72 representing human knowledge of precession can be found in ancient history. For instance, the Egyptian prince Gaythelos is said to have spoken 72 languages, Jesus had 12 disciples (constellations of the zodiac) and another 72 disciples,[9] 72 languages were confused by the Tower of Babel, Confucius also had 72 disciples, the number of steps on Jacob's ladder is 72, there are 72 immortals in the history of Taoism, and the Egyptian god Osiris was enclosed in a coffin by 72 followers of his evil brother Set.[10] These recurring nods to the number 72 don't make any sense unless we understand the symbolism of precession.

In ancient belief systems it was agreed that humans lived in 5,000-year stages. Viewing the past as a Golden Age, we can clearly see how we have degenerated into a Dark Age. Despite being told that we are at the height of our development, one quick glance at the world shows things are getting worse by the minute. This is not a Golden Age. Golden Ages are times of enlightenment when civilizations reach high points in architecture, spirituality, and benevolence. This is considered to decline slightly in the Silver Age, further deteriorating in the Bronze Age, and reaching extreme levels of chaos, corruption, and ignorance in the Iron Age or Dark Age. Then, the cycle works its way back up to the next Golden Age. December 21, 2012 marked the end of a 26,000-year cycle that put humanity at the bottom of the barrel of the Dark Age. Physically, we are heading deeper into the Dark Ages; meanwhile our consciousness, along with the universe, is expanding in the spiritual realm, seeking another Golden Age.

The ancient Egyptians' knowledge of the stars was at its height in previous Golden Ages. While it is possible to conceive of an age of enlightenment that would have organically reached heightened levels of technology, required to investigate star systems, it is more probable to imagine that a halfway encounter took place.

As a global society we have exchange programs across all fields. It is a common practice to study outside one's own field of expertise. Many exchange students opt to remain, for one reason or another, in the host country. Military postings, for example, result in commingling with locals. The technology available during Egypt's ancient Golden Age could have very well included interstellar travel. Therefore, it is not far-fetched in the least to propose that the knowledge that blossomed in ancient, Golden Age Egypt was the result of a long-term interstellar exchange. Pinpointing the time when this could have taken place is the real trick.

Geologist Robert M. Schoch claimed that the weathering on the Sphinx and the Sphinx enclosure were formed by runoff from rain. This claim was met with absolute silence from the academic world; nobody uttered a peep, essentially accepting the claim as valid. The last time Egypt had rains like that was anywhere from eight thousand to eleven thousand years ago.[11] These dates are in conflict with the established view that Pharaoh Khafra built the Sphinx in 2,500 BCE (see plate 1). It is interesting to note that according to *Travel Cairo,* "It is not known by what name the original creators called their statue, as the Great Sphinx does not appear in any known inscription of the Old Kingdom, and there are no inscriptions anywhere describing its construction or its original purpose. The commonly used name Sphinx was given to it in classical antiquity, about two thousand years after the accepted date of its construction."[12]

The controversy appears to indicate that the Sphinx and the surrounding Giza complex are extremely ancient, far older than the establishment dares to admit. A good way to judge how old these monuments can possibly be is to examine the migration of the Nile River. Using a geologic mapping program on a computer, we can see that the riverbed migrated all the way from the west beyond fifty kilometers, then passed across the plateau, and went right up to the pyramids.[13]

Based on geological time, it would take tens of thousands of years for the Nile to make that migration. We can compare that to places

Figure 1.4. The Great Sphinx, pyramids of Giza (July 17, 1839). From David Roberts, Egypt & Nubia, From drawings made on the spot by David Roberts and lithographed by Louis Haghe, *vol. 1, part 18, 1846–1849.*

like the ancient city of Tiahuanaco in Bolivia that almost certainly was on the edge of Lake Titicaca and now is fifty miles away.[14] Precession changes the whole idea of how ancient these places could have been. It takes thousands of years for a river to make this tilting journey (see plates 2 and 3).

Today, the oases of El Kharga and Faiyum run parallel to the Nile, but 100 kilometers west. It seems that the river migrated all the way from there to its current course. In 2010 evidence of a huge ancient harbor was found near the Bent pyramid. The harbor connects to one of the pyramid's temples by way of a 140-meter-long causeway and lends further credence to theories concerning the Nile's migration. This discovery was made by a joint venture of the Cairo department of the German Archaeological Institute and the Free University of Berlin. Dr. Nicole Alexanian of the German Archaeological Institute believes the area surrounding the pyramid complex was filled with water and that it provided a perfect harbor for ships to enter the canals that appear to have surrounded the Giza Plateau,[15] postulating that in Egypt's ancient past the waters of the Nile were in sync with the pyramid complex. This discovery points to an advanced age when elements of water, in conjunction with certain types of stone and crystal, all were blended to create the stone used in the pyramid fields. This Golden Age has been lost in the mists of time, but looking at myths with fresh eyes in a fast-paced digital world, we can recognize greater forces at play.

Upon closer study of Egypt's most mysterious character, Thoth, an interesting picture emerges. Thoth was highly worshipped in the Egyptian pantheon. Late-period (700–323 BCE) writings describe him as a god, holding the heart and tongue of Ra. In the 1908 edition of *The Americana: A Universal Reference Library,* Thoth is described as

> one of the most interesting figures in Egyptian mythology . . . he is the god of time and its divisions; he is the measurer, and god of measurements. He is the conductor of the dead. He is also the god of human intelligence, to whom are attributed all the productions of human art . . . all the literature of Egypt is attributed to him— all the writings that relate to the different sciences, mathematics, astronomy, medicine, music. Thoth is also credited with the invention of alchemy and magic.[16]

In the earliest Egyptian writings, Thoth wasn't a god but a flesh-and-blood ruler, known as an important teacher of humankind who supposedly left behind a great library of knowledge and science for future generations' edification. Phoenician historian Sanchuniathon wrote in the thirteenth century BCE that Thoth was once the ruler of a western island kingdom before the Egyptian priests turned him into a god.[17] Sanchuniathon and his writings were thought to have been invented by the Greeks until excavations in Syria in 1929 revealed Phoenician writings supporting his claims, made centuries before by the Greek transla-

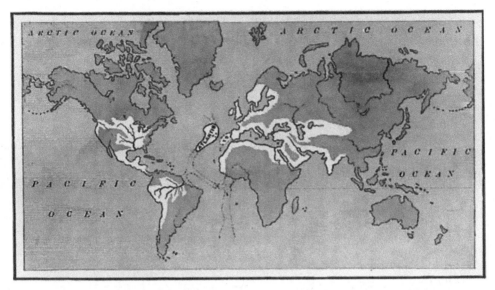

Figure 1.5. Map of the Atlantean Empire, from Atlantis: The Antediluvian World *(1882). Courtesy of the estate of Ignatius Donelly.*

tions from Philo of Byblos. These writings give us a detailed account of Thoth's arrival and influence on ancient Egypt.[18] The western island Thoth may possibly be ascended from is an Atlantis-type of lost civilization. The Atlantis theory has always been ridiculed by academia but on July 2, 2012 things got exciting when the *Daily Mail* published an article about a team of research divers from St. Andrews University who discovered underwater mounds and traces of a village in Britain swallowed by the sea more than 8,500 years ago.[19]

The Egyptians grasped an advanced level of astronomy and mathematics that we are only now beginning to understand. If Thoth was from Atlantis or some other form of lost civilization, one possible explanation is that Thoth may have descended from an interstellar race that once visited Earth eons ago. Possibly, he inherited a profound amount of knowledge and a mastery over the energies that naturally occur in the atmosphere. If this superior knowledge was shared with the ancients, it was ultimately destroyed and forgotten with the passage of thousands of years, which surely included other catastrophic events. It is conceivable that the ancients living in an advanced Golden Age of a distant past understood the cataclysm that results from the Earth's cycles, or greater cycles that affect other planets, and even other star systems. It stands to reason that any lofty civilization able to discern that future cycles of time bring about cataclysmic events would be plunged into the depths of collective despair. Why? Because humanity, with a complete disconnection from our spiritual nature, would be powerless to avert that disaster. Yet the ancients would have prepared a trigger—magnificent structures strategically built to withstand global catastrophes, skillfully aligned with the stars, engineered to be superconductors of energy, and encoded with symbols to awaken humanity from the depths of the Dark Ages. However, the building of the pyramids is not attributed to Thoth. This possibly dates the construction of these structures to a time before Thoth.

The Golden Age and the subsequent Silver Age marked the time during which the average person no longer had the capacity to live in a state of heightened awareness. The ancients lived in a society far more enlightened and benevolent than ours, but that almost-divine state that exists only in a Golden Age was beginning to fade. As humankind descended into the Silver Age, more of an emphasis was placed on what we refer to as "sacred sites" and "sacred structures."

As civilization began to lose touch with its individual, inner source of finely tuned awareness, a movement to stabilize this source through external, energy-driven locations began. Many of these structures in Egypt inspire awe and wonder, and even today exude a palpable and measurable energy force field. The Great Pyramids certainly are not, nor were they ever intended as, tombs. Despite the shouts coming from accepted Egyptologist dogma, there isn't a single shred of evidence supporting the notion that the pyramids were actually built by the Egyptians. Notorious for illustrating everything from applying makeup to what happens in the afterlife, ancient Egyptians are uncharacteristically and strangely mute on how they constructed the pyramids.

2

PYRAMIDS OF
THE BAND OF PEACE

*The pyramids themselves, doting with age, have forgotten
the names of their founders.*

THOMAS FULLER, ENGLISH HISTORIAN AND AUTHOR.
ONE OF THE FIRST ENGLISH WRITERS ABLE
TO LIVE BY HIS PEN

THE PYRAMIDS OF EGYPT have been mysterious and curious monuments for some time now. Alexander the Great saw them; so did Julius Caesar and Napoleon. Neither the pyramids nor the Sphinx contain hieroglyphs. There are no markings anywhere, in any structure of the Giza Plateau, that point to their origin or purpose, and they appear to be so old as to have been built before the biblical Flood. Arab historians contend that the pyramids were meant to house the accumulated knowledge of a lost civilization. The word *pyramid* in Arabic means "ultimate age or size,"[1] recalling the Golden Age and once again offering evidence that a flood may have been responsible for bringing an end to this era.

Arab historian Muhammad ibn Ahmad Biruni writes in *The Chronology of Ancient Nations,* "People are of the opinion that the traces of the water of the Deluge and the effects of the waves are still visible on these two pyramids halfway up, above which the water did not rise."[2] Add to this the curious history of an ancient city in Iran also dealing with a post-deluge world (see plate 4).

King Tahmurath of Persia, a mythical figure who was the third shah of Iran and ruled in a time before the deluge, was warned in a dream to build a safe haven for all scientific books that might be destroyed during the coming floods. This myth turned into reality as strange monuments were uncovered in Isfahan, exactly the site where Tahmurath had decided to build. In *The Chronology of Ancient Nations,* Muhammad ibn Ahmad Biruni writes:

> In favour of this report we may state that in our time in Jay, the city of Ispahan, there have been discovered hills, which, upon being excavated, disclosed houses filled with many loads of that tree-bark, with which arrows and shields are covered . . . bearing inscriptions of which no one was able to say what they are, and what they mean.[3]

Observations made by researchers over the years point out the hundreds of thousands of marine fossils and seashells preserved in the walls of the pyramids and surrounding the base of the monuments.[4] Joseph Jochmans writes in an issue of *Atlantis Rising,* "Legends and records likewise speak of the fact that, before the Arabs removed the pyramid's outer casing stones, one could see water marks on the stones halfway up the pyramid's height, in about the 240-foot level, which would be 400 feet above the present Nile level."[5] He adds that geologists, "are hard pressed to explain why there existed a fourteen-foot layer of salt sediment around the base of the pyramid, a layer which also contained many seashells, and the fossil of a sea cow, all of which were dated by radiocarbon methods to 11,600 B.P. [Before Present] plus or minus 300 years."[6]

Charles Piazzi Smyth was an astronomer royal for Scotland in the mid-1800s, and a pioneer in the field of pyramidological research. In

Figure 2.1. Scrapbook page with one photograph showing the Egyptian pyramids during a flood, annotated with information about the pyramids. Courtesy of William Vaughn Tupper.

1867, Smyth published *Life and Work at the Great Pyramid During the Months of January, February, March, and April, A.D. 1865.* Based on his firsthand experience, he cites clues pertaining to the extreme age of the pyramids. In a chapter detailing materials found inside the pyramids, Smyth writes at length about the amount of salt discovered:

> This substance is so abundant, i.e., in dense plates, an inch thick often in the horizontal passage and Queen's chamber and so scanty everywhere else that the Arabs believe both that it exists nowhere throughout the pyramid except in these two named localities, and that it is to be found there simply because the builders put "salt stones" into that particular part of the building. Yet there are

incrustations of salt in large superficial extents, through to small thickness, developed on the walls of the grand gallery.[7]

Smyth goes on to describe discoveries of sea salt incrustations on other pyramids, notably made by his colleague Sir William R. Wilde, the eminent Irish surgeon and polymath. Although now overshadowed by his son Oscar's fame, W. R. Wilde was one of the most respected historians of folklore and ancient myths of his time. He helped establish the museum of the Royal Irish Academy and wrote the catalogues of its collection.[8] He traveled the world, writing splendid accounts of his voyages.

Wilde discovered what he hoped was monatomic gold in what we refer to as the second pyramid, but after having the substance analyzed by scientists he was disappointed that it was nothing more than common sea salt.[9]

No one has found signs of water erosion within the pyramids, yet there is proof of marine life and salt. This means the pyramids were not completely submerged. Water erosion around the Sphinx has been attributed to rain, but considering ancient records that describe water marks halfway up the pyramids, it seems more likely that the Sphinx was completely underwater for a long period, and that the evidence of

Figure 2.2. Several native men stand in a flooded palm grove.
From A. B. De Guerville, New Egypt, 1906.

sea life within the pyramids is the result of waves lapping at its highly protective casing. If the floods of 9000 BCE were the last catastrophic water events in Egypt, and the pyramids exhibit signs of having survived them, it must mean that the pyramids and the overall Giza complex must date from a period before the flooding occurred.

Researcher David Wilcock adds more intrigue to the antiquity of the pyramids, noting that:

> In approximately 440 B.C., Herodotus wrote that the pyramids' casing stones were highly polished—with joints so fine they could scarcely even be seen with the naked eye. The thirteenth century Arab historian Abd-al-Latif said that despite their polished appearance, these stones were inscribed with mysterious, unintelligible characters—enough to fill ten thousand pages. . . . William of Baldensal visited the pyramid in the early 1300s and described these strange inscriptions as being all arranged in long, careful rows of strange symbols.[10]

Unfortunately, the casing stones have been reused, stolen, destroyed, and eventually lost in the cruel march of time.

This desert pyramid field is situated at the geodesic center of the world and rests at the mouth of the Nile Delta, clustering at six distinct sites known as the Band of Peace. Most people are familiar with the Giza Plateau and the Sphinx but are not aware of their connection to the other sites that run parallel to the fertile band of the Nile. Some sites are unknown, isolated in the middle of the desert; other sites are known but are only partially excavated. This leaves much history still buried in the sand. The sheer, grand scope of the area is hypnotic and stimulates our wonder and curiosity. All the sites show evidence of sophisticated engineering, advanced technology, and monumental architecture (see plate 5).

The ruined Abu Rawash pyramid is located five miles north of the Giza Plateau and built on top of a mountain. Abu Rawash is almost never visited. It is easy to see why. One look at this pyramid and the theory of pulling stones with a rope to get them up on top of a pyramid is debunked, in that the stones would first have to come up a sizable mountain, before being hauled up a pyramid. This site is somewhat isolated and abandoned, and many people do not even know it is there. There's no gatehouse, there's no guard, there's nobody there at all. It is meant to be largely forgotten because it undermines the theory about how the pyramids were built.[11] Inspecting the site, one can see clear evidence of small stones that are newer, medium stones, and then the ancient large stones. It is a familiar pattern in the ancient Egyptian sites (see plate 6).

The builders of the pyramids used a combination of limestone and granite, both important stones in the ancient world. Although very little granite remains at Abu Rawash, a stunning artifact does exist. A square slab of pink granite is propped up by a few smaller stones. This unbelievably smooth granite slab is four feet long and three feet wide and arcs upward toward the top of the stone. Looking closely, one can clearly see evidence of cutting marks produced by what had to have been a sophisticated cutting tool.[12] Granite is the hardest rock on Earth, and it is impossible to cut it without diamond-tipped tools. It is therefore inconceivable to maintain, as modern Egyptologists do, that this great complex was built with nothing more than copper chisels, stone hammers, dolerite pounding rocks, and human-man brute strength. It is hard to imagine Stone Age tools constructing the Giza acropolis, especially when visiting the so-called unfinished pyramid. The megalithic remains are mind-boggling.

The experience of walking into this hollowed-out pyramid with no top is both spooky and fascinating. Strangely, the stones have been blackened. This makes one wonder whether it was truly unfinished or the top was blown off. The evidence points to high heat of some kind. At the bottom of the pyramid is a large circular pit, dug into the ground. Chunks of massive limestone blocks are scattered around the pit. It seems as if this area was used as a smelting facility. In 1995 a joint team of French and Swiss archaeologists began excavations at Abu Rawash. This team, led by Michel Valloggia, discovered a copper axe blade while drilling deep in the deposit foundations.[13]

The necropolis at Abu Rawash is the farthest northern point in the Band of Peace. The *Band of Peace* refers to an area consisting of twenty-two pyramids that go from north to south within the vicinity of the Giza Plateau. All the pyramids along the Band of Peace trace the shape of the River Nile. As recent discoveries prove, the Nile once flowed right in front of the pyramids and the causeways of all the sites touched the river itself. Considering that the Nile is the lifeblood of Egypt, just as rivers all around the world are vital to the cultures living alongside them, it seems obvious that important sacred structures would be built directly on the river, not eight miles away from it.

The pyramids of the Giza Plateau astonish us to this day. The Great Pyramid covers thirteen acres, and was constructed of 2.3 million stones, weighing up to two hundred tons each.[14] Why was this massive, megalithic complex even built? We may need to reconsider what we've been told about the pyramids and what we think we've seen. For example, instead of thinking that the Egyptians put the causeway at an angle because the Sphinx was in the way, let's consider another reason. At summer solstice, the Sun rises along the causeway in front of the Great Pyramid and moves across the sky, setting between the second and the Great Pyramid, making it hotter in the summertime. In the winter, the Sun rises in line with the grand causeway by the second pyramid and sets between the second and third pyramids, making a short trajectory, resulting in cooler weather. It appears that the causeways are deliberately pointing toward the rising Sun on the summer and winter solstices.[15]

Orthodox Egyptologists insist that the pyramids were tombs, despite never once finding any mummies buried in a pyramid. They just chalk it up dismissively to ancient grave robbers. The Great Pyramid stands exactly at the center of the largest landmass on the planet, yet

*Figure 2.3. People gathered at the base of the Great Pyramid in Egypt.
Courtesy of Félix Bonfils.*

we had no idea of the position of continents until six hundred years ago. It is impossible to have known this with the use of rudimentary tools and, therefore, laughable to accept that a pharoah would have had the means to measure the world, find the geodesic center, and build his tomb there.

A quick Google search of the words *Abu Garab* would likely yield a bunch of links and pictures of the infamous prison in Iraq. This is a shame because the real Abu Garab in Egypt is one of the most amazing places in the world. It makes one wonder if the powers that be intentionally did this to confuse us. Abu Garab in Egypt is an isolated area off the beaten path. Taking a camel ride south from the Giza Plateau, one would come up over a sand dune and see these other crumbled pyramids that are now a pile of rubble.

Abu Garab was once home to Egypt's largest obelisk, but nothing remains now except a fractured base. There is something here that, thankfully, couldn't be carried away—an awe-inspiring and mystical crystal altar made of quartz.[16] A magnifying glass reveals little bits of crystal flaking right off it. This altar is highlighted by what seems to be the precise laser slice on the side of the solid piece of quartz. The whole thing looks like a giant crystal compass (see plate 7).

Short distances away are huge crystal basins that have perfectly drilled holes in them (see figure 2.4). The Egyptian Department of Antiquities lined these up with the idea of bringing them to the Cairo Museum, but they didn't know what they were, so they decided just to leave them in place. They claim the perfectly drilled holes are insignificant and the basins were used for animal sacrifices. But quartz crystal emits natural harmonic energy, so it seems highly unlikely that these basins were used for blood sacrifice. A much more logical explanation would hold that they served as a source of energy in ancient times.

It is unlikely that anyone knew more about this area than Hakim Awyan, an indigenous wisdom keeper, born near the village of Abusir, located practically at the base of the pyramids. Hakim was trained in Europe as an archaeologist; he was a certified Egyptologist and a tour guide. His unparalleled passion and knowledge of the area were reflected in the documentary series *The Pyramid Code*. Hakim lived his whole life (1928–2008) in the area known as the Band of Peace. The Giza Plateau was his front yard, and he describes it wonderfully:

Figure 2.4. Mysterious large crystal bowls.
Courtesy of Soundofallthings.com.

1936–37 the Sphinx was covered in sand up to the neck and there was my playing yard. There are tunnels. I used to walk in these tunnels. In water, I used to crawl sometimes because it is narrow. At Abu Garab we have a crystal altar—a round disk in the middle of four—a symbol of Hotep and the word *Hotep* means "peace" and "food." This round disk, it is a lid on a shaft about 180 feet deep to the level of the ocean. And there is still running water in there. You can feel it while you're in the area. These instruments were not found in a line like you see today, the nine of them, but they were found around the area and there are still some more to be found.[17]

Hakim was unique among Egyptian tour guides in that he spoke conversational English. When the first wave of new age hippies began to descend upon Egypt in the late 1960s, Hakim was there to greet

Figure 2.5. Perfect hole drilled in a crystal basin at Abu Garab.
Courtesy of Soundofallthings.com.

Figure 2.6. Strange rock floor with indented features at Abu Garab.
Courtesy of Soundofallthings.com.

them, not with traditional academic mumbo jumbo, but with the real wisdom of the indigenous Egyptians. Stressing the importance of meditation and teaching about the inherent energies of sound and water, Hakim led these tours for over fifty years and was known as the father of meditation, a title that was at first meant to slander and discredit him.

Despite Hakim's illustrious credentials, the Egyptian Antiquity Council, fearing he was teaching sacred indigenous customs to Westerners, shunned him. Hakim courageously continued these teachings as part of a world heritage, not a heritage solely belonging to Egypt. Over the years, Hakim became the most respected source in the study of the pyramids. His influence was so far-reaching that in the late seventies even the iconic rock group the Grateful Dead paid him a visit when they came to Egypt to play in front of the Great Pyramid. The fortunate rockers were even allowed to spend a night in the king's chamber. While inside the king's chamber, the zoned-out musical vagabonds recorded themselves singing and were afterward astonished by the acoustics produced.[18]

The ancient village of Abusir, where Hakim grew up, is a place where the specter of ancient priests and priestesses training as high-level initiates can easily be imagined. Just as we have monks, nuns, and priests nowadays, the ancients trained initiates in ritual practices that served the highest good of humankind. Hakim's teachings followed this tradition, and his knowledge of the pyramids was vast. The pyramid field at Abusir has black granite floors.[19] Similarly, the temple to the east of the Great Pyramid also has this same kind of beautiful black floor. There are also massive red granite blocks, perfectly cut and situated all over, not to mention rows of mighty granite pillars. It appears that Abusir played a role in relation to the stars, as its layout is directly linked to the star system Pleiades.[20] Corresponding exactly with the seven stars are the seven sun temples found in the Abusir pyramid complex. The Pleiades also provide clues to where to look concerning possible interstellar starseed contact. This is a topic we will discuss at length in future chapters.

Saqqara is home to the famous step pyramid of Djoser, which is flanked by large chunks of quartz crystals and an ancient courtyard with a quartz floor. The remains of a quartz floor can also be found at Giza in the temple to the east of the second pyramid. Traditional Egyptology tells us that Sneferu built the entire site.[21] At Dahshur, for example, there are three pyramids with three "burial chambers" in each—nine in all. Assuming that the established story that the pyramids are tombs were correct, why would Sneferu have needed so many of them? Sneferu would have had nine different possibilities and options for where he would have been buried, which makes no sense.

But if we set aside the notion that these pyramid sites along the Band of Peace were tombs, a more sensible, uplifting, and appropriate explanation emerges. Let's consider an explanation based on visible evidence of their construction. The pyramids would be impossible for us to duplicate, even with today's tools and materials. The chambers in the pyramids are harmonically tuned to a specific frequency or musical tone. It has been documented that sound healing techniques can restore the body to the correct harmony, meaning that these pyramid cavities could be used for healing. These theories dovetail with the claims of Raymond Rife, an early twentieth-century scientist and inventor. Rife proved that by using harmonic frequencies, cancer-causing agents can be destroyed by locating the unique frequency of that agent.[22] Because his discoveries were not profitable for the pharmaceutical and medical industrial complexes, his work was suppressed. Unfortunately for humankind, Rife is a forgotten man, but his amazing research validates what the ancient Egyptians seemed to know about healing thousands of years ago.

Another outstanding feature of the Saqqara complex is the famous Bent Pyramid. This intriguing structure has two angles and the best-preserved limestone outer sheath of any pyramid in Egypt.[23] The casings of the other pyramids were looted by later generations, who took the materials to build their own temples. The official line about this curious oddity among traditional Egyptologists is that the Egyptians

Figure 2.7. Pharaoh Sneferu's Bent Pyramid in Dahshur, Egypt.
Courtesy of Ivrienen.

were "practicing" building pyramids, and they started building at one angle and changed their minds partway through.

Indigenous wisdom keeper Hakim makes sense of the situation by explaining, "Now, when you come to the word *Sneferu, sne* means 'double' and *nefer* is 'harmony,' so it is double harmony. It is not a name of a person but it is the energy we get from these constructions."[24] Hakim believes the chambers in the pyramids were harmonically tuned to different frequencies or musical tones and teaches, "The Bent pyramid has two chambers for two different sounds."[25] Each chamber in each pyramid, then, could be exemplifying sound technology with distinctive tones, creating huge fields of harmonic resonance capable of reaching far distances.

At Dahshur, we have the Red Pyramid, the Black Pyramid, and the Bent Pyramid, each of which is covered in white tura limestone— red, white, and black. The second pyramid still glimmers red, and the third pyramid has remnants of black stones. These outer casings covered the entire surface of the pyramids. The stone construction we see today is the inner structure of the monuments. The sight of these pyramids at the height of their splendor must have been breathtaking. With respect to the odd-shaped and crumbled Black Pyramid, Egyptologists say that the pyramid builders were experimenting and they miscalculated, so the pyramid broke apart. Another pyramid with similar construction a hundred kilometers south of the Band of Peace is known as the Maidum Pyramid.

Figure 2.8. Corbeled ceiling in a chamber of the Red Pyramid. Courtesy of Jon Bodsworth.

Figure 2.9. Passage from the second back to the first chamber in the Red Pyramid. Courtesy of Jon Bodsworth.

Figure 2.10. Maidum Pyramid.
Courtesy of Jon Bodsworth.

Known in Arabic as the "false pyramid," the Maidum Pyramid[26] is instantly recognizable as being odd. Near the pyramid is a mastaba belonging to an unknown noble. A mastaba is a type of ancient Egyptian stone tomb. Following a narrow tunnel deep in this particular mastaba leads to a more spacious opening, where we find what the Egyptologists claim is the world's oldest red-granite sarcophagus. No official further explorations have been documented. Examining the desert grounds outside the pyramid, one can see specs of black decorating the sand surrounding the entire area, like glittering bits that survived an ancient catastrophe. The ground is coated with black-colored flints; a closer inspection shows them to be blackened on the top, but when they are flipped over, the bottom is a different color.

Maidum is not the only place that looks as though it had withstood an explosion. There is a giant crack in the solid stone of the Red Pyramid.[27] It would have taken a huge force to crack the solid rock. There is also a crack in the subterranean chamber of the Great Pyramid, and there is another one in the Grand Gallery, near the entrance to the king's chamber, as well as chemical burns staining the walls in the Red Pyramid.[28] Old photos of the king's chamber in the Great Pyramid show the stone black, but after the room was cleaned and restored the walls are now pink granite. The granite sarcophagus has a broken corner, and the wall next to it has a giant crack. There is evidence that a great force or explosion occurred there. Is the Department of Antiquities erasing evidence under the guise of restoration? Our history of Egypt comes to us from Herodotus, a Greek historian in the fifth century BCE. He wrote from his perspective with help from local people, and we have been repeating his story ever since.[29] For Egyptology to survive the surge of irrefutable evidence that describes the potent and advanced technology at play in ancient times, Egyptologists must hitch their wagon to the more sensible and accurate theories that have been progressively proposed over the last fifty years.

For thousands of years, the pyramids and the Sphinx stood as sentinels in the open desert. Yet, in the last couple of years, a twenty-mile wall, fourteen feet high, has been installed around the enormous site of the Giza Plateau. Visitors to the famous pyramids of Giza will find about a hundred armed guards patrolling the pyramids at night, and

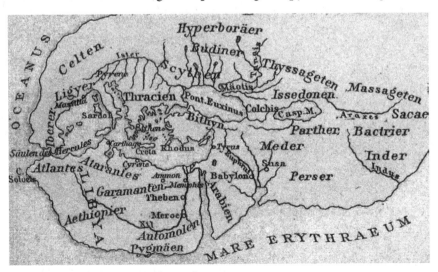

Figure 2.11. The ancient world of Herodotus. Courtesy of Putzger's Historischer Schul-Atlas, 1877.

applications to conduct academic research on site, while appearing to be initially considered, are almost all routinely refused. Unlike in times past, tourists are now being restricted from taking photographs in the Egyptian Museum. The monuments of Egypt are world heritage sites. Access for legitimate scientific researchers is being systematically restricted. This indicates that there is something they do not wish the public to know.

Much of ancient Egypt remains undiscovered, but new findings are being made thanks to advancements in satellite and infrared-camera technology. In a BBC program, aired on May 24, 2011, journalist Frances Cronin notes:

> Seventeen lost pyramids are among the buildings identified in a new satellite survey of Egypt, [along with] more than one thousand tombs and three thousand ancient settlements. . . . The work has been pioneered at the University of Alabama at Birmingham by U.S. Egyptologist Dr. Sarah Parcak. The team analyzed images from satellites orbiting 700km above the Earth, equipped with cameras so powerful they can pinpoint objects less than 1m in diameter on the Earth's surface. Infrared imaging is used to highlight different materials under the surface.[30]

These satellite images show traces of buried structures that may never be excavated. In the name of protecting sacred sites, Egyptian authorities are preventing the world from learning the truth about our ancient past. Despite strict regulations on what kind of research is allowed, there is still an extraordinary amount of evidence that shows that the ancient Egyptians had sophisticated knowledge that has been lost. We do not have the technology to build the pyramids now—not even close. Ours is not the most evolved civilization humanity has ever produced, and that is one of the blinders that has stopped us from imagining that the ancients could have been far smarter than we are.

Another controversial object that Egyptologists reject as coming from ancient times is the artifact commonly known as the Baghdad Battery, which generates a mild electrical charge.[31] Similar ancient artifacts have been found in other areas of Egypt, and it would appear that the Egyptians documented the existence of these artifacts as well. Re-creations of these objects have been made and have successfully generated electric current.

During the past twenty years, physicists have been researching subtle energy, which is believed to be a universal life force running within and between all things. Though this study is lambasted as being esoteric, these pioneering physicists have made major breakthroughs in our understanding of this mysterious form of energy. One of the champions of subtle energy is Dr. Claude A. Swanson, who graduated from Princeton University and trained at MIT. With a PhD in physics, Swanson has been studying this phenomenon intensely and believes that in the last twenty years of research a lot of experiments have been done showing that there's a certain type of energy that's unknown to our current science. Known as ley lines, these invisible energy fields can be found crisscrossing the entire world. Temples were built in certain areas where ley lines intersect, and only kings or royals could be buried on such lines.[32]

Ley lines are believed to be energy currents that invisibly surround the Earth. Certain types of rocks, such as granite and crystals, are used to channel these energies, creating natural energy fields. First mentioned in 1870 by William Henry Black, during a speech given to the British Archaeological Association in Hereford, England, they were made famous in the 1920s by the writer Alfred Watkins, who published some of the first paranormal books ever written (see plate 8).[33] His book *The Old Straight Track* (1925) remains the bible of ley-line enthusiasts, who, while not supported by archaeologists, have continued to demonstrate the existence and significance of these alignments up to the present day. As a photographer, Watkins was responsible for the important invention of the Bee Meter to measure the intensity of light, one of which was used by Captain H. G. Ponting Scott's photographer in the Antarctic.

Since Watkins's time, ley lines have entered pop culture as a prominent theme in books, television, and role-playing games the world over. Ley lines seem to be activated by certain types of geology. This might explain why massive granite stones are prominent at Giza as well as other areas of the ancient world.

The possibility that the pyramids hold clues to ancient electricity became more evident with the discovery of crude, red-colored diagrams that clearly detail electrical devices and cables.[34] The builders of ancient Egypt designed these structures and built them in such a way as to further concentrate the naturally occurring subtle energies. The cores of the pyramids found at Giza are made out of a type of limestone called dolomite, perfect for conducting electricity because of its high magnesium content. But the outer limestone that sheathed the pyramid completely in its day is the white tura limestone, which has almost zero magnesium content and is a much poorer conductor of electricity. It's intriguing that these outer stones are joined so precisely that all these thousands of years later it is impossible to get a razor blade between them. Basically, what we have is a highly electrically conductive core wrapped in what is a very effective insulator. With a little help from the granite found in the passageways, the pyramid could become radioactive and ionize or electrify the air. This explains the copious amount of granite found at Giza. The outer stones, then, were used to interact with the pyramids, turning them into powerful, electrically charged machines.

Invisible, subtle energy surrounds us all the time and is measurable by science. Even to the completely untrained mind, occurrences in our natural environment support the existence of a unifying energy. Not visible to the naked eye, that we are aware of, so-called orbs are often captured in photographs. They are written off as dust or other particles in the air, but that does not change the fact that they seem to occur more often in particular places and at particular times. We do not know what orbs are, but my personal guess is that they're balls of ionized or electrified air that tend to cling together. A good analogy would be ball lightning, where it is simply so electrified that the molecules are excited enough to glow.

Nikola Tesla was certain that there is a ubiquitous form of naturally occurring energy on the planet. He discovered that the Sun ionizes electricity present in the ionosphere. He also created ways to harness those energies. Tesla wanted to capture this natural energy and make it available free to the public. Unfortunately, Thomas Edison, who had registered more than a thousand patents and whose work was sponsored by the powerful banking system, endeavored to produce and distribute electricity by creating a regulated monopoly for profit.

Between 1901 and 1917, the Tesla Tower was built on Long Island, New York, as a wireless broadcasting system for telephone and electrical signals. Interestingly, it was constructed on an aquifer with descending passageways and tunnels beneath it. At the time, few understood how it worked. J. P. Morgan, who seemed to have taken an interest in Tesla's work until the first experiment using the tower, dropped further funding. So even though many saw Tesla's genius, he was still driven into obscurity, where he starved to death alone and penniless.[35]

The possibility of creating free wireless energy has always existed on our planet, and still exists today. The idea that we have to rely solely on

Figure 2.12. Nikola Tesla on the cover of Time *magazine 18, issue 3 (July 20, 1931).*

fossil fuel–based energies is an old, outdated one, designed to benefit a small, concentrated group of individuals. The energy we use now is generated by combustion and is nonrenewable. Called *explosion energy*, it produces exhaust and pollution, scars the Earth, and decimates our environment. It is a characteristic of a Dark Age, as is our collective acceptance of these methods as proper. By contrast, *implosion energy*,[36] like that generated by solar panels and wind power, is clean, renewable, and very simple to produce—all you need are tunnels, running water, and beams from the Sun.

In addition to the limestone aquifers underneath the pyramids, there is evidence of a network of human-made tunnels. If the pyramid fields of the Band of Peace and the network of underground tunnels are still there, they do not generate energy the way they used to, as little as a hundred years ago. Most likely, this is due to the extreme age and subsequent damage to the monuments. Looking again at the quartz objects found throughout the Band of Peace, it is clear that at least one of their ancient roles was to provide crucial energy on a grand scale.

Today, quartz crystal is used as the basis of all kinds of modern technology. It is most commonly used in crystal oscillators. Technological devices use oscillating frequencies from tiny quartz crystals that vibrate at specific speeds with a signature vibration for each device. AM/FM radios, CDs and DVDs, computer processors, and ethernet rely on quartz crystals. It appears that the ancients were tapping into this technology and using it on a much larger scale in a way we can only begin to imagine.

There are many theories as to what the pyramids could have been used for. Most of these theories revolve around destruction and war machines. There is proof of an ancient, powerful destructive force, as indicated by the cracks in stones and blackened shards spread through the desert. Could such an explosion have occurred during the decline into the Silver Age, when the original knowledge had already been lost? Were the ancient Egyptians experimenting with this energy long after the original providers of this wisdom had vanished? Were the original engineers of the pyramids from an Earth-like planet somewhere in the realms of Orion's belt?

On one hand, we have evidence of a principled civilization attuned to the naturally occurring healing properties of vibrating sounds and a high degree of scientific and mathematical understanding. On the other hand, we have gigantic structures with harmonic cavities, presumably designed to generate energy. It is not beyond the realm of possibility to conclude that the Giza Plateau was a broadcast facility, transmitting a renewable form of energy throughout the planet. Following through on this thesis, we might posit that, over time, the pyramids ceased to fulfill their original purpose, as natural and human-made catastrophes around the world damaged and decommissioned these sites. But according to this hypothesis, the ancient pyramids were essentially machines that emitted grand-scale signals—perhaps even capable of reaching similar frequencies in deep space—to other key points in other areas of the world. The energy that was transmitted and shared was presumably intended to keep us at an enhanced state of expanding consciousness before our descent into the Dark Ages.

However ingenious the ancients were, they knew Mother Nature would always have the last word, and over time the true intention of the pyramids has been obscured. Eventually, wisdom keepers created mystery schools that preserved what was remembered of this ancient knowledge. But the strong, unyielding arm of religion deemed them "satanic," so they went underground, later to be misunderstood and manipulated by unscrupulous religious leaders determined to be the rulers of us all.

From predynastic to dynastic times, the ancients maintained a deep reverence for nature. They were astonishingly creative and artistic. From clues left on temple walls, it is clear that our Egyptian ancestors accessed altered states of consciousness. Their primary concern was how we arrive on Earth, and what happens when we leave our earthly bodies. They described everything bodily in terms of biology and everything spiritual in terms of cosmology. Our human ancestors, empowered by the full capacity of their senses, left clues embedded in symbols that have multiple layers of meaning. The capacity of advanced humans in a Golden Age must have seemed godlike. Beyond that, no conclusion other than this seems plausible: in the far reaches of time, humans were not alone on planet Earth.

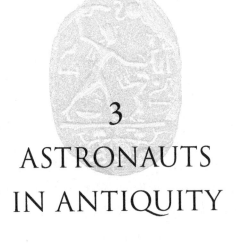

3

ASTRONAUTS
IN ANTIQUITY

There's a Starman waiting in the sky
He'd like to come and meet us
But he thinks he'd blow our minds

DAVID BOWIE, ROCK MUSICIAN

BEFORE GOING INTO THE EIGHTEENTH DYNASTY and the
era of Akhenaten and Nefertiti, let us first familiarize ourselves with
the construct of the ancient astronaut. The majority of modern minds
don't give credence to ancient writings. The records found in the world's
oldest manuscripts and carved on stone or clay tablets contain fantastic
and legendary tales that are, for many, simply too incredible to believe.

With the arrival of the space age, humanity began to understand
that incidents once considered ancient miracles and supernatural beliefs
now have explanations based on high technology and advanced mathematics. Early humans were not capable of adequately describing something they did not understand because they didn't know what they were
seeing. Even today the great majority of people are not aware that there
are things we don't even know that we don't know. If we accept this
simple concept, it becomes easier to unravel what actually occurred in

41

antiquity, as described by our own time line of ancient scriptures. In the world's oldest writings, including hieroglyphs and petroglyphs, we find consistent commonalities among stories of spaceships and alien visitations. Over the next few chapters, we will point out some references to this, shed light on where the theory of the ancient astronaut comes from, and consider who is responsible for this seismic shift in thinking.

Some assert that the French works of Louis Pauwels and Jacques Bergier, the Italian works of Peter Kolosimo, the work of Robert of Charroux (inspired by Pauwels and Bergier), and even early twentieth-century American horror master H. P. Lovecraft all serve as the origin of the idea of ancient astronauts in antiquity. But only one man actually brought this theory to the mainstream. Looking up at the Great Pyramid in Egypt, nineteen-year-old Erich von Däniken knew he was facing something that would totally and irrevocably undermine the foundation of his religious upbringing in Switzerland. The Christian holy scriptures he had been studying since he was a child perplexed von Däniken. His epiphany came when he couldn't understand why God would need to create earthquakes and smoke every time he wanted to speak. Had this god just been misunderstood by the ancients, who were unable to grasp that they were actually seeing a rocket and an astronaut?

More than fifteen years after his first visit to the Giza Plateau, von Däniken was working as a manager at a fancy Swiss resort and preparing to publish his thesis. In 1967 his ancient astronaut theory was first published in German and a year later translated into English as *Chariots of the Gods?* The impact was meteoric. Von Däniken became famous almost overnight. His theory struck a nerve with the people and his book was in worldwide demand. Needless to say, the establishment was not happy. Von Däniken was convicted of fraud and thrown into prison for three years.[1] This is enough to shut anybody up, but von Däniken is no ordinary man. He refused to be broken or bought off, and to the dismay of the world's academics, he continues to write books that are sold all over the globe. They bashed him at every opportunity, but this stubborn man did not go away.

Influential documentaries and more books followed, and despite being called out on a few exaggerations (including a nonrusting iron pillar in India and a gigantic subterranean tunnel system in Ecuador) von Däniken[2] has managed to sell over sixty million copies of his books, translated into thirty-two languages. Although relegated unfairly to the realm of pseudoarchaeology, von Däniken's theory is more popular and better accepted than ever, thanks in part to the success of the History channel's *Ancient Aliens* series—one of the highest-rated shows on cable. These high ratings prove that more and more people are ready and willing to start accepting and looking into the clues of extraterrestrial visitations in humanity's past.

Zecharia Sitchin is another famous name associated with the ancient astronaut theory. Sitchin has written a collection of works, including the immensely popular book *The 12th Planet,* first published in 1976. This book claims that aliens came from a distant planet called Nibiru and created humankind in order to mine for gold.[3] Sitchin backed up these claims by pointing out that he was a master linguist and perhaps the only living person in the world able to decipher the ancient dead cuneiform language. He sparked a whole new interest in aliens and ushered in many ideas that eventually wound up in mass culture, thanks

Figure 3.1. Zecharia Sitchin. Courtesy of Lapavaestacaliente.

to popular movies, such as *Stargate* and *Cowboys & Aliens,* plus video games like *The Conduit.* The validity of his analysis has not, of course, been proven. Sitchin may have been one of a rare handful of people capable of translating Sumerian text back in the 1970s, but how will his translations hold up in the twenty-first century?

Most of what we know about the Sumerian language stems from the Akkadian/Semitic translations. Sumerian itself is the world's oldest written language and has no known associates in the linguistic family tree. It simply appeared from nowhere and vanished into fragmented Akkadian.[4] Everything scholars have been able to piece together about this language is sadly inaccurate. Supposedly, in the early nineteenth century, the Sumerian language was deciphered. But that only added an extra layer to the mystery, when the confused scholars found it to be different from both the Indo-European and Semitic language groups. Despite this, linguists have established a framework of the dead language aided by the available Akkadian texts handed down by ancient scribes. And according to them, there are no mentions of aliens or spaceships in ancient Sumerian writings.

Michael S. Heiser holds an MA and a PhD in Hebrew Bible and Semitic languages from the University of Wisconsin–Madison. He claims that Sitchin's theories are wrong and that anybody can prove this by going to Oxford's online electronic text corpus and typing a word into the search category.[5] Of course, nothing suspicious, other than Oxford's uninspiring website, comes up. There are other online Sumerian libraries that are also quick to dismiss Sitchin's theories as false. When engaging in these translation wars, one might forget the whole point of what we are looking for—in this case, certain words that are out of place even in the Akkadian translations. And scholars agree that these words do indeed exist; one of them—the mysterious *Elohim*—doesn't seem to be properly understood by any of its translators, whether ancient or modern.[6] So we're confronted with a line in the sand on what to believe, considering that none of us are going to spend years of our lives learning a language of which only 10 percent is known.[7]

The one thing Sitchin's popularity clearly accomplished was to etch in our modern consciousness the belief that an alien presence appeared in our midst in ancient times. In movies such as *Independence Day* and *War of the Worlds,* Hollywood reinforces the notion that this alien presence was malicious. These movies convey the subliminal message that alien life is bent on our destruction. No big-budget script in Hollywood relating to an alien invasion of Earth gets made without first receiving the approval of the Pentagon. It would appear that, at the highest level of government, there is an interest in propounding the idea that anything alien is unfriendly and dangerous. This, in turn, gives credence to those who claim there is a plan by the New World Order to stage a fake alien invasion and then swoop in with an international, unified armed force as the saviors, thus leading to the fabled endgame, centuries in the planning, known as One World Government. Despite being a major influence in the field of alien research, and providing us with valuable knowledge concerning ancient history, Sitchin's credibility will always be called into question, especially considering that his office was, of all places, in Rockefeller Center!

So far, we have seen how influential—whether negative or positive (depending on your individual beliefs)—von Däniken's and Sitchin's works have been concerning the subject of ancient astronauts. Both have sold millions of copies of their works and have thumbed their noses at academia for decades. But their sales are dismal in comparison to the all-time champion of best-selling literature. The Holy Bible is the undisputed, undefeated, number-one bestseller of the Western world. For most of us, our earliest memories involve our grandmothers and some type of church. And while the verdict may still be out as to whether the Sumerian tablets spoke of rockets and alien commanders, it may come as a shock to learn what the Bible has to say about our earliest ancestors.

Even the most butchered translations of the Christian holy texts contain verses that strongly support the ancient astronaut theory. The Christian passages are a great starting point for learning how to break

Figure 3.2. *Annunciation with Saint Emidius* (1486).
Carlo Crivelli's fifteenth-century painting
details a saucer-shaped object emitting a beam of light.

down what to look for when searching ancient records for clues. They're easily accessible and familiar to most readers. We will examine some of the relevant passages in the Bible and pinpoint what to look for as we peer through our new lens of alternative thinking and bring to bear our understanding of how modern technology works.

One of the most frequently used terms to describe spaceships in the Bible is the word *cloud*, which makes sense, considering how they must have been perceived spaceships as moving at that time. The Greek variant of the Hebrew word for *cloud* is "`anan,*"* which is defined as "a cloud (as covering the sky), i.e., the nimbus or thundercloud."[8] The various descriptions of the clouds always pictured them as dark, which tells us these were not normal, white clouds but abnormal, metallic-colored clouds. These clouds had erratic flight patterns and the ability to glow at night and therefore cannot be related to the clouds any of us see each time we step outside.

All passages below are from the 1769 Oxford King James Bible:

And Moses went up into the mount, and a cloud covered the mount. And the glory of the LORD abode upon mount Sinai, and the cloud covered it six days: and the seventh day he called unto Moses out of the midst of the cloud. And the sight of the glory of the LORD [was] like devouring fire on the top of the mount in the eyes of the children of Israel. And Moses went into the midst of the cloud, and gat him up into the mount: and Moses was in the mount forty days and forty nights. (Exodus 24:15–18)

Then a cloud covered the tent of the congregation, and the glory of the LORD filled the tabernacle. And Moses was not able to enter into the tent of the congregation, because the cloud abode thereon, and the glory of the LORD filled the tabernacle. . . . For the cloud of the LORD [was] upon the tabernacle by day, and fire was on it by night, in the sight of all the house of Israel, throughout all their journeys. (Exodus 40:35–38)

And on the day that the tabernacle was reared up the cloud covered the tabernacle, [namely], the tent of the testimony: and at even there was upon the tabernacle as it were the appearance of fire, until the morning. So it was always: the cloud covered it [by day], and the appearance of fire by night. And when the cloud was taken up from the tabernacle, then after that the children of Israel journeyed: and in the place where the cloud abode, there the children of Israel pitched their tents. (Numbers 9:15–17)

The burden of Egypt. Behold, the LORD rideth upon a swift cloud, and shall come into Egypt: and the idols of Egypt shall be moved at his presence, and the heart of Egypt shall melt in the midst of it. (Isaiah 19:1)

Who [are] these [that] fly as a cloud, and as the doves to their windows? (Isaiah 60:8)

Descriptive passages associated with rocket or space-age technology can be found as well. Earthquakes and billowing smoke, similar to that spewed by NASA rockets as they rise into the sky, accompanied the fast-moving metallic "clouds" described above. Even with limited knowledge of stealth bombers and helicopters, we can read the Bible verses below with fresh technological insight:

Then the earth shook and trembled; the foundations of heaven moved and shook, because he was wroth. There went up a smoke out of his nostrils, and fire out of his mouth devoured: coals were kindled by it. He bowed the heavens also, and came down; and darkness [was] under his feet. And he rode upon a cherub, and did fly: and he was seen upon the wings of the wind. And he made darkness pavilions round about him, dark waters, [and] thick clouds of the skies. Through the brightness before him were coals of fire kindled. The LORD thundered from heaven, and the most High uttered his voice. And he sent out arrows, and scattered them; lightning, and discomfited them. And the channels of the sea appeared, the foundations of the world were discovered, at the rebuking of the LORD, at the blast of the breath of his nostrils. (2 Samuel 22:8–17)

And it came to pass on the third day in the morning, that there were thunders and lightnings, and a thick cloud upon the mount, and the voice of the trumpet exceedingly loud; so that all the people that [were] in the camp trembled. And Moses brought forth the people out of the camp to meet with God; and they stood at the nether part of the mount. And mount Sinai was altogether on a smoke, because the LORD descended upon it in fire: and the smoke thereof ascended as the smoke of a furnace, and the whole mount quaked greatly. (Exodus 19:16–18)

Figure 3.3. Woodcut: Ezekiel's vision from
the Zürich Bible (ca. 1538).
Courtesy of Hans Holbein der Jüngere.

The book of Kings details the close encounters and eventual abduction of the prophet Elijah, who disappeared into a spaceship that roared off toward heaven:

> And it came to pass, as they still went on, and talked, that, behold, [there appeared] a chariot of fire, and horses of fire, and parted them both asunder; and Elijah went up by a whirlwind into heaven. (2 Kings 2:11)

Even a passage related to the Exodus describes a UFO guiding the way in the dark of night with a powerful beam of light:

> And the LORD went before them by day in a pillar of a cloud, to lead them the way; and by night in a pillar of fire, to give them light; to go by day and night. (Exodus 13:21)

The most supportive scientist behind the notion of the ancient flying machines is former NASA engineer J. F. Blumrich. In his classic book *Spaceships of Ezekiel,* Blumrich paints a vividly descriptive narrative picture of Ezekiel, the mysterious prophet of the Old Testament. Published in 1974, *Spaceships of Ezekiel* opens with an indirect homage to Erich von Däniken. The NASA engineer and skeptic was at home relaxing by the fire when he received a phone call from his son away in college. His son had just finished reading an amazing book and wanted to send his father a copy immediately. It can't be understated how profound *Chariots of the Gods?* was to college students in the late 1960s and the 1970s. Blumrich recalls that fateful evening when his phone rang:

> It all began with a telephone conversation between Long Island and Huntsville. Our son, Christoph, mentioned that he had just read a fascinating book about visits from outer space. Its title: *Chariots of the Gods?* Its author: a certain von Däniken. For me, an engineer

who began his career in aircraft design in 1934, and who was working on large rockets and spacecraft, such books provide wonderful entertainment, and no more: they describe exciting events that occurred at times and in places that cannot be checked. So, when the [book] arrived, I read, smiled, grinned, and laughed—until I found the passage in which von Däniken writes about the prophet Ezekiel. Here were technical statements and claims right in the fields of my own professional knowledge! Suddenly it seemed very easy—I would take a Bible and would explain why a certain von Däniken was wrong. How sure I was! I soon lost my grin, became profoundly curious, and what followed was a wonderful experience, unusual in every respect, an undertaking which was done exclusively in my spare time, since NASA my employer, is not engaged in such matters. Hardly ever was a total defeat so rewarding, so fascinating, so delightful![9]

Blumrich's book is full of sketches and mechanical designs that fully illustrate his opinions as to what type of crafts were flown during the age of Ezekiel. There are references not only to motherships but also helicopters and fast-moving jets. It appears that a fully formed space platoon was interested in showing Ezekiel the proper workings of their crafts by bringing him along for a ride.

The *Book of Ezekiel,* which on its own stands as one of history's most astonishing works of literature, expands to mind-blowing proportions when reinforced with Blumrich's technical prowess. This iconic passage, describing an alien military reconnaissance mission, is once again from the 1769 Oxford King James Bible. This section details a fleet of helicopters detaching from another ship and how Ezekiel struggled to explain what he saw:

And I looked, and, behold, a whirlwind came out of the north, a great cloud, and a fire infolding itself, and a brightness [was] about it, and out of the midst thereof as the colour of amber, out of the midst of the fire. Also out of the midst thereof [came] the likeness of four living creatures. And this [was] their appearance; they had the likeness of a man. And every one had four faces, and every one had four wings. And their feet [were] straight feet; and the sole of their feet [was] like the sole of a calf's foot: and they sparkled like the colour of burnished brass. And [they had] the hands of a man under their wings on their four sides; and they four had their faces and their wings. Their wings [were] joined one to another; they turned not when they went; they went every one straight forward . . . their appearance [was] like burning coals of fire, [and] like the appearance of lamps: it went up and down among the living creatures; and the fire was bright, and out of the fire went forth lightning . . . The appearance of the wheels and their work [was] like unto the colour of a beryl: and they four had one likeness: and their appearance and their work [was] as it were a wheel in the middle of a wheel. When they went, they went upon their four sides: [and] they turned not when they went. As for their rings, they were so high that they were dreadful; and their rings [were] full of eyes round about them four . . . and the likeness of the firmament upon the heads of the living creature [was] as the colour of the terrible crystal, stretched forth over their heads above. And under the firmament [were] their wings straight, the one toward the other: every one had two, which covered on this side, and every one had two, which covered on that side, their bodies. And when they went, I heard the noise of their wings, like the noise of great waters. (Ezekiel 1:4–28)

Even using the transliterations that are available to us, we can begin to understand what early historians had to say regarding ancient beings flying high above earthbound mortals. The Hindu records of prehistoric India are an inexhaustible source of data in relation to the ancient astronaut theory. Sanskrit legends compiled over two millennia ago provide some of the oldest available accounts of mythical spaceships, atomic wars, and a space opera history that would put *Battlestar Galactica* to shame. Some of the passages found in India's national epic *The Mahabharata* speak of large celestial chariots equipped with wings of lightning that soar through the skies like fading comets (see plate 9).

These descriptions can be found throughout the Vedic literature, which may constitute the earliest form of science-fiction writing or a physical history that stretches far beyond the academic acceptance of humanity's known history. Hindu conceptualizations of time stretch back billions of years, intertwined in a cyclic procession of endless creation and eventual destruction. Indian sages chronicled tales of great wars with fabulous weapons, such as the "flame of Indra,"[10] that had the ability to decimate entire regions over three thousand years ago. W. Raymond Drake, a British student of the great "anomalous phenomena" pioneer Charles Fort and a contemporary of Erich von Däniken, spent decades researching the ancient astronaut theory. His tireless combing of ancient manuscripts resulted in eleven books that document the exploits of ancient aliens exploring various corners of the globe.

In his most famous work, *Gods and Spacemen in the Ancient East,* he recounts the fascinating love story of the Hindu deity Rama:

The Ramayana, telling in magic imagery the quest of Rama for his stolen wife Sita, has thrilled the people of India for thousands of years; generations of wandering story-tellers have recited its 24,000 verses to marveling audiences captivated by this brilliant panorama of the fantastic past, the passions of heroic love, tragedies of dark revenge, aerial battles between Gods and Demons waged with nuclear bombs; the glory of noble deeds; the thrilling poetry of life, the philosophy of destiny and death. This wonderful epic of the Ramayana, the inspiration of the world's great classic literature, intrigues us most today by its frequent allusions to aerial vehicles and annihilating bombs, which we consider to be inventions of our own 20th century impossible in the far past. Students of Sanskrit literature soon revise their preconceived ideas and find that the heroes of Ancient India were apparently equipped with aircraft and missiles more sophisticated than those we boast today.[11]

Using the Hindu examples of the flying vimanas and epic wars with futuristic technology, depicted in the Vedic literature, plus the space-themed biblical stories, we can compare the references in our ancient texts to spaceships and strange alien beings—whether humanoid in appearance or not. If we apply this same method to ancient Egyptian scrolls and papyri, the picture that emerges is exhilarating.

4

CLOSE ENCOUNTERS
OF THE SUN DISKS
AND SKY CULTS

Our passionate preoccupation with the sky, the stars, and a
God somewhere in outer space is a homing impulse. We are
drawn back to where we came from.

ERIC HOFFER, AMERICAN SOCIAL PHILOSOPHER
AND AUTHOR

NOW THAT WE HAVE SHOWN how to interpret certain Bible
passages as reflections of early humans' misunderstanding of how modern technology works, we can apply the same techniques to the ancient
Egyptian texts. But we do not need to look back five thousand years
or more to find evidence of humanity's perplexity concerning metallic vehicles roaming the sky. A phenomenon anthropologists call "cargo
cults"[1] began to appear in remote South Pacific islands after the end of
World War II. Aboriginal Indians formed these sky cults after being
showered with material gifts by American and Japanese pilots. These
islanders had never seen airplanes before. So imagine the shock and joy
at seeing a loud bomber fly by and drop boxes full of food and other

goods. Then imagine their confusion once the planes vanished and the goods stopped falling from heaven.

In 1871 the Russian baron Nikolai Miklouho-Maclay and his fellow explorers became the first white settlers in Madang, New Guinea.[2] When they arrived in their mammoth steamships, the native black Indian population somehow believed the Russians were their long-dead ancestors, now returning as gods. The baron impressed the natives with "magical" inventions like dynamite, chewing gum, and lanterns. After the Russians left, the natives prayed for their return, and finally, in 1884 more white men came ashore. The smiling faces of the natives didn't last long as the Indians quickly learned that these strangers didn't bring any goods. The German settlers rounded up the natives and put them to work on their newly formed plantations. The Indians would eventually rebel against their taskmasters but found that they were no match for another "magical" invention the white man had developed— the Winchester fast-reloading rifle.

Over a period of decades, progress between the black native islanders and white missionaries and industrialists from various countries began to sour race relations in the remote South Pacific islands. Most native islanders believed that white men inside a volcano somewhere in Australia were holding their gods hostage. These beliefs continued until World War II, when the Japanese began occupying most of the Pacific islands. Showered with goods, the islanders now believed that the Japanese were going to rescue their gods and drive away the whites from the islands. The Japanese were happy to go along with these beliefs, considering that they were fighting for their lives against the Allied forces.

After being given weapons, the native population was ready to attack any foreign troops not wearing Japanese uniforms. Their enemies were now wearing GI camouflage, and they were preferably white. Imagine how awestruck and disoriented they must have been after watching John Frum's American fighter plane skid recklessly across the ground, smashing through palms and low-lying brush until safely halting after sliding across miles of jungle grass. With smoke billowing from the plane's engines, Frum emerged from the cockpit. The natives ran up to the smoldering plane and stared curiously at Frum. After climbing out of the plane, John Frum pulled off his helmet, revealing African features similar to those of the local Indians. John Frum was an African American fighter pilot; to the black native islanders, this was a *huge* revelation.[3]

Once the islanders saw Frum as a hero and his plane as a symbol of a sky cult, it didn't take long for a cult to grow up around him. Frum initially gave out candy bars and socialized with the natives until he was rescued. After he promised to return and then never appeared again, the islanders turned John Frum into a deity. The cult of Frum began to take hold right after the war ended. The natives constructed bamboo radio shacks, complete with wooden antennas and vines to represent electric cables. In these shacks they repeated phrases they must have heard during the war, including popular military jargon like, "Roger, Foxtrot, Bravo, Over and out."[4] They even made a landing strip and built replica airplanes out of palms and straw and have yearly celebrations dedicated to John Frum's return, where they paint *USA* on their chests and hoist a stick representing the American flag opposite the bamboo rifles slung over their shoulders.

The modern sky cult sheds light on the many psychological elements underlying how we have always viewed unfamiliar technological devices. If primitive natives had trouble understanding World War II bomber planes in the 1940s, then how can we expect ancient humans not to have had the same problems? When the South Pacific natives failed to understand how airplanes worked, it prompted them to worship the airplane. This is tied to our ancient belief in magic, and a desire to relegate something that we don't understand to the supernatural realms. The sky cult seen in modern times makes it easier for us to understand what the ancients were describing thousands of years ago.

What is known today as *The Egyptian Book of the Dead* was called by the ancient Egyptians *Reu nu pert em hru,* commonly translated as, "The

Figure 4.1. The worshipping area for the sky cult that grew up around African American U.S. pilot John Frum. Courtesy of Charmaine Tham.

Chapters of Coming Forth by Day." This book was an important guide, full of funerary rites and instructions in preparing ancient Egyptians for life after death. But it was only made available during a later period of history, when the priesthood began selling this "How to Survive the Underworld" manual. Once the priests discovered how much money people were willing to pay for access to the afterlife, a cycle of mass control through religion was started that continues to the present day.

The Egyptian Book of the Dead contains some of the world's oldest written knowledge and goes far deeper than just simple spells and old-time remedies. Collections of funerary chapters first appeared in Egyptian tombs around 1600 BCE. The most famous example of this, the Papyrus of Ani, is now kept in excellent condition at the British Museum in London. This famous papyrus represents a small portion of the museum's massive archives of Egyptian texts. Many sections of *The Book of the Dead* have never been seen publicly and are up to 3,500 years old. Yet we do not have scholars poring madly over these documents round-the-clock in an attempt to decipher them. Considering that over 70 percent of ancient Egypt still sleeps under the hot desert sands, and that the indigenous teachings of Egypt are different from those found in the European trans-lations of the past few hundred years, most scholars acknowledge that we only know 30 percent of its contents, at best. There is certainly plenty of room for growth. Despite the different translations, the overall core of the Egyptian texts can still be properly decoded.

Our search for clues that lead to the ancient astronaut theory in Egypt begins with the translations made by respected Egyptian linguist E. A. Wallis Budge in the book *Egyptian Literature Comprising Egyptian Tales, Hymns, Litanies, Invocations, the Book of the Dead and Cuneiform Writings*, published in 1901.[5] Below are varied descriptions of spaceships that can be found in Egyptian writing. The mainstream view is that these are merely different kinds of boats that are meant to float on water. But if the ancient Egyptians saw the Nile as the Milky Way, then why not assume that they're talking about celestial boats, rather than boats travers-ing the water? Obviously, Egyptians had boats to sail on, but given the extreme antiquity and importance of their writing, it seems more logical that they are describing scenes involving ancient space platoons, possibly older than those that visited during the days of Rama and Ezekiel.

Reading with our twenty-first-century minds, we will find the quotes below (from Budge's book, cited above) both poetic and clear. These early Egyptian writings, especially the ones concerned with the gods hiding in their space stations or ports, are also, without a doubt, describing fast-moving jets and space vehicles able to travel to the stars:

> May the soul of Osiris Ani, the triumphant one, come forth with thee into heaven, may he go forth in the Motet boat. May he come into port in the Sektet boat, and may he cleave his path among the never-resting stars in the heavens. (Hymn to Ra: Papyrus of Ani No. 10,470, sheet 20)

Thou passest over the sky, and every face watcheth thee and thy course, for thou hast been hidden from their gaze. Thou dost shew thyself at dawn and at eventide day by day. The Sektet boat, wherein is thy Majesty, goeth forth with might; thy beams [shine] upon [all] faces; [the number] of thy red and yellow rays cannot be known, nor can thy bright beams be told. The lands of the gods, and the eastern lands of Punt must be seen, ere that which is hidden [in thee] may be measured. Alone and by thyself thou dost manifest thyself [when] thou comest into being above Nu [i.e., the sky]." (Hymn to Ra: Papyrus of Ani No. 10,470, sheet 20)

The hidden places adore thee, the aged ones make offerings unto thee, and they create for thee protecting powers. The divine beings who dwell in the eastern and western horizons transport thee, and those who are in the Sektet boat convey thee round and about." (Hymn to the Setting Sun: Papyrus of Mut-hetep No. 10,010, sheet 5)

Here's a verse that describes our "divine" alien ancestors lifting off and creating a billow of smoke and fire, in a scene similar to a NASA rocket launch:

I am the oar made ready for rowing, wherewith Ra transported the boat containing the divine ancestors, and lifted up the moist emanations of Osiris from the Lake of Fire, and he was not burned. (Preservation from Scalding: Papyrus of Nu No. 10,477, sheet 12)

There's an astonishing verse about the God Osiris dwelling in what appears to be a scientific chamber for the purpose of cloning. Our knowledge of stem cells and DNA cloning has reached the point where we can read the verse below with a whole new understanding. Whether or not this hypothesis is too far-out to believe still doesn't take away the staggering and unmatched quality of the poetry:

Figure 4.2. Ani before Osiris. From James Wasserman, The Egyptian Book of the Dead: The Book of Going Forth by Day, *1994.*

I have sat in the birth-chamber of Osiris, and I was born with him, and I renew my youth along with him . . . I fill the office of priest in the regions above, and I write down there [the things] which make strong the heart . . . I snuff the wind of the East by his head, and I lay hold upon the breezes of the West thereby . . . I go round about heaven in the four quarters thereof." (Beating Back the Crocodile: Papyrus of Nu No. 10,477, sheet 5)

Here is one of the most profound and mysterious descriptions of alien visitation ever written. Excerpted from Budge's *Egyptian Literature,* it is visually and mentally stimulating, alluding to cloning as well as offering an understanding of the time lapses that occur during long celestial voyages:

> I am he who cometh forth, advancing, whose name is unknown. I am Yesterday, and Seer of millions of years is my name. I pass along the paths of the divine celestial judges. I am the lord of eternity, and I decree and I judge like the god Khepera. I am the lord of the Ureret crown. I am he who dwelleth in the Utchat [and] in the Egg, in the Utchat and in the Egg, and it is given unto me to live [with] them. I am he that dwelleth in the Utchat when it closeth, and I exist by the strength thereof. I come forth and I shine; I enter in and I come to life. I am in the [Utchat], my seat is upon my throne, and I sit in the abode of splendor (?) before it. I am Horus and [I] traverse millions of years . . . I open the door in heaven, I govern my throne, and I open up [the way] for the births [which take place] on this day. I am (?) the child who marcheth along the road of Yesterday. [I am] To-day for untold nations and peoples. I am he who protecteth you for millions of years, and whether ye be denizens of the heavens, or of the Earth, or of the south, or of the north, or of the east, or of the west, the fear of me is in your bodies. I am he whose being has been moulded in his eye, and I shall not die again. My moment is in your bodies, but my forms are in my place of habitation. I am he who cannot be known, but the Red Ones have their faces directed toward me. I am the unveiled one." (Abolishing the Slaughterings: Papyrus of No. 10,477, sheet 6)

Here, again from Budge's book, are more descriptions of space fleets and their divine commanders, who not only have mastered the art of cloning and space travel but also know how to keep themselves hidden from humanity:

> I am Yesterday, To-day, and To-morrow, [and I have] the power to be born a second time; [I am] the divine hidden Soul who createth

Figure 4.3. Hathor with Rocket.
From James Wasserman, The Egyptian Book of the Dead:
The Book of Going Forth by Day, *1994.*

the gods, and who giveth sepulchral meals unto the denizens of the Tuat (underworld), Amentet, and heaven. [I am] the rudder of the east, the possessor of two divine faces wherein his beams are seen. I am the lord of the men who are raised up; [the lord] who cometh forth from out of the darkness, and whose forms of existence are of the house wherein are the dead. Hail, ye two hawks who are perched upon your resting-places, who hearken unto the things which are said by him, who guide the bier to the hidden place, who lead along Ra, and who follow [him] into the uppermost place of the shrine which is in the celestial heights! I am the divine envoy [?] of the house of him that dwelleth in his possessions, and I have come from Sekhem to Annu to make known to the Bennu bird therein concerning the events of the Tuat [underworld]. Let me journey on in peace; let me pass over the sky; let me adore the radiance of the splendor [which is in] my sight; let me soar like a bird to see the companies [?] of the Khus in the presence of Ra day by day, who vivifieth every human being that walketh upon the regions which are upon the earth. (*Coming Forth by Day:* Papyrus of Nebseni No. 9,900, sheets 23 and 24) (See plate 10.)

This verse contains astounding technical descriptions and is packed with words that can only be referring to space-age vehicles. Note also the references to cloning:

I have risen, I have risen like the mighty hawk [of gold] that cometh forth from his egg; I fly and I alight like the hawk which hath a back four cubits wide, and the wings of which are like unto the mother-of-emerald of the south. I have come forth from the interior of the Sektet boat, and my heart hath been brought unto me from the mountain of the east. I have alighted upon the Atet boat, and those who were dwelling in their companies have been brought unto me, and they bowed low in paying homage unto me and in saluting me with cries of joy. I have risen, and I have gathered myself together like the beautiful hawk of gold, which hath the head of a Bennu bird, and Ra entereth in day by day to hearken unto my words; I have taken my seat among those firstborn gods of Nut. (*Of Performing Transformations:* Papyrus of Nu No. 10,477, sheet 10)

Behold me now, for I make this mighty boat to travel over the Lake of Hetep, and I brought it away with might from the palace of Shu; the domain of his stars groweth young and reneweth its former strength. I have brought the boat into the lakes thereof so that I may come forth into the cities thereof, and I have sailed into their divine city Hetep. The god Horus maketh himself to be strong like unto the Hawk which is one thousand cubits in length and two thousand [cubits in width] in life; he hath equipments with him, and he journeyeth on and cometh where the seat of his heart wisheth in the Pools thereof and in the cities thereof. He was begotten in the birth-chamber of the god of the city, he hath offerings [made unto him] of the food of the god of the city, he performeth that which it is meet to do therein, and the union thereof, in the matter of everything of the birth-chamber of the divine city. When [he] setteth in life like crystal he performeth everything therein, and these things are like unto the things which are done in the Lake of double fire, wherein there is none that rejoiceth, and wherein are all manner of evil things. The god Hetep goeth in, and cometh out, and goeth backward [in] that Field which gathereth together all manner of things for the birth-chamber of the god of the city. (*Of Sekhet-Hetepet:* Papyrus of Nebseni No. 9,900, sheet 17)

There's a curious verse that appears to describe a first-person narrative of witnessing a spaceship and implies that this individual was taken on a space flight, or was allowed to fly along with a fleet. A peculiarly stated word in the last line suggests that ancient apes' DNA and ours might have been experimented with at some point in the past. It's no secret that our DNA has much in common with primates'. For the ancient Egyptians to refer to apes as being divine reflects their knowledge of humankind's genome:

> [Hail], ye bright and shining flames that keep your place behind Ra, and which slay behind him, the boat of Ra is in fear of the whirlwind and the storm; shine ye forth, then, and make [ye yourselves] visible. I have come [daily] along with the god Sek-hra from the bight of his holy lake, and I have seen the Maat [goddesses] pass along, and the lion-gods who belong unto them. I have made a way in front of the boat of Ra, I have lifted myself up into his divine Disk. I am he who dwelleth among the gods, come, let [me] pass onward in the boat, the boat of the lord Sa. Behold, O Heru-ur, there is a flame, but the fire hath been extinguished. I have made [my] road, O ye divine fathers and your divine apes! (*Sailing in the Great Boat*: Papyrus of Nu No. 10,477, sheet 28)

The *Litany of Ra* is the most esoteric of all the ancient Egyptian writings. The rite specified in this text originated in Thebes from the walls adorning the tombs of the pharaohs and maybe one-quarter has been discovered. Edouard Naville translated these passages from texts published in France in 1875 and today housed in the British Museum:

> Homage to thee, Ra! Supreme power, the only one, the courageous one, who fashions his body, he who calls his gods [to life], when he arrives in his hidden sphere . . . Supreme power, he who shines when he is in his sphere, who sends his darkness into his sphere, and who hides what it contains . . . he who lights the bodies which are on the horizon, he who enters his sphere . . . he who descends into the spheres of Ament, his form is that of Turn . . . the urn 7 of the creatures, the only one, that unites the generative substances, its form is that of Horus . . . the brilliant one who shines in the waters of the inundation, his form is that of Nun and comes

forth continually from his highly mysterious cavern . . . he who calls the bodies into the empyrean, and they develop, who destroys their venom, his form is that of the transformer . . . the being with the mysterious face, who makes the divine eye move, his form is that of Shai . . . he who unites the substances, who founds Amto, his form is that of one who joins substances . . . he who invents secret things, and who begets bodies, his form is that of the invisible [progenitor] the master of the hooks [who struggles] against his enemies, the only one, the master of the monkeys . . . he who sends the flames into his furnaces, he who cuts off the head of those who are in the infernal regions, his form is that of the god of the furnace. Supreme power, the master of the light, who reveals hidden things, the spirit who speaks to the gods in their spheres, his form is that of the master of the light. They sing praises in thy honor, spirit Keschi in thy seventy-five forms which are in thy seventy-five spheres. The royal Osiris knows them by their names, he knows what is in their bodies, all their hidden essences. The royal Osiris speaks to them in their forms, they open to the royal Osiris, they display the hidden doors to his spirit which is like thy spirit, thou Greatest them, thou Greatest the royal Osiris; the development of his body is like thine because the royal Osiris is one of thy companions, who are in their spheres, and who speak in their caverns, those who are blessed through thy creation and who transform themselves when thou commandest it. The royal Osiris is like one of those who speak in their hidden spheres. God of the disk with the brilliant rays, the brilliant triangle which appears in the shining place . . . he enters into the interior of his white disk, he lights the empyrean with his rays, he creates it, he makes the souls remain in their bodies, they praise him from the height of their pedestal. He receives the acclamations of all the gods who open the doors, the hidden essences who prepare the way for Ra's soul, and who allow the King of souls access to the fields. He traverses his disk himself.[6]

Figure 4.4. Resurrection chamber relief, Sethos I Temple, Abydos.
Courtesy of Olaf Tausch.

The lines of this litany contain a wide array of mysterious topics far beyond what we can imagine, let alone what primitive humans could. If we apply what we know about technology today, some of the descriptions in this document appear to be of multiple spaceships working in conjunction with one another to express profound metaphysical poetry, philosophies, scientific equations, and most significant of all an understanding of gene manipulation and cloning techniques. The roots of these predynastic alien mysteries can be traced all the way to the beginning of Egyptian mythology, where a celestial goddess known as Hathor claimed that she was indeed an alien from a distant galaxy.

5

HATHOR

OF THE PLEIADES

THE CULT OF HATHOR predates the historical period in Egypt and is so ancient that its beginnings date back to predynastic, matriarchal times in ancient Egypt. The worship of Hathor has been a staple of Egyptian history since its beginnings, and there were more festivals in her honor than in the honor of all other deities. Seen as a cosmic goddess who came from the sky and accompanied the sun god Ra as a "dweller in his disk"[1] she was known as his female counterpart and the "mother of light," responsible for one of the first acts of creation.

Hathor became associated with fertility and procreation and was sometimes depicted as a white cow feeding all the other gods with her divine milk. Other representations of Hathor show her and the goddess Nuit holding up the Milky Way, with their legs placed on calculated celestial alignments, equinoxes, and solstices, corresponding to landmarks in Egypt. Hathor's face has been depicted artistically as a uterus, with her horns resembling fallopian tubes, similar to the

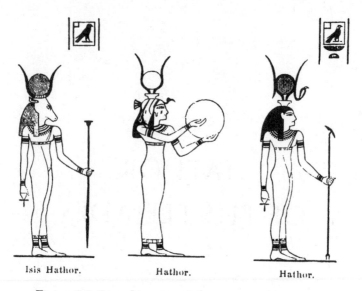

Figure 5.1. Line drawings of the Egyptian god Hathor.
From Karl Baedeker, Handbook for Traveling: Lower Egypt, with
the Fayum and the Peninsula of Sinai, *part 1, 1885.*

headpiece Madonna wore during the 2012 Super Bowl halftime show in Indianapolis. In a way these kinds of artistic representations showcase an archaic understanding of ancient matriarchal symbolism, now overlooked in modern history with its emphasis on patriarchal rule.

Figure 5.2. Hathor. Museum Carnuntinum, lower Austria. Head of the Egyptian goddess Hathor (3rd century). Courtesy of Wolfgang Sauber.

Figure 5.3. This rare bas-relief shows King Necho II, right, facing the cow-goddess Hathor, who wears a vulture headdress topped by a sun disk and cow horns. The inscription above the goddess may once have read, "I grant you every country in submission."
Courtesy of Walters Art Museum, Baltimore, Maryland.

Figure 5.4. Depicted above the god is a head of Hathor with a winged sun disk. Gems with magical icons and words were believed to be protective. Courtesy of Walters Art Museum, Baltimore, Maryland.

In the lore of the Seven Hathors or, as the Greeks called it, the Seven Fates, Hathor guides her celestial herd—a group of seven stars in the Taurus constellation known as the Pleiades. Also known as the Seven Sisters, the Pleiades are the closest array of stars visible to the naked eye (see plate 11). Since the Egyptians were keen observers of the heavens, it stands to reason that they mythologized Hathor's celestial homeland. The Pleiades comprise a strange star system that continues to fascinate humankind. Curiously, NASA's "flagship" supercomputer—capable of calculating in sixty seconds what would take over a year to compute if everyone on the planet did one calculation per second, for eight hours a day—is named after them.[2] A mind can only begin to fathom the meaning behind the code word of NASA's pride and joy. If Hathor and her companion, the sun god Ra, descended from the Pleiades, it makes sense that when they cruised on their solar boat or spacious disk that this "'disk" was meant to represent a spaceship and not the actual Sun. Because if they were indeed only talking about the Sun, then what would be the reason for Hathor to make such a ruckus while morphing into a hawkish hybrid, capable of flight?

The distinguished Egyptologist and director general of excavations and antiquities for the Egyptian government Gaston Maspero of Paris spent decades researching, cataloguing, and writing about ancient Egypt and Asia. His voluminous series on the ancient world's history provides some of the best and most credible information available on the tangled history of predynastic Egypt. He describes Hathor's colorful visit from heaven in such a way that if Maspero would have been privy to our understanding of the ancient astronaut theory he would have stopped dead in his tracks after writing, ". . . in the form of a human-headed sparrow-hawk of lapis-lazuli, accompanied by her divine cycle to come and unite herself to the statue,"[3] in describing Hathor's return to Earth.

A verse from the Papyrus of Nebseni describes a longing for the goddess Hathor, who has recently flown off in her spaceship toward Heliopolis:

Figure 5.5. Bas-relief of Hathor taking off in her ship.
Dendera Hathor temple complex. Courtesy of Csorfoly Daniel.

In a clean place shall I sit on the ground beneath the foliage of the date-palm of the goddess Hathor, who dwelleth in the spacious Disk as it advanceth to Annu (Heliopolis), having the books of the divine words of the writings of the god Thoth.[4]

The Temple of Hathor at Dendera was the central location of the cult of Hathor and houses many curious features that have been covered up for centuries. There is even an older temple beneath the present one that stretches into a maze of underground crypts and vaults. Curiously, these deep underground crypts contain no soot marks, which would have indicated the presence of fire torches—the only means of illumination that would have been available at that point in history, according to the time line elite Egyptology has established. What light source were these ancients able to use while constructing the elaborate hieroglyphs and the famous round Dendera zodiac? (See plate 12.) Is it possible that these engineers didn't need light to carry out their work? Unfortunately, the zodiac found on the ceiling in a small room on the second floor

Figure 5.6. Temple of Dendera. From David Roberts, Egypt & Nubia, From drawings made on the spot by David Roberts and lithographed by Louis Haghe, *vol. 1, part 36, 1846–1849.*

of Hathor's main temple is a replica commissioned by Napoleon after he invaded Egypt and hauled the original one back to France, where it resides permanently at the Louvre Museum in Paris. The present zodiac replica has been damaged to the point that it is barely recognizable. This zodiac and the accompanying walls of astonishing hieroglyphs have left archaeologists baffled for over a century as to what they mean. In later chapters we will discuss in greater detail the other mysterious frescoes that adorn Hathor's temple.

Scenes depicted on the walls of Hathor's temple span a range of fields, including biology, unknown technology, cloning, astronomy, astrology, planetary systems, and large cycles of time. If the Seven Hathors represented the Pleiades, as evidence appears to indicate, it means the initiates had knowledge beyond our galaxy, again pointing to interstellar travel and exchange of knowledge with alien beings. Interestingly, this knowledge would surface again during the Amarna period—one of the most important ages in humanity.

Figure 5.7. Hathor Temple complex entrance. Courtesy of Csorfoly Daniel.

Figure 5.8. The ceiling of the pronaos of the Dendera Temple;
a UFO can be seen flying through sky in this bas-relief. Courtesy of LassiHu.

During the Amarna period, the arts and sciences flourished to a point we have yet to reach. We can't even understand how such heightened talents were possible. This magnificent leap in cultural evolution happened at a time when a mysterious race known as the Shemsu Hor was operating behind the scenes of the Egyptian priesthood. Who were the Shemsu Hor? The truth of what really happened during this fateful era of humanity has been debated, been pondered, and driven people mad ever since. We will see that Pharaoh Akhenaten and his bloodline represented the last stand of a truly free humanity with widespread access to a sacred and ancient knowledge taught by and handed down from an advanced, interstellar race far back in antiquity. The battle to possess this information would turn out to be an epic confrontation between good and evil with repercussions still felt today.

6

REPTOIDS AND
THE SHEMSU HOR

Come not between the Dragon, and his Wrath.
WILLIAM SHAKESPEARE, *KING LEAR,* ACT 1, SCENE 1

THE FIRST PHARAOH in Egyptian recorded history was Menes-Narmer, who ruled about three thousand years before the Common Era. Menes-Narmer's reign was chosen as the starting point because that is as far back as we can trace to the beginning of human civilization. Our civilization was born from the destruction of the previous one. As chronicled on the Palermo stone, there was a civilization prior to the present one that went back anywhere between twenty and thirty thousand years and had a good grasp of astronomy, engineering, biology, bioengineering, chemistry, and sacred geometry—all of which required advanced knowledge of mathematics and applications of that knowledge that we do not have today. Logic tells us the time before Menes was the last Golden Age.

Mainstream academia treats Egypt's prepharaonic past as if it had never existed because it disappeared quite suddenly, as did many other similarly ancient cultures throughout the world. It is typically referred to as a "lost" civilization, but our world, our universe, and the galaxy beyond are cyclical. Every cyclical process has an end, and life-forms dwindle, become extinct, or evolve.

The fragmented influence of the last Golden Age reached the Egyptian culture some time later. The Egyptian civilization and culture appear to have suddenly sprung up out of nowhere. Even Egyptologists who adhere to mainstream thinking, such as the distinguished Cambridge Egyptologist Dr. Toby Wilkinson, admit that "they don't seem to have an ancestry, they don't seem to have any period of development, they just seem almost to appear overnight. This has left people pondering, and of course it has been fertile ground for the unorthodox who suggest it was all planted by aliens."[1]

These mysterious rulers of previous Golden Ages are the "divine" beings the ancient Egyptians believe their civilization came from. These claims of divine lineage are regarded as myths and are derided by official Egyptologists. The recent uproar concerning Dr. Alaaeldin Shaheen of Cairo is a good example of how official Egyptology adheres to the time line that it has compiled, even in the face of contradictory evidence. Dr. Shaheen, one of Egypt's premiere archaeologists, was overheard during a press conference saying that aliens had built the pyramids and that his research team had found evidence of alien technology on the Giza Plateau. This news quickly spread through Internet conspiracy chat rooms and caused a furor in academic circles. Shortly thereafter, Dr. Shaheen replied with a token rebuttal, claiming that he never made such a ludicrous statement. But in his response was a thinly veiled admission that even if he did discover that aliens had been involved in Egypt's past, as an Egyptologist with a doctorate and dependent on grants from universities, it would be career suicide to publicly assert that.

His official response, in an e-mail to investigative journalist Andrew Collins reads: "Kindly be informed that I did not give such stupid statement[s] about aliens and pyramids. As [I am] Egyptologist I could [not] say such stupid words and ideas."[2]

More double standards can be found by studying the so-called father of Egyptology himself: Manetho, an Egyptian high priest who studied at the famous library of Alexandria and wrote a thirty-volume history of Egypt. Written in Greek, the *Aegyptiaca* was compiled during the third century BCE, supposedly for Ptolemy I, II, or III during their reigns as kings of Egypt. Historians don't know exactly which Ptolemaic king Manetho originally wrote his book for but have narrowed it down to one of the three, using dating techniques and historical clues now available. Manetho had a mixed background, with one parent being of Egyptian heritage and the other Greek, and spent his entire life in Egypt. He had an advantage over the scholars of his time in that he could speak and read both Greek and Egyptian, making his translations much more accurate. He compiled a predynastic kings list that stretched deep into the Golden Age, when Thoth roamed ancient Egypt, anywhere from 33,894 to 23,642 BCE. The list of the predynastic kings found on the Palermo stone validated the controversial list that Manetho first wrote about.[3]

Manetho's list is what Egyptologists use when teaching their official time line and chronology of Egyptian history. It's disturbing that Egyptologists would use Manetho's dating to establish the officially recognized time frame of the pharaoh dynasties, but completely ignore the mysterious rulers of the predynastic epochs he cites. This "official" listing completely disregards the history already written because it goes against the time line academic institutions contend is the truth. Simply put, scholars claim to know the history of Egypt better than the ancient Egyptians who wrote it.

Manetho's works would eventually be superseded by Herodotus, and Manetho's original manuscripts would become lost to time. Thankfully, Eusebius, Caesar's bishop in Palestine, and the Byzantine scribe Syncellus, also studying in Palestine, followed in Manetho's footsteps, providing more proof of predynastic genealogies of the ancient Egyptians.[4] Manetho wrote that the original Sky Gods lived long lives and reigned for hundreds of years more than thirty thousand years ago, but his assertions would fade out of history and be replaced by stories of semidivine kings who still lived long lives as much as twelve thousand years in the past. These semidivine kings would come to be known as the Followers of Horus or, more traditionally, the Shemsu Hor, a term coined by researcher Schwaller de Lubicz.[5] The word *Shemsu* likely comes from the Akkadian *shamash*, which means "serpent," and *Hor* derives from *Horus*, the hawk-headed god of the rising and setting Sun.

According to the oral traditions of the indigenous Egyptians, the Shemsu Hor were present during the Golden Ages of the original divine kings, and they remained long after these kings ascended back into the stars. The Shemsu Hor inherited the sacred knowledge of the Giza Plateau and continued to use the pyramids in the Band of Peace and the surrounding energy fields as they were meant to be used. They reestablished, maintained, and rebuilt temples and foundations in sacred locations that had once been populous areas and cities of the original divine kings. Thousands of years before the last major flood, the Shemsu Hor maintained the most ancient cities in Egypt, cities so illustrious and steeped in Egyptian mythology that the very roots of their alien history lay in plain view but somehow remain shrouded in mystery.

Heliopolis, meaning "city of the Sun," was one of the largest religious and science centers of ancient Egypt and was the original home of the sun god Ra. It's also where the famed Phoenix, or Benu Bird (spaceships), would return to every twelve thousand years or so.[6] Before its destruction by invading Persians in 525 BCE, Heliopolis was the main center of knowledge in antiquity and the source of our solar calendars.

A popular tourist destination, it was once visited by some of the most distinguished scholars of the past, including Pythagoras, Herodotus, Solon, Thales, Democritus, Opheus, and Homer. Plato lived in Heliopolis for thirteen years, and while there, we assume, he learned the legend of Atlantis from the Egyptian priest Solon, who knew about it from studying the vast annals of the city's ancient history.[7] This metropolis eventually vanished, with nothing to testify to its existence except the beautifully carved, massive obelisks that survived the ages. There's a good chance that half of Heliopolis's predynastic splendor lies buried under Cairo, where new temples are still being discovered.[8]

Lost megalithic wonders swallowed by the desert are also what

Figure 6.1. Heliopolis. This drawing is by German artist Karl Richard Lepsius during an 1845 scientific expedition for the King of Prussia.

we find when studying the remaining ruins of the other major city of ancient Egypt believed to have divine roots—the awe-inspiring and majestic locale known as Abydos (see plate 13).

Abydos means the "hill of the emblem." Although some scholars replace *emblem* with the word *symbol,* both these words refer to the sacred head of Osiris.[9] Is it possible that before being murdered, Osiris was the lead alien commander on Earth, where he took on a human form and helped establish civilization? According to Egyptian mythology, the eldest son of the sun god Ra, Osiris was sent to live among the humans and teach them the ways of goodness. After his death, his body was cut into fourteen pieces and separated. The fourteen pieces of Osiris are a reference to the sun's passing through the zodiacal cycles of a precessional Great Year, the normal twelve constellations of the zodiac, plus the extra two in the forms of Ophiuchus and Orion.[10] Isis gathered the scattered remains and, with the help of her sister Nephthys, plus Anubis and Thoth, somehow magically resurrected Osiris and made him rise again after three days.

The story of Osiris is so old that it has inspired countless knock-offs. It echoes the biblical story of Cain and Abel and the life of Jesus.

Gerald L. Berry describes the power this ancient tale has wielded over the ages. It has prompted legends once based on historical events that happened tens of thousands of years before in the Golden Age:

> Osiris . . . was successively god of the Nile, a life-giver, a sun-god, god of justice and love, and finally a resurrected god who ruled in the afterlife. . . . The most popular legend about Osiris is one of a resurrected god. He was killed by Set, the god of darkness . . . Osiris was then resurrected and went to live on high. Osiris became the first of a long line of resurrected deities—Tammuz, Mithras, Balder, Christ. Every spring the life of Osiris was re-enacted at Abydos in a stirring passion play, dating back to the eighteenth or nineteenth century before Christ. This play is the earliest record in history of drama.[11]

From the earliest times, Osiris has been related to the constellation Orion. In addition, the pyramids at Giza align with this very constellation, providing yet another clue in understanding the alien mysteries of ancient Egypt. Abydos was the original home of the divine kings, and the ancient Egyptians believed the tomb of Osiris was located under one of the many splendid temples built there. Supposedly, the temple of the Osirian once housed the body of the god Osiris, and his sacred head was encased in glass, held up on scepters, and paraded around by priests during ancient ceremonies.[12]

The temple of the Osirian sits at the rear of a much larger temple complex attributed to Seti I and was discovered in 1903. More than half of its impressive structure is still buried under the sand. To complicate matters even more, the Osirian is also flooded by an ancient water source that has turned the pools surrounding the stone columns an oozy shade of green (see plate 14). The Osirian's underground megalithic chambers of Osiris are rumored to be the most ancient of all Egyptian ruins. The massive megalithic blocks that compose the Osirian are similar to those found on the oldest parts of the Giza Plateau, like the Valley and Sphinx temple and the Chephren funerary complex.

Figure 6.2. Line drawing of the Egyptian god Osiris. From Karl Baedeker, Handbook for Traveling: Lower Egypt, with the Fayum and the Peninsula of Sinai, *part 1, 1885.*

Figure 6.3. The Shrine of Osiris; Osiris is being put back together for his resurrection. From Amelia B. Edwards, A Thousand Miles Up the Nile, *1890.*

Figure 6.4. Temple of the Osirian. Courtesy of Merlin-UK.

Figure 6.5. Another view of the Temple of the Osirian.
Courtesy of Merlin-UK.

Some of the enormous red granite blocks and pillars used in the Osirian's construction weigh up to one hundred tons apiece. The roof of the Osirian is composed of these massive stone pillars. Placing these stone pillars atop the complex is a feat of unparalleled engineering; even our most advanced crane technology could not duplicate it. Although it has been rebuilt numerous times over the years, the remaining temple complex of Seti I is also impressive. Still standing are massive megalithic blocks, all pointing to construction dating back to the Golden Age. The temple of Seti I at Abydos represents some of the finest masonry seen in all of Egypt and includes an amazing assortment of beautifully carved reliefs and hieroglyphs. The most famous are the brazen images of a helicopter, a submarine, a tank, and what appears to be Luke Skywalker's Tatooine cruiser.

First discovered during an archaeological expedition in 1848, the mysterious glyphs on a ceiling beam high above the temple grounds were copied and passed around scholarly circles in Europe. However, since flight had yet to be invented by the Wright brothers, these bizarre hieroglyphs were quickly stored away and forgotten until curious tourists began snapping photos of Seti's temples in the early 1990s and posting them on the Internet. These images are instantly recognizable, especially the helicopter, but the consensus of skeptics and Egyptologists is that the glyphs are re-carved inscriptions of an overlaid royal cartouche. Claiming that Ramses II carved over the panel of Seti I with his own inscriptions, essentially doubling the original hieroglyphs.

Egyptologists claim these glyphs are nothing more than illusions, resulting from years of re-carving and weathering that over a period of time creates an overlapping effect known as *palimpsests,* which look nothing like the original hieroglyphs. However, one of the oldest Arab newspapers, *Al-Sharq Al-Awsat,* published several photographs taken by Egyptologists at a different temple in Karnak that show the exact same features as a helicopter.[13] These suppressed pictures put to rest the palimpsest theory. What are the odds that two exact palimpsests of strange hieroglyphs, showing machines apparently capable of flight,

Figure 6.6. Hieroglyphs showing seemingly modern aircraft and vehicles depicted on a riser in a temple in Abydos, Egypt. Courtesy of Olek95.

would be found hundreds of miles apart from each other? The actual hieroglyphs speak for themselves. The images are undeniable.

How many more hieroglyphs of these helicopters and submarines still lie unseen, buried beneath the Egyptian sands? The fact that these hieroglyphs are found in an area with roots stretching back to the Golden Ages proves that in the archaic past high levels of technology were the norm. Certainly, these myths had once been real and the impact on the human psyche over the millennia has forced humankind to occasionally remind ourselves of this extraordinary history. Deep in their past, the ancient Egyptians saw flying vehicles, and the memory survives to this day. We have proof of this knowledge, although it's another anomaly Egyptologists would rather not discuss:

Numerous wooden models of glider airplanes have been found in Egyptian tombs. One example was found in 1898 at the Saqqara ruins and catalogued by the Cairo Museum as item #6347, but misidentified as a "bird." That plane, which dated to 2000 BCE, along with several others, was reexamined in 1969. They all incorporated a direct dihedral angle of wing attachment, with aerodynamically designed proportions that were ideal for flight.[14]

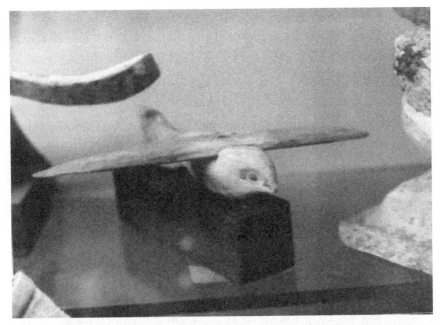

Figure 6.7. Glider model from the ruins of Saqqara. The model resembles a bird but with a vertical tail, no legs, and straight wings. Courtesy of Dawoudk.

Figure 6.8. Side view of the glider. Courtesy of Dawoudk.

These advanced, space-age feats were understood by the Shemsu Hor, who ruled when the ancient lands of Egypt were tropical and lush. These semidivine kings received a legacy designed to maintain humanity's consciousness at a level of uplifted, creative awareness, in tune with nature and the psychic realms of the universe. Unfortunately, the Shemsu Hor cycled out of the Golden Age and into a Dark Age that saw the world destroyed by epic floods of the last great cataclysm. The Shemsu Hor who managed to survive this catastrophe relocated underground and remained undetected while the various other life-forms on Earth took thousands of years to repopulate and rebuild civilization. After nearly being wiped out, the semidivine Shemsu Hor were forced to reevaluate their future and the future role that humanity, who were inferior to them in knowledge, would play in their plans to regain the lost technology. The Shemsu Hor were beings who shared Earth with humans, but were not like us. Perhaps much superior in intellect, this race, known as the followers of Horus, had a different form.

The myths of ancient reptilian beings appear in all the cultures of the world. The haunting image of the serpent or snake is ubiquitous within Egyptian iconography, representing something we have misinterpreted for hundreds of years. The Shemsu Hor were either reptilian or human-reptilian hybrids. The topic of the reptilian alien is the most lauded, criticized, and hated aspect of the ancient astronaut theory. David Icke made it famous,[15] but it was already a subject of speculation and discussion since at least medieval times, when brave knights went on quests to slay dragons.

Let's take a closer look at the origin of the world's most controversial conspiracy theory and determine if it is possible that the Shemsu Hor were indeed reptilian and if there are clues in ancient Egypt to corroborate this conjecture. According to David Icke's theory, the reptilian alien species originated in Thuban, also known as Alpha-Draconis, which is a star system in the constellation of Draco.[16] However, if we take into account evolution, the reptilians may not have needed to travel millions of light-years to reach our world: they might have evolved into an intelligent species over vast periods right here on Earth.

Figure 6.9. Russian poster (1914); St. George killing the dragon. Courtesy of Viktor Vasnetsov.

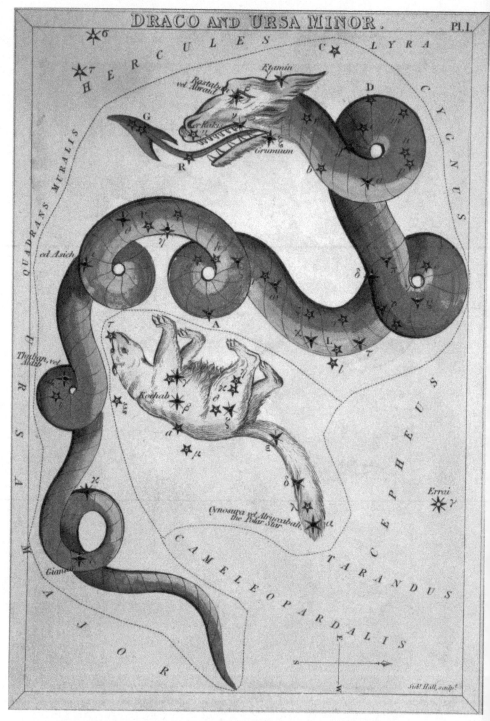

Figure 6.10. Draco sketch (1825). Courtesy of Sidney Hall.

Scientists who support Darwinian evolution admit that our earliest ancestors were reptiles and that mammals evolved from them millions of years ago. According to the theory of evolution, the relationship between reptiles and mammals could be viewed as a matter of Which came first—the chicken or the egg? Mainstream theory holds that mammals proliferated and evolved into intelligent beings with dominion over the animal kingdom because our greatest threat, the dinosaurs, were killed by an unknown and still-debated cataclysm. The problem is that we still have reptilian species around today so old that they might as well be labeled living dinosaurs, such as the Komodo dragon.

Another ancient and permanent link humans share with reptiles lies in that mysterious slush of watery neuronal space we call our brains. The reptilian and human brains both share a few key similarities. The most primitive part of our brain, the stem, performs the same functions as and is similar to the brain stems of reptiles. Sitting at the top of our spinal cord, this part of the brain is even called the "reptilian brain,"[17] or the R-complex (reptilian complex), and is said to govern the more dinosaurian functions, such as aggressiveness, territoriality, and mob-rule behavior. This area of the brain is much older than the recent additions that make up the higher parts of the modern brain, such as the limbic system and the neocortex, or outer layer. How the brain evolved is another mystery.[18]

It is interesting that the limbic area of the brain is responsible for reasoning, love, and knowing the difference between good and evil, which is exactly what ancient creation myths claim the serpent provided to humanity. Reptiles and humans also function in a similar way when it comes to vision, respiration, eating, and circulation. Paleontologist Dale Russell suggests that if the *Troodon* dinosaur hadn't perished in the Cretaceous–Tertiary extinction event* sixty-five million years ago,

---

*The Cretaceous–Tertiary extinction event is famously believed to have killed the dinosaurs at the end of the Cretaceous period. A large-scale mass extinction of animal and plant species believed to be caused by an asteroid or meteor strike combined with volcanic activity, the event marks the end of the Mesozoic era and the beginning of the Cainozoic era.

its brain would have developed six times faster than all other known brains of the ancient era. This would have happened because the encephalization quotient of the brain weight, when compared to that of other species with the same body weight as the *Troodon,* was perfectly proportioned for speedy, exponential growth. In addition, the *Troodon* already had a brain six times larger than any of its known dinosaur contemporaries.[19]

Russell postulates that, over millions of years, this "dinosauroid"[20] would have become sapient and intelligent long before humans. It is possible that the reptiles didn't all die during the so-called dinosaur extinction event and over millions of years evolved into intelligent beings. These beings could have developed technology on their own, traversed the skies themselves, and possibly even had a close encounter with alien species deep in the remote past. Famed biological scientist Ronald Breslow, PhD, released a study on April 12, 2012, suggesting that "alien worlds could be full of super-intelligent dinosaurs"[21] and that humans were only able to triumph on Earth because an asteroid wiped out ours.

Maybe at some point their DNA, along with ours, was tampered with by another set of unknown aliens. No one knows for certain, but there's plenty of evidence indicating that a species of intelligent reptiles might have also evolved at one point during Earth's long history. Recently, Associate Professor Sheila Coulson, from the University of Oslo, found an image of a python engraved on a six-meter-long stone in Botswana. The python was an important player in South African creation myths. According to those myths, the python once appeared intelligent and upright. The carved image and other artifacts found within the cave systems near the discovery have proved to be at least seventy thousand years old.[22] These ancient ritual grounds of the python date from a staggering thirty thousand years earlier than the oldest discoveries in Europe.

Our genetic memories and the events of long ago are replete with dragons, snakes, reptiles, vipers, and descriptions of various other

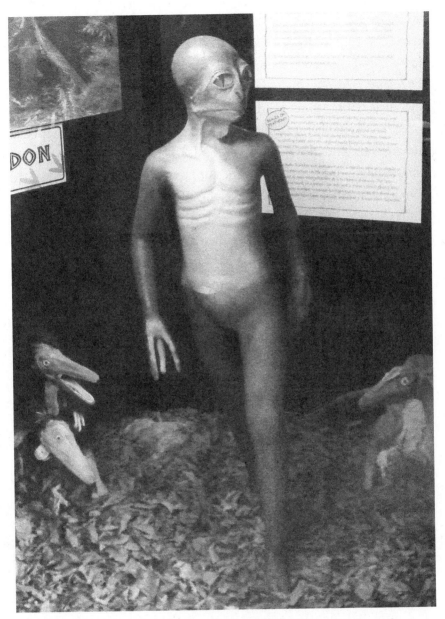

Figure 6.11. In 1982 paleontologist Dale Russell, curator of vertebrate fossils at the National Museum of Canada in Ottawa, conjectured a possible evolutionary path that might have been taken by bipedal predator dinosaurs, like the one pictured here, had they not all perished sixty-five million years ago. A few scientists have embraced Russell's idea, but many are highly skeptical. Courtesy of FunkMonk.

fork-tongued monsters and hybrids. John the Baptist, in Matthew 3:7, referred to the mysterious sect called the Pharisees as a "generation of vipers"[23] and the "Jinn" of Middle Eastern folklore were an ancient race of serpents that predated all other demonic or angelic beings on Earth. The ancient kingdoms of Mexico, including the Toltecs, Mayan, and Aztec, all claim that a "serpent"[24] gave them wisdom and enlightened humankind. The Hopi, Cherokee, and other Native American tribes believe their culture came from ancient "snake-brothers"[25] that emerged from underground labyrinths and civilized humanity. The Chinese have similar legends of the "dragon kings"[26] that emerged from the waters of the four corners of Earth to bring them civilization.

Cecrops I, a native of Egypt and the founder of Athens, was the "first to establish civil government and marriages among the Greeks"[27] and was described by some writers as a monster—half-man and half-

Figure 6.12. The Pergamon Altar; the Gigantomachy frieze depicts the struggle of the gods against the children of the primordial goddess Gaia, who were snake-footed giants. Courtesy of Claus Ableiter.

serpent. Images seen carved in various coins and on the famous frescoes of the Greek-Turkish town of Pergamum depict giant human warriors with legs of snakes.[28] Boreas was the Greek god of winter and the north wind, who, according to the historian Pausanias, "appears as serpent-legged on the famous coffer of Kypselos."[29] On another vase, Boreas is shown as a "huge winged monster, half man and half a double snake."[30]

British Lieutenant-General Sir Henry D'Oyley Torrens wrote a travel book in 1862 after exploring the historic regions of Hindostan, which included Ladak, Kashmir, and the Himalayan regions of China. In the book he describes a curious legend recounted to him during a trek past the village of Bourwa, more than seven thousand feet high,

Figure 6.13. Cecrop, the serpent-king of Athens. Illustration from a vase found at Palermo. This image comes from Hermann Julius Meyer, Meyers Konversations-Lexikon *encyclopedia, fourth edition, 1885–90.*

Figure 6.14. Melian relief in clay, about 460 BCE. On the left, Gaia offers Erichthonius to Athena; on the right is Cecrops. From Wilhelm Heinrich Roscher, Ausführliches Lexikon der griechischen und römischen Mythologie [Concise Dictionary of Greek and Roman Mythology], *1884.*

near the Rotung Pass of the Himalayas. After passing by a causeway of stones, one of the guides pointed out to Torrens that they were now in a sacred area, the place of a famous event immortalized in Hindu mythology. On this high mountain an army of serpents had an outpost assigned to guard the giant race the Hindus called the Rakis from the wrath of the gods. Apparently, this snake army was no match for the gods, and the giant Rakis were forced out of hiding and slain. According to Torrens, the gods, "took the field, utterly routed the Rakis, and slew them a giant. The fossils so plentifully strewed over the Sewalik, or lowest ranges of the Himalayas, are the bones of the slain Rakis!!!"[31] It's an amazing tale that not only focuses on the serpent race but also on Earth's other most mysterious lost race—the giants.

The ancient Indian scriptures include a race of reptilians known as the Naga that had "hoods and the body of a man, the lower extremities being like that of a reptile."[32] The Naga descended from the Sarpa, an earlier serpent race found in Hindu texts. Writers of Marco Polo's era described the Syrictae of India as a nomadic tribe with snakelike nostrils in place of noses and "after the manner of snakes they have their legs and feet limmer, wherewith they crawl and creep."[33] The original Naga have been described in the *Mahābhārata* as having the ability to shapeshift into human form, and the texts even share other ancient beliefs in a serpent race that lived underground for long periods of time.[34]

In the Haggadah, a tenth-century Jewish manuscript, the scribes clearly record that the serpent was not merely a snake, but stood erect and was highly intelligent:

> Among the animals, the serpent was notable. Of all of them, he had the most excellent qualities, in some of which he resembled man. Like man, he stood upright upon two feet, and in height, he was equal to the camel . . . His superior mental gifts caused him to become an infidel . . . In punishment for tempting Eve, God said, "I created you to be king over the animals . . . but you were not satisfied. . . . I created you of upright posture.[35]

Figure 6.15. Buddha under the Nagas, Nong Khai, Thailand.
Courtesy of jpatokal.

The serpent is also a prominent character in other ancient texts. In 1945 a peasant in the Egyptian town of Nag Hammadi found a sealed jar with twelve leather-bound papyrus codices stuffed inside. Named after the town in which they were discovered, the Nag Hammadi Texts are similar to the Dead Sea Scrolls and are considered to be key early Gnostic histories of Christianity. The controversy that surrounds their translation is justified since the tree of knowledge story it contains is much different from the version found in Genesis. These ancient texts describe Adam and Eve as a race of humans that the gods were experimenting with. On a particular occasion, a council of seven gods approached Adam and Eve in the Garden of Eden, warning them not to eat fruit from the tree of knowledge. The gods then frightened the young human prototypes with the boisterous spectacle caused by their spaceships flying back up into the sky.

Now terrified, Adam and Eve were approached by

the one who is wiser than all of them, this one who was called "the beast"... And when he saw the likeness of their mother Eve, he said to her, "What is it that God said to you?" "Don't eat from the tree of knowledge," she said. "He not only said, 'Don't eat from it,' but 'Don't you touch it lest [you] die.'" He said to her, "Don't be afraid! You certainly shall [not die]. For [he knows] that when you eat from it your mind will be sobered and you will become like God, knowing the distinctions which exist between evil and good men. For he said this to you, lest you eat from it, since he is jealous." Now Eve believed the words of the instructor. She looked at the tree and she saw that [the fruit] was beautiful and magnificent, and she desired it. She took some of [the] fruit and ate, and she gave to her husband also, and he ate too. Then their minds opened. For when they ate, the light of knowledge shone for them... when they saw their makers, they loathed them since they were beastly forms. They understood very much.[36]

This rebellious act by the reptilians to give humans knowledge can be compared today with the selling or trading of national security secrets. This one, of particularly grave importance, angered the gods who, after finding out, immediately retaliated by returning to the Garden of Eden to hack off the arms and legs of the serpent. Adam and Eve hid while the gods roamed in their spaceships, causing the typical noise and shuddering associated with their technologically advanced landings.

The symbolic meaning of the tree of life is usually associated with DNA and the intertwined helixes that compose it. But an alternative viewpoint, based on the reverence in which it was held by the ancients of all civilizations, is that the tree of life refers to cannabis. Adam and Eve were created so as not to be able to distinguish truth, and ultimate truth is the knowledge of God. This knowledge places its holder above the ills of mortal humans. Cannabis acts like a robot override, in that it opens the mind's eye. It is curious that only after consuming the fruit of the tree did Adam and Eve realize they were naked!

The ancient cannabis plant has been used in religious ceremonies and for personal reasons for thousands of years and is known by many different names. Rastafarians refer to it as "Ganja"; they believe it is the "healing of the nations" and attribute its holiness to its having been found growing on King Solomon's grave. Recently, the world's oldest weed stash was discovered in a tomb deep in China's Gobi Desert. Two pounds of still-green herb were discovered by a team of stunned archaeologists who no doubt must have had a good laugh at the 2,700-year-old haul.[37]

Hieroglyphs of the marijuana leaf exist in Egypt but are rarely pointed out to tourists. In fact, it's not mentioned or even admitted, and according to Egyptologists, the recognizable image of the hemp/marijuana leaf is nothing more than the Seshat emblem, a hieroglyph associated with a star that has nothing to do with pothead fantasies. It's interesting to note, however, that the Seshat image is one of the oldest hieroglyphs found in ancient Egypt and represents the goddess Seshat, who wore the Seshat emblem of a long-stemmed, seven-petal flower on top of her head. Seshat was the goddess of writing; the hieroglyph represents the feminine side of artistic expression and implies the power of

Figure 6.16. Seshat, goddess of knowledge and writing, at Luxor. Courtesy of Karen Green.

Figure 6.17. Seshat. Karnak Temple in Luxor. Courtesy of Steve F.-E.Cameron.

relating hidden mysteries and secrets to the masses. The goddess Seshat makes these mysteries understandable with the help of the Seshat flower, a powerful conductor of creative forces.[38]

Dr. Rick Strassman, a specialist in psychiatry and psychopharmacology research, was the first person in America to use psychedelic or entheogenic substances on humans after a twenty-year ban on such practices. He discovered that users of the drug dimethyltryptamine (DMT) have encounters with reptilian entities; sometimes these reptiles are more humanoid in appearance, other times they are more beastlike. The main trigger for these encounters is DMT, which the brain produces naturally before death and is the main ingredient in the shamanic plant potion ayahuasca.[39]

The ayahuasca plant, commonly found in Brazil, is known to be at least twenty times more powerful than LSD, and some believe the psychedelic effects caused when drinking ayahuasca open other realms not visibly detected within the reality of our closed minds (see plate 15).[40] The beings perceived in these extradimensional realms, accessed by psychogenic drugs, seem to be intelligent and offer another layer of mystery to the already puzzling topic of the alien question. The fact that everyone who takes ayahuasca will sooner or later come across some form of reptilian entity or projection proves that humans and reptiles are far more closely related than what we have been led to believe.[41]

The strong reptilian presence in our genetic memory has made the reptile/dragon or dinosaur image popular throughout the ages, including the twenty-first century, when these beliefs are broadcast worldwide over the Internet. Contemporary cinematic and graphic displays in pop culture, tied to the alien subtext phenomenon called the "reptilian agenda," have a tremendous fan following. The reptoid is featured in many popular movies, comics, and television programs, and while some of these appearances are imaginative and fun, others are clearly more sinister.

One of the most popular and innovative shows of the 1990s was *Dinosaurs,* a family program on ABC, set in 60,000,003 BCE and featuring a cast of intelligent, upright walking dinosaurs. Humans on the show were portrayed as dumb cave dwellers, whom the dinosaurs believed would never develop intelligence. The show revolved around the Sinclairs and is a stereotypical portrayal of the working-class American family. When Jim Henson developed the series, he wasn't thinking of typical Americana but rather taking a potshot at an ancient aristocratic and elite Scottish family, also known as the Sinclairs.

The Sinclairs own the famous oil company, whose gas stations have the dinosaur logo seen all over the world (see figure 6.18). Originally, their family name was St. Clair, and before changing their name they traced their ancestry to the Knights Templar. Although it's generally believed that at this point in history the Templars have ceased to exist, there is plenty of Templar symbolism found at the mysterious Rosslyn Chapel in Scotland to defy this assumption. Built by the Sinclair family, this chapel is a holy temple of the elites, showcasing images of cactus and corn decades before Columbus's first trip to the New World. The masons of this church obviously had knowledge far beyond what's historically

Figure 6.18. Sinclair logo, featuring a dinosaur, at a gas station in upstate New York. Courtesy of Doug Kerr.

accepted.[42] The founders of the Sinclair oil company were directly related to the ancient Templar builders of Rosslyn Chapel and the Earls of St. Clair, an aristocratic family that had dragons on the family crest.[43]

Jim Henson was a Hollywood insider, and there's reason to believe that he might have been blowing the whistle a little. The television show *Dinosaurs* was a huge success, but unfortunately, Henson never got to enjoy any of it. He died before it ever aired. His sudden death shocked fans around the world. Mysteriously, the day before he died he was negotiating a contract with the Disney Corporation (whose parent company is ABC) but refused to give up the rights to his much-loved creation *The Muppets*. Jim Henson died the next day, and Disney got the rights anyway.[44]

Other examples of reptilians or reptoids in pop culture are the Sleestaks of *Land of the Lost,* the evil King Koopa in the *Super Mario Brothers,* and the secret reptoid rulers that Hall of Fame wrestler Rowdy Roddy Piper sees when he puts on a special pair of sunglasses in *They Live.* Piper also fights for the survival of the human race against reptoid invaders in the cult classic *Hell Comes to Frogtown.* In *Enemy Mine* Dennis Quaid befriends the alien son of a reptilian pilot from the constellation Draco, where the invading enemies of humankind, known as Dracs, come from. In *Dreamscape,* another cheesy 1980s movie, Dennis Quaid gets caught up in a secret CIA psychic assassins experiment and ends up doing battle with a shape-shifting reptoid in the film's climactic fight scene. Dennis Quaid gets extra credit not only for starring in *Enemy Mine* and *Dreamscape* but also for completing his reptilian hat trick with *Dragonheart,* a film about a Templar's friendship with the last dragon from the constellation Draco.

Thulsa Doom, the evil shape-shifting villain in *Conan the Barbarian* (see plate 16), reigns as the shape-shifting Serpent King in a film filled with heavy reptilian and occult symbolism. The Narns are another reptoid species of warriors in the nerd-cherished television series *Babylon 5.* The most blatant show depicting the reptilian *and* New World Order agendas is unquestionably *V,* a no-holds-barred television psychological operation (psyop) that debuted to record ratings in 1983 and spawned a loathed remake in 2010 (see plate 17). There is a staggering amount of New World Order propaganda mixed in with prophetic warnings found in *V,* the original miniseries, its follow-up *V: the Final Battle,* and the short-lived nineteen-episode television series (with a budget of over $1 million per episode). Considering that the series is over thirty years old, it makes us wonder if an alien invasion scenario has been stalled or if it is indeed just around the corner.

In the comic book *The Amazing Spider-Man #6,* published in 1963, Dr. Curt Connors experiments with reptilian DNA in hopes of regenerating an arm he lost in the Vietnam War. His experiment works but with a disastrous side effect: it turns Connors into a reptilian humanoid monster. Connors would return as the lizard reptoid in later cartoon versions of *Spider-Man* and was even the main antagonist in the 2012 summer blockbuster movie starring Andrew Garfield.[45]

Other notable reptoids found in comic books are the Skrulls, a shape-shifting race of aliens who battled the *Fantastic Four;* Sauron, a ferocious humanoid pteranodon that battles the *X-Men;* and the *Teenage Mutant Ninja Turtles,* who resemble the Kappa of Japanese reptilian folklore, and in *Jake Long: American Dragon,* the main character shape-shifts from human into a dragon form. It's interesting to note that *long* is the Chinese term for "dragon."

Saurod and the Snake Men are all reptoid bad guys, hell-bent on destroying the planet Eternia and He-man in *The Masters of the Universe.* Slithe and the Lizard Men are enemies of the *Thundercats,* battling for supremacy on a planet that's ruled by a form of magic called "technology," amassed by an ancient mummy who lives in a pyramid. In the pilot episode of *Conan the Adventurer,* the evil Serpent Man plans on enslaving the human race and battles Conan for a mysterious sword made out of a "star metal" powerful enough to open portals and stargates between dimensions.[46] A race of reptoids created the all-important seven dragon balls in the popular Japanese cartoon *Dragon Ball Z,* and intelligent anthropomorphic dinosaur reptoids rule in the forgotten favorite *Dinosaucers.*

The most open nod to the reptilian agenda is found in perhaps the most popular animated program of the 1980s, *G.I. Joe,* a TV show that not only covers this topic but also spans the staggering animated blueprint of the New World Order's plan for global domination.[47] The main enemies of the righteous, freedom-loving Joes are the evil and shadowy group known as Cobra, an international cabal of bankers and egomaniacs striving to take over the world and bring it under the control of one government. The tactics they use to achieve this goal are fomenting wars and then selling arms to both sides of the conflict, staging false flag attacks, destroying famous landmarks, using various mind-control techniques, instilling a constant state of fear in the populace, installing puppet leaders and presidents, and manipulating stock markets.[48]

The leaders of this secret terrorist organization are Serpentor, a menacing reptoid super-soldier specifically built with advanced DNA, and Cobra Commander, another reptoid who hides his serpentine face under a reflecting silver facial shield and blue helmet (see plates 18 and 19). Cobra Commander traces his ancestry back to a secret underground civilization known as Cobra-La. It was this group of reptilian hybrids that had advanced scientific technology and once ruled the planet before being partially destroyed and having to go underground during the last ice age.[49] This was heavy-duty stuff in an animated program that always ended with positive and honorable messages, culminating in "And now you know, and knowing is half the battle."

There are plenty of other places where the reptilian agenda theme shows up in pop culture. The theories concerning the origin of such reptilian motifs are complex, and those advancing these theories add an exciting subculture of their own to the puzzling enigma of the followers of Hor, right into this century. Undeniably, the reptilian influence in both ancient and modern culture has been profound: it's encoded in our brain's genetic memory and accessed through psychogenic drugs that give rise to visions of extradimensional reptilian figures.

Rock icon and poet extraordinaire Jim Morrison famously declared, "I am the Lizard King. I can do anything.[50] His lyrics were inspired by an extradimensional encounter Morrison had with a lizard figure while tripping on mescaline in the hot desert sands of southern California. Jim Morrison believed the lizard was his totem and wrote an epic postapocalyptic poem in honor of the ancient snake called, not surprisingly, the "Celebration of the Lizard." This was originally planned to be recorded as the entire side 1 of an album but later split into performance pieces, poetry outtakes, and various songs.

Morrison loved snakes and had them as pets during certain points in his life. He also had a deep understanding of the bond we all share with reptiles, whether physical or extradimensional. He said:

I've always liked reptiles. I used to see the universe as a mammoth snake, and I used to see all the people and objects, landscapes, as little pictures in the facets of their scales. I think peristaltic motion is the basic life movement. Swallowing, digestion, the rhythms of sexual intercourse. We must not forget that the lizard and the snake are identified with the unconscious, with the forces of evil. There's something deep in the human memory that reacts very strongly to reptiles. Even if you've never seen one, the snake embodies everything we fear.[51]

It appears the most recent roots of this genetic fear of snakes took full effect after the last ice age, when floods destroyed the lush tropical lands of Egypt, wreaking havoc and turning wetlands into desert sands. The ancient predynastic cities were mostly destroyed, but some of the megalithic wonders, including the pyramid complex at Giza, remained. The Shemsu Hor, an ancient race of reptilian hybrids, dwindled in number during this stage but still possessed thousands of years of knowledge and experience, compared to the vastly primitive Egyptians, who lived simple lives thousands of years ago. The Shemsu Hor began to plant the seeds of our eventual modern-day world, but instead of molding a society that was fully creative, in tune with nature and using the pyramids as a tool to raise humanity's consciousness, as it had been in earlier ages, the remaining Shemsu Hor went the opposite route. This, perhaps, because the pyramids could no longer function as the machines they were meant to be.

The reasons for the turnaround are unclear. What we do know is that the Shemsu Hor morphed into the Brotherhood of the Snake and envisioned an easy rule and a smooth transition for guiding our future role as slaves to money. The Brotherhood of the Snake used the pharaohs as puppet rulers while wielding the real power behind the scenes. They advanced and built the Egyptian empire into a warrior nation, whose powerful military conquered distant lands with bloodshed and violence—a far cry from the original matriarchal teachings of the indigenous Egyptians.

7

CLOSE ENCOUNTERS
OF THUTMOSE III

It is no coincidence that the century of total war coincided with the century of central banking.

RON PAUL, AMERICAN PHYSICIAN, AUTHOR,
AND FORMER MEMBER OF CONGRESS

AFTER THE LAST GREAT FLOOD, the Shemsu Hor slowly began to rebuild their culture. It's likely that they survived for long periods underground and emerged sometime afterward to view the altered landscape. They would have noticed that the terrestrial civilization had a long way to go before reaching the high level of achievement their ancestors had enjoyed. Thousands of years passed, and life on Earth plodded along. During this time sub-Saharan Africa was dense with vegetation, and drawings of this tropical paradise adorned the cave walls at Tassili n'Ajjer, a mountain range in the Algerian regions of the Sahara Desert (see figure 7.1). Scenes on these walls depict strange animals and humans joined by unmistakable images of floating aliens wearing space-suits and helmets.

It appears that either the Shemsu Hor in Africa were able to re-create some of their lost technology from the pieces that survived or

Figure 7.1. Ancient horn-headed alien giant petroglyph (from 10,000 BCE), found in Tassili National Park, Algeria.

they were visited by other Shemsu Hor from different areas of the globe. It is also possible that an interstellar version of the Shemsu Hor or other alien species visited our planet after the cataclysm and made contact with the indigenous Shemsu Hor. Maybe this cataclysm was of universal proportions and affected other planets. If so, this would certainly draw the attention of intelligent alien species that might be monitoring the galaxy in a sort of space federation as depicted on *Star Trek* or merely out of curiosity. Plausible theories are endless and may seem too far out, but it's important to keep an open mind when analyzing an extremely ancient and crucial period in history.

The means by which the Shemsu Hor achieved their goal of regaining lost technology on Earth remains a mystery, but somehow they did so. Early in Egypt's eighteenth dynasty (1539–1295) they made their mark on human civilization. The human society that was developing in Egypt was beginning to emerge as a civilizing force. Similar cultures evolving near the Nile, in the greater Middle East, and in Asia were also developing at a rapid pace. The Egyptian empire prospered, and the pharaohs' obsession with the ancient gods was at an all-time high. Their ponderings about these mysterious forebears of civilization must have been similar to ours, since they weren't around during the original Golden Ages, either. And like us, all they had to guide them were bizarre myths and legends.

The Shemsu Hor infiltrated the Amun priesthood and, over time, slowly turned it into the Brotherhood of the Snake. The pharaoh who ruled Egypt during this time was Akhenaten's great-great-great grandfather, Thutmose III (1504–1426). This pharaoh possessed all the qualities of a great ruler, and more important to the Shemsu Hor, he seemed to be military minded—a big advantage if they planned on turning human society into patriarchal rule. This movement was stalled temporarily, largely due to the matriarchal reign of Queen Hatshepsut, a female monarch. Hatshepsut's era (1479–1458) was notable for its lack of wars, as she restored the original divine principles to Egyptian society. Her philosophy promoted worship of the creative mother principle; she also taught her subjects how to live in harmony with both the sacred feminine and the masculine dualities of human beings.[1] This ancient way of living and worship served no purpose to the Shemsu Hor. If we take a look around our current society, it still doesn't serve the purposes of the power elite.

Queen Hatshepsut was an obstacle to the Shemsu Hor, and she mysteriously "disappeared" during an outing one evening with Thutmose III, who eventually tried to chisel her out of history (see figure 7.2).

With the uncooperative Queen Hatshepsut out of the way, Thutmose III seized full power in Egypt. Thutmose came of age at the perfect time for the Shemsu Hor to orchestrate a spectacular aerial showing that would subjugate him and future pharaohs to the reptilian overlords. This defining moment in history (1482)—found in the annals of the Nile civilization—had a profound impact on Thutmose III and undoubtedly spooked the Egyptian people who witnessed the UFO encounter. This encounter is not only depicted in the walls of Karnak but also documented. The well-known Tulli Papyrus describes this event, which was recorded by the pharaoh's scribes during the eighteenth dynasty. This controversial document, originally part of the

Figure 7.2. Chiseled limestone bust of Hatshepsut.
Courtesy of Henri Chevrier.

Royal Annals of Thutmose III, has sparked countless debates within academic circles concerning its authenticity.

The original papyrus was written in hieratic, which is a simple style of cursive writing that was used for everyday purposes. The Italian-Russian Egyptologist, Prince Boris de Rachewiltz, an accomplished scholar and the heir of Ezra Pound's "vast library of rare medieval magick manuals,"[2] laboriously studied and translated the papyrus that he acquired, among other assorted documents and papers belonging to Professor Alberto Tulli.

Rachewiltz, in the 1930s one of the world's most sought-after Egyptologists, was the man responsible for saving this slice of forgotten history. He complained about the disastrous state of the papyrus, noting that both the beginning and ending were missing, along with several pieces of untranslatable text. With no expectations out of the ordinary, Rachewiltz stumbled into translating the eighteenth-dynasty UFO encounter. As soon as the translation was published, it was embroiled in controversy.

Professor Tulli was the director of the Vatican's Egyptian Museum, and it's likely he obtained the papyrus on the black market, since the Vatican has no official listing of its purchase. However, the Vatican has acknowledged its existence in response to an official inquiry, headed by Dr. Edward U. Condon, in a U.S. government–supported investigation into UFOs in 1966. Apparently, officials at the Pentagon were so curious about the Tulli Papyrus that they sent an inquiry to Dr. Walter Ramberg, the head scientist at the U.S. Embassy in Rome, asking for proof of its existence.

Ramberg replied with discouraging news:

> The current director of the Egyptian Section of the Vatican Museum, Dr. Nolli, said that Prof. Tulli had left all his belongings to a brother of his who was a priest in the Lateran Palace. Presumably the famous papyrus went to this priest. Unfortunately the priest died also in the meantime and his belongings were dispersed among heirs, who may have disposed of the papyrus as something of little value.[3]

Legend has it that Professor Tulli acquired the papyrus at a Cairo bazaar in 1934 from Phocion J. Tano, a respected antiquities dealer, and then asked Dr. Etienne Drioton at the Cairo Museum to translate the cursive hieratic text into simple hieroglyphics, a common practice that makes the document easier to read. Dr. Drioton would later be named director general of the Department of Egyptian Antiquities and would write several books on ancient Egypt that are still highly influential and referenced as authoritative works by esteemed scholars and authors. When Professor Tulli died in 1952, these translated documents came into the possession of his brother, Gustavo, who then handed them over to the distinguished Egyptologist Rachewiltz.

Phocion J. Tano, the man who originally sold Tulli the manuscripts, was the former proprietor of the Cairo Antiquities Gallery, and a renowned collector and student of history. Tano's many years of experience and his good standing within Cairo's academic circles would have been shattered if he had come within shouting distance of fake or hoax manuscripts. As a matter of fact, given the highly distinguished careers of everyone involved with the history of the Tulli Papyrus—Tulli, Tano, Drioton, Rachewiltz—it is doubtful any one of these men would have risked his reputation for a hoax that would not benefit any of them.

The main proponent of the hoax theory is an Italian professor, Franco Brussino, of no notable background, who claims that Tulli copied select pieces from Alan Gardiner's *Egyptian Grammar,* a book published in 1927. Brussino misses the point: many Tulli-like phrases are common and can be found by looking at the Budge translations from the *Book of the Dead,* which is more than likely where Gardiner got his source material. This has only added another layer to the cover-up,[4] considering that Brussino's case falls apart instantly when we question why anyone would fake a papyrus detailing close encounters of the third kind decades before the subject of UFOs was even considered.

The great lengths to which skeptics have gone to undermine the authenticity of the Tulli Papyrus are absurd and rather suspicious. Rachewiltz, the man responsible for translating the papyrus, was one of the foremost experts in Egyptology in his time. He authored several scholarly works that are still used in university curriculums today.

At the core of the mystery of the papyrus are the references it makes to Circles of Fire. This also happens to be the traditional glyph translation for *island* and is similar to the Hebrew translations of the nimbus or thundercloud, as discussed in previous chapters. These Circles of Fire, or islands, not only resemble solid formations—unlike circles, which have gaping holes—but also are located in the sky, high above the Egyptians, so these islands clearly have nothing to do with land-based, geographical formations.[5]

What the scribes witnessed were fiery disks blazing across the sky, high above the Egyptian people, who watched in stunned amazement. Thutmose III ordered that a description of this event be recorded for posterity. The encounter didn't end there. The number of disks began to increase as the days passed, eventually culminating in a large fleet of UFOs that hovered above the pharaoh's empire. Before this fleet disappeared into the southern horizon on a winter night more than 3,500 years ago, the commanders made contact with Pharaoh Thutmose III. When he met the gods of this space fleet at a private location in the desert, he was introduced to the Shemsu Hor and given the opportunity of a lifetime. But before they could be certain that Pharaoh Thutmose III was indeed the leader they had in mind, they had to make sure by initiating him into the mysterious ways of heaven.

This meant that Thutmose was given a ride by the Shemsu Hor into Earth's upper atmosphere, like other prophets before him; namely, Elijah and Enoch. Below is Rachewiltz's original translation of this bizarre event, first published in 1953:

> In the year 22 third month of winter, sixth hour of the day . . . the scribes of the House of Life found it was a circle of fire that was coming in the sky [though] it had no head, the breadth of its mouth [had] a foul odour. Its body 1 rod long [about 150 feet] and 1 rod large. It had no voice . . . Their hearts become confused through it, then they laid themselves on the bellies . . . They went to the King . . . ? to report it. His Majesty ordered . . . has been examined . . . as to all which is written in the papyrus-rolls of the House of Life His Majesty was meditating upon what happened. Now, after some days had passed over these things, Lo! They were more numerous than anything. They were shining in the sky more than the sun to the limits of the four supports of heaven. . . . Powerful was the position of the fire circles.[6]

The prominent anthropologist R. Cedric Leonard also translated the papyrus with similar results, yielding a more fluid translation:

In the year 22, of the third month of winter, sixth hour of the day . . . among the scribes of the House of Life it was found that a strange Fiery Disk was coming in the sky. It had no head. The breath of its mouth emitted a foul odor. Its body was one rod in length and one rod in width. It had no voice. It came toward His Majesty's house. Their heart became confused through it, and they fell upon their bellies. They [went] to the king, to report it. His Majesty [ordered that] the scrolls [located] in the House of Life be consulted. His Majesty meditated on all these events which were now going on. After several days had passed, they became more numerous in the sky than ever. They shined in the sky more than the brightness of the sun, and extended to the limits of the four supports of heaven . . . Powerful was the position of the Fiery Disks.[7]

Part of this encounter, found in the annals of Thutmose III, was written on the walls of Karnak and offers a firsthand narrative. Although the wall hieroglyphs are missing the portions relating to the fiery disks, the temple walls of Karnak do illustrate the pharaoh's meeting with the Shemsu Hor and the flight afterward. In the writings the pharaoh associates the Shemsu Hor with the sun god Ra because of the great technological magic they had performed for him.

In *Divine Encounters* Zecharia Sitchin describes the fateful meeting after "Amon-ra appeared in his glory from the horizon." Thutmose III arrived as the hand-picked future monarch of Egypt, chosen with some help from the Shemsu Hor's "working of miracles." Sitchin writes about the pharaoh's space odyssey, which made him "full with the understanding of the gods." This is mentioned briefly between numerous accounts of wars and plundering on the walls of Karnak:

He opened for me the doors of Heaven; He spread open for me its portals of horizon.

I flew up to the sky as a divine Falcon, able to see his mysterious form, which is in Heaven, that I might adore his majesty. [And] I saw the being-form of the Horizon God in his mysterious Ways of Heaven.[8]

Brad Steiger, the world-renowned author of the influential *Worlds before Our Own* and more than 170 other books, is probably the planet's most popular and beloved scribe of unexplained phenomena. Steiger says, "This encounter, which took place over 3,400 years ago, shows that aliens did not just recently start exploring our planet" and that "the report of Thutmose III proves that ancient astronauts visited Earth long ago."[9]

Another interesting aspect of the Tulli Papyrus is the similarities in prose style it shares with the book of Ezekiel, supposedly written nine hundred years later. Drawing on these similarities, we might posit that the Tulli Papyrus might have served as an inspiration to the Hebrew scribes who rewrote sections from the Annals of Thutmose III, replacing Egyptian characters with Jewish ones. Some examples of these prose similarities include:

Egyptian = Ezekiel
the House of Scribes = the House of Israel
was coming in the sky = the heavens were opened
it was a circle of fire = wheel of fire
it had no head = heads with four faces [everything had "four faces"]
It had no voice = I heard a voice that spake
toward the south = out of the north
the brightness of the sun = and a brightness was about it
His Majesty ordered . . . written in rolls = God spread a roll before
    me and it was written . . .
in the land of Egypt = I am against pharaoh, king of Egypt
Fishes . . . fell down from the sky = thee and all the fishes: thou
    shalt fall upon the open fields[10]

The main problem, of course, is that the Tulli Papyrus is nowhere to be found. Most likely, it is in private hands. This is the ultimate issue concerning this astounding document, which has been sought after by both scholars and officials at the highest levels of government.

After taking his flight and receiving the stamp of approval from the Shemsu Hor, Thutmose III catapulted to instant fame as a warmongering pharaoh. An accomplished charioteer, archer, athlete, and soldier, he organized huge armies that marched thousands of miles, obliterated his foes, and captured new lands and kingdoms. He has been compared to Napoleon and Alexander the Great as one of the few people in history to expand the borders of their empire to encompass the entire known world. Most certainly, he was aided in accomplishing this feat by the technology of the Shemsu Hor. Unlike Napoleon and Alexander the Great, Thutmose III never lost a battle nor was he poisoned to death while still in his prime (see plate 20). Through the course of sixteen military campaigns, Thutmose III conquered Palestine, Syria, and Nubia, and his impact on Egyptian culture was profound.

Thutmose III was seen as more than a pharaoh; he was celebrated in Egypt as a national hero. Egyptologists today regard him as the greatest pharaoh who ever lived. He created the largest empire seen in Egypt and attempted to erase all trace of the memory of Hatshepsut's brief return to matriarchal rule. He did all this while the Shemsu Hor quietly pulled the strings behind the curtains, like the wizards they were. While Thutmose III propelled his empire into a superpower, through wars and conquest, an advanced civilization sprang up in Egypt.

Thutmose III constructed over fifty new temples and built magnificent tombs and obelisks, showcasing the sophisticated craftsmanship that suddenly evolved during his reign. During this era groundbreaking advances were made in art and design, including astounding works of relief architecture, sculpture, painting, and glass making, all of which stand apart from the works of previous pharaohs (see plate 21). This swift leap forward points to the Shemsu Hor and the Golden Age knowledge they alone had. This knowledge gave them full control of the destiny of Egypt—or so they thought.

Through the spoils of war and the reign of their puppet ruler, Thutmose III, the Shemsu Hor created a wealthy society that began to use gold and silver instead of the usual barter system of disposable goods and agricultural resources.[11] These victories allowed the Brotherhood of the Snake to establish a central banking system, carefully disguised beneath the rule of the Amun priesthood. The founding of this central bank—fronted by the priesthood and run behind the scenes by the Brotherhood of the Snake, a.k.a. the Shemsu Hor—was the watershed moment in the reign of Thutmose III. This central bank helped work out the kinks in the banking system and established the blueprint for how society was to be run in the postdiluvian world.

The Shemsu Hor began setting up their new empire by taking over the Amun priesthood and installing pharaohs who served as puppet rulers. This bit of theater got the people to believe that power rested in the hands of the pharaoh, not the priests. They never knew that the real rulers were behind the scenes. This is a time-tested practice that keeps citizens under tight control by letting them believe they, or their leaders, hold the reins, when another entity is actually pulling the strings behind the scenes.

Over time, the celebrated Thutmose III died and was replaced by another puppet pharaoh who continued the practice of expanding borders, central banking, and patriarchal rule. The Shemsu Hor operated behind the pharaoh's throne while the Amun priesthood blossomed into the dominant power of ancient Egypt.

A hundred years went by, and society flourished, as the various pharaohs who succeeded Thutmose III played out their roles according to the Shemsu Hor script. The Brotherhood of the Snake's plan of total domination was going smoothly until a pesky child prodigy came along. Developing conscientious opinions and ideas that didn't accord with the Brotherhood of the Snake's plans, this particular pharaoh grew up to be a royal pain to the establishment and sparked a civil war so intense that what we call our modern world was born from its ashes.

8

AKHENATEN VERSUS THE BROTHERHOOD OF THE SNAKE

There's a plot in this country to enslave every man, woman, and child. Before I leave this high and noble office, I intend to expose this plot.

PRESIDENT JOHN F. KENNEDY,
SEVEN DAYS BEFORE HE WAS MURDERED
ON NATIONAL TELEVISION

BEFORE AKHENATEN BEGAN HIS QUEST to develop what is known as the first monotheistic culture in recorded history, the Brotherhood of the Snake was the unchallenged authority of Egypt. They governed the people through politics and religion, respectively; that is, through puppet pharaohs and the Amun priesthood. They molded, shaped, and reshaped the world at their whim and experimented with the antediluvian knowledge that was now their legacy. The crocodile-headed god Sobek secretly represented the Brotherhood of the Snake and was worshipped alongside Ra as a deity of creation.

Sobek, a god associated with Egyptian creation myths, was said to have been the first to emerge from the water of chaos, and he is thought

*Figure 8.1. Aamerut praying to the reptilian god Sobek.
Courtesy of Rama.*

to have helped build and destroy previous civilizations.[1] Sobek was initially associated with fertility, but during the reign of the Brotherhood of the Snake, he became known as a mighty military deity and his name was added as a suffix on receipts related to precious metals, minerals, and money (see figure 8.2). Even the origin of the word *messiah* stems from Sobek and his reptilian relatives, sometimes referred to as either messeh or mus-hus. As noted in *The Dragon Legacy*:

It was from the practice of kingly anointing with the fat of the messeh that the Hebrew verb *mashiach* [to anoint] derived, and the Dragon dynasty became known as Messiahs [anointed ones].[2]

Figure 8.2. Sobek. Courtesy of Hedwig Storch.

The Brotherhood of the Snake made sure their ancient genealogies survived the progression of millennia by having symbols of their existence embedded in our awareness. Their mark can still be found on the caduceus rod that's encircled by two snakes on the seal of the American Medical Association. It is no coincidence that the pharmaceutical industry, comprising the biggest and most powerful corporate conglomerates in the world, cleverly assigns the R_x tag to every bag or bottle of medicine we buy. Though it's supposed to mean "treatment" and is used as a doctor's shorthand scribble, R_x represents the eye of Horus and is pronounced "Rex," which is the ancient meaning of the word *king* or *monarch*.[3] This is another clue to who really rules the world.

The Brotherhood of the Snake ran Egypt during the eighteenth dynasty, a time of exceptional cultural advancements. Imagine their shock when one of their own turned on them and threatened to expose their fraudulent system. This individual has become the most misunderstood and controversial figure in all of history, with a life so mired in disinformation and complicated truths that he remains the world's hardest puzzle to solve. Of all the characters in the past, one man stands out like a sore thumb. At times he has been called Akhnaton, Ikhnaton, Amenophis, or Amenhotep IV, but to most he is simply known as Akhenaten.

Figure 8.3. Casting of Akhenaten's head found in the workshop of the sculptor Djehutimes at Amarna. The original is in the Egyptian Museum in Cairo. The photo was taken at VAM Design Center, Budapest, at the Treasures exhibition. Courtesy of HoremWeb.

He's more popular than ever, thanks to the conspiracy theories of "Freeman," a researcher who correctly predicted the terrorist attacks of 9/11. Freeman claims that President Barack Obama was cloned in a laboratory from the DNA of Pharaoh Akhenaten. Freeman's fantastically wild DVD, *Obama Cloning and the Coming Space War,* is informative, funny, and utterly original.[4] One can't type Akhenaten's name into a search engine anymore without inevitably crossing paths with Obama and links that lead to YouTube footage showing them merging together, forming the grandest of conspiracies. This so-called conspiracy becomes even more bizarre when we examine the ancient representations of Akhenaten's family and the striking similarities they share with Obama's clan. Placing reproductions side by side, Michelle Obama looks exactly like Akhenaten's mother, Queen Tiye, and the Obamas' two daughters, Malia and Sasha, resemble Akhenaten's daughters by Nefertiti. This odd bit of pop culture only makes Akhenaten's legacy even more confounding.

Born as the youngest son of Amenhotep III and his chief queen, Tiye, and named Amenhotep IV, this young man grew up in the royal palace with no expectations of being a future ruler, since that job had already been promised to his older brother, Crown Prince Thutmoses, a high priest of Memphis.[5] The historical records of Amenhotep IV's youth are so sketchy that we know almost nothing about his early days. However, he appears to have been the black sheep of the family.

It's possible that the future pharaoh inherited genetic memories of matriarchal philosophies taught before the age of the warrior pharaoh who dominated Egypt at the time of his birth. He had four sisters and was close to his mother. Perhaps they played a key role in shaping his views, which must have been looked down upon by his combatant pharaoh father and his Shemsu Hor–worshipping older brother. Amenhotep IV was never shown in any family portraits, and there is no record of his attending any public events with his father, Pharaoh Amenhotep III, a man known as "the magnificent," whose forty-year reign was characterized by unbridled prosperity and artistic grandiosity, as well as by wars as he was influenced by the Shemsu Hor.

Figure 8.4. Relief of King Amenhotep III in limestone. Theben West, New Kingdom, eighteenth dynasty, ca. 1360 BCE. His features aren't elongated, as Akhenaten's were, and there are snakes interwoven in his headdress. Egyptian Museum, Berlin. Courtesy of Andreas Praefcke.

Amenhotep III was responsible for the groundbreaking temple building during Egypt's peak as an artistic and international powerhouse. He was the Shemsu Hor's favorite pharaoh, and they must have shared with him the secrets of Golden Age megalithic building. We can draw this conclusion because Amenhotep III is credited with constructing the massive pylon and colonnade extensions found at the temples of Karnak and Luxor, the Colossi of Memnon statues, and, most likely, the unfinished obelisk at Aswan (see figures 8.5 and 8.6).[6]

These granite blocks, some weighing over four hundred tons apiece, would be impossible to duplicate today. This means that either these

Figure 8.5. Colossi of Memnon, guarding the passage to
the Theban necropolis. West Bank section of Luxor, Egypt.
Courtesy of Przemyslaw Idzkiewicz.

Figure 8.6. This unfinished obelisk is the largest known ancient obelisk
located in Aswan. Courtesy of Olaf Tausch.

works were constructed before the floods or that Egyptian high priests, under the guidance of the Shemsu Hor, shared these advanced building secrets with Amenhotep III. No matter what the truth is, there they stand in defiance of our theories. When Amenhotep III died of what most experts believe were natural causes, Egypt was at the peak of its power and dominated the international landscape as the most respected and feared country in the known world.

No one knows how Amenhotep IV felt about his father's death, nor is it known how his brother, Thutmoses, died unexpectedly shortly thereafter. These sudden departures wound up leaving the throne in the hands of the impressionable Amenhotep IV, a young man who seemingly didn't want anything to do with the responsibility of being pharaoh. The deaths of Amenhotep III and his eldest son, Thutmoses, meant nothing to the Brotherhood of the Snake, since they maintained control of the political and religious power centers through the Amun priesthood. They saw the mental and charismatic potential that the young pharaoh possessed and figured the people of Egypt would easily accept the new ruler.

Amenhotep III's younger son had no choice but to step into his father's shoes, even if these were big ones, and he became the tenth pharaoh of the eighteenth dynasty. Things were going fine for the Brotherhood; the first few years of Amenhotep IV's reign passed without incident. He was a favorite of the Egyptian people, and the young pharaoh's charisma, the likes of which had never been seen before, made him the world's first teenage celebrity. But despite the easy living and fanfare, something happened to the young boy-king that made him change his mind about everything.

It's assumed that his relationship with Nefertiti blossomed during this time and that he began to carefully examine what was going on behind the scenes of the Amun priesthood. Had he figured out the great game? Did Nefertiti and members of her mysterious bloodline persuade the pharaoh that he was the real ruler and not the priesthood? Did he have genetic memories of past Golden Ages, and did he realize that the

Amun priests weren't using the sacred knowledge for the proper reasons? These questions have haunted historians for over 150 years and, unless we can develop a time machine, it's likely we'll never know the true answer to these questions.

What we do know is that during Amenhotep IV's early reign as pharaoh, Egypt was the richest nation on Earth, and most of this wealth was controlled by the Amun priesthood. The priesthood represented a form of organized religion, using the Egyptian deities as tools to sow fear and enslave the population.[7] The more deities to worship the better, meaning there would be more things to buy and, of course, more things to create. Since religion was the "big business" of the time, it's likely that over 75 percent of the Egyptian population earned their living in connection with the worship of gods.

The practice of buying different statues and spells for the purpose of protection or the guarantee of a nice spot in the afterlife was a popular and much encouraged tactic that kept the riches flowing into the hands of the Amun priesthood. The ancient religious practice of instilling fear into a population worried about their souls, in order to acquire money from them, is a profitable one that has been repeated throughout history. This tradition may go unimpeded for ages, but no matter how well organized the plan is, the unknown element may throw a wrench in the works. For instance, the German Martin Luther rebelled against the Catholic Church in the 1500s for selling salvation certificates by defiantly nailing his challenge to this practice on the church's front door.[8] This bold act shook up the religious power structure and caused a wave of paradigm shattering and bloodshed. The young Amenhotep IV did something similar in ancient Egypt.

Making the brash move to take the power out of the hands of the Amun priesthood, Amenhotep IV changed his name to Akhenaten, meaning "Amun is satisfied" or "Effective spirit of Aten," and began to close down the temples run by the Brotherhood of the Snake. Intent on restoring the religion of predynastic Egypt, in which the people worship only the Sun, Akhenaten disregarded the other deities; these were

Figure 8.7. This stone block, which portrays Akhenaten as a sphinx, was originally found in the city of Amarna. This object is now located in the Kestner Museum in Hanover, Germany. Courtesy of Hans Ollermann.

important to the Amun priesthood only as revenue streams. This radical shift in thinking shocked the Brotherhood of the Snake and threatened to put them out of business for good. Knowing the danger his actions posed to his life, Akhenaten began taking steps to get as far away as possible from the Amun priesthood. He decided to establish an entirely new metropolis for himself called Horizon of the Aten, now known as Amarna, a city constructed halfway between Memphis and Thebes.

The celebrated biographer Arthur Weigall wrote the first and most influential biography of Akhenaten in 1910 and imagined how the young pharaoh must have seen the lands belonging to the future site of Amarna:

> Down the river it would seem that the young pharaoh now sailed in his royal dahabiyeh, looking to right and left as he went, now inspecting this site and now examining that. At last he came upon a place that suited his fancy to perfection. It was situated about 160

miles above the modern Cairo. At this point the limestone cliffs upon the east bank leave the river and recede for about three miles, returning to the water some five or six miles farther along. Thus a bay is formed which is protected on its west side by the river in which there lies a small island, and in all other directions by the crescent of the cliffs. Upon the island he would erect pavilions and pleasure-houses. Along the edge of the river there was a narrow strip of cultivated land whereon he would plant his palace gardens, and those of the nobles' villas. Behind this verdant band the smooth desert stretched, and here he would build the palace itself and the great temples. Behind this again, the sand and gravel surface of the wilderness gently sloped up to the foot of the cliffs, and here there would be roads and causeways whereon the chariots might be whirled in the early mornings. In the face of the cliffs he would cut his tomb and those of his followers; and at intervals around the crescent of these hills he would cause great boundary stones to be made, so that all men might know and respect the limits of his city. What splendid quays would edge the river, what palaces reflect their whiteness in its waters! There would be broad shaded avenues, and shimmering lakes surrounded by the fairest trees of Asia. Temples would raise their lofty pylons to the blue skies, and broad courts should lie stretched in the sunlight. In Akhnaton's youthful mind there already stood the temples and the mansions; already he heard the sound of sweet music.[9]

During the fifth year of his reign, Akhenaten began building Amarna in hopes of establishing a treasury for the Egyptian state based on the country's private reserves of gold. This would take the source of the financial power away from the Amun priesthood, essentially putting an end to their central banking scheme.

Let the chronicles of history show that Pharaoh Akhenaten was the first revolutionary to challenge the powers of the banking establishment. Akhenaten dismantled the Old World Order that had been in

Figure 8.8. Small Temple of Aten at Tell el-Amarna.
Courtesy of Einsamer Schütze.

place for over a thousand years and confiscated the wealth of the Amun priesthood, closing their temples and leaving most abandoned and in ruins. During his reign, he also began to wipe out the gods associated with the Amun priesthood and obliterated hundreds of images of deities found on temple walls, obelisks, and tombs.

While at Amarna, Akhenaten established a cult based on Aten, the sun god Ra, and made the official logo a rayed disk with outstretched hands of sunbeams. The arts at Amarna flourished, and for a few years Akhenaten, Nefertiti, and the royal family enjoyed a private renaissance of art and thought in their personal Camelot beneath the scorching Sun. Akhenaten attempted to usher in a new Golden Age, based on the knowledge he gained from the Shemsu Hor, genetic memories, or from his personal gut feeling that what was going on was not the way things were supposed to be.

What sets him apart from most people in history is that when he encountered evil, he didn't choose to make a backroom deal to benefit himself, but rather confronted it head-on. Plus, he was pharaoh. He already had it all—and discarded the material for ideals and principles.

It's likely that Akhenaten was truly the last man who understood the Golden Age secrets of the universe—secrets like free energy, antigravity, stargates, wormholes, and quantum mathematic theories that we're still searching to understand.

But while Akhenaten attempted to impart and communicate these ancient secrets, the streets of Egypt were tossed into anarchy and disarray. According to author and theologian Ralph Ellis:

> Egypt had been a relatively stable society for thousands of years, both before and after this rebel pharaoh, the capital cities, temples, gods, arts, and social grades of the empire had changed little. Akhenaton would change them all. His whole career was out of the ordinary.[10]

While Akhenaten and Nefertiti were being depicted on groundbreaking art within the confines of Amarna, the outside world was in tumult. By upsetting the long-established balance of power between the priesthood and the pharaoh, Akhenaten plunged the country into massive unemployment and was no longer viewed as a charismatic leader, but rather as a sadistic dictator. His life was now in danger not only from the Brotherhood of the Snake but also from Egypt's general population. As the years passed, armed military guards heavily surrounded Akhenaten's Amarna, a city transformed into an isolated compound.

As his reign entered its twelfth year, the people were extremely disillusioned with their pharaoh, now viewing him as an evil villain or a "heretic king,"[11] resulting in large expressions of public unrest.

Akhenaten might have been an amazing artist, poet, and philosopher, but he wasn't a ruler. Toward the end of his reign, for the first time in Egyptian history, his cabinet was not composed of priests, but entirely of army generals:

> It is apparent that during the Eighteenth Dynasty the personnel surrounding the king included a significant number of high-ranking army officers . . . A central feature of Akhenaton's government is

Figure 8.9. Akhenaten, Nefertiti, and their children.
Courtesy of Gerbil.

that his immediate entourage was drawn directly from the military . . . If we take the reliefs at face value, then it could be argued that the city of Akhenaton was virtually an armed camp! Large platoons march at double speed, or stand at ease, and it is noticeable that these forces are never very far away from the figure of Akhenaton. There are soldiers under arms standing in front of the palaces and the temples, and in the watchtowers which border the city.[12]

While Akhenaten continued his reign under heavy military protection, the rest of Egypt wasted away, due to the upheaval caused by ousting the Amun priesthood:

The temples of the gods and goddesses, beginning from Elephantine down to the marshes of the Delta, had fallen into neglect. Their shrines had fallen into desolation and become terraces overgrown with weeds. Their sanctuaries were as if they had never been. Their halls were a trodden path. The land was in confusion.[13]

And from the Stele of Tutankhamen, discovered in Karnak in 1905 and translated in 1923 by E. A. Wallis Budge:

> The whole country was in a state of chaos, similar to that in which it had been in primeval times [i.e., at the Creation]. From Abu [Elephantine] to the Swamps [of the Delta] the properties of the temples of the gods and goddesses had been destroyed, their shrines were in a state of ruin and their estates had become a desert. Weeds grew in the courts of the temples. The sanctuaries were overthrown and the sacred sites had become thoroughfares for the people. The land had perished, the gods were sick unto death, and the country was set behind their backs.[14]

Akhenaten sent the military out to gather resources and make sure the Amun priesthood had been run into the ground. Unfortunately, these unmatriarchal tactics were necessary if Akhenaten's determination to end the Amun priesthood were to be taken seriously. However, when fighting fire with fire, those participating in the fight eventually get burned. Military corruption intensified, and commando raids of terror swept across Egypt in Akhenaten's name:

> The temple walls were mutilated by the Atenites, the priesthoods were driven out, and all temple properties were confiscated and applied to the propagation of the cult of Aten. The figures of the great gods that were made of gold and other precious metals in the shrines were melted down, and thus the people could not consult their gods in their need, for the gods had no figures wherein to dwell, even if they wished to come upon the Earth. There were no priests left in the land, no gods to entreat, no funeral ceremonies could be performed, and the dead had to be laid in their tombs without the blessing of the priests.[15]

Figure 8.10. Scarab showing a pharaoh executing the enemy. Courtesy of Henry Walters.

By eliminating the power of the Amun priesthood, levying taxes upon the people, and emptying the coffers of Egypt to pay for the construction of his dream city and other Theban temples, Akhenaten bankrupted and ruined Egypt. But he did accomplish his goal of crushing the Brotherhood of the Snake and the Amun priesthood. Akhenaten effectively destroyed an integrated system of politics, economics, family banking dynasties, and religion that had been entrenched in Egypt for at least seventeen hundred years.

His actions are comparable to Jesus's, when he stormed the temples of Jerusalem and kicked out the moneychangers or bankers, but on a grander scale, since Akhenaten was a ruler. Another similarity the Bible shares with Akhenaten is Psalm 104, which is an almost exact copy of a hymn to Ra that Akhenaten wrote when he was twenty-one years old. Preserved from the Papyrus of Hu-nefer, Akhenaten's hymn left biblical archaeologists who recognized the similarities with Psalm 104 astounded, since it is in conflict with the belief that the Bible was written as the true and only word of God. Psalm 104 stands out as the only passage in the Bible that ascribes to the Lord characteristics of the Sun.[16] The fact that Akhenaten's poetry can still be found in one of the world's most popular books is a testament to his principled and swift mind and how far ahead of the times he truly was.

Unfortunately, being misunderstood is the fate of all true genius and not only was Akhenaten misunderstood, he also had a sizable bounty placed on his head. It was only a matter of time before the hangman came to collect. More than fifteen years after Akhenaten began his revolution, he found himself isolated and alone to face the uncertain end of his reign in Amarna. Nefertiti's disappearance[17] during the final years of his reign suggests that Akhenaten sent her away to foreign lands in order to save his family. It's likely that the beautiful Nefertiti served as the inspiration of the future myths of Mary Magdalene and the bloodlines of the Holy Grail (see plate 22).

It's also probable that Akhenaten's story eventually morphed into the Hebrew tale of Moses. However, it is wrong to assume that Akhenaten was Moses, as some thinkers, like Sigmund Freud, propose.[18] Why? Because instead of fleeing to the desert in an exodus, Akhenaten stayed in Amarna. He had built the city and empire in an ultimate act of rebellion, and despite feeling the noose tightening around his neck, he remained there to the end.

All his youthful dreams and arrogance came full circle to crush his naïve heart:

> It was an era which, though starting off well enough, had degenerated rapidly into mayhem and widespread religious persecution, an orgy of wanton destruction and almost total economic collapse. For the events he set in train, Akhenaten could never be forgiven: with a ruthlessness not seen in Egypt before or since, Amarna, both as a city and a concept, was razed and all trace of Pharaoh's existence systematically expunged.[19]

Akhenaten's vision of a future Egypt free from the clutches of the Brotherhood of the Snake was an illusion. His kingdom crumbled, and Hittite warriors took advantage of the chaos, swooping down on

Egypt, violently sacking towns, and conquering the pharaoh's outposts in Syria and Palestine. As his empire was decimated by foreign invaders Akhenaten did nothing to stop the assault. Heartbreaking pleas from generals, asking for help, can be read in the Amarna Letters, transcribed from a series of clay tablets that are some of the most important surviving relics from the Amarna era. Akhenaten ignored the cries for help, already knowing that his reign was over and there was nothing left worth fighting for.

His revolution failed:

> The tribute having ceased, the Egyptian treasury soon stood empty, for the government of the country was too confused to permit of the proper gathering of the taxes, and the working of the gold-mines could not be organized. Much had been expended on the building of the City of Horizon, and now the King knew not where to turn for money. In the space of a few years Egypt had been reduced from a world power to the position of a petty state, from the richest country known to man to the humiliating condition of a bankrupt kingdom. Surely one may picture Akhnaton now in his last hours, his jaw fallen, his sunken eyes widely staring, as the full realisation of the utter failure of all his hopes came to him.[20]

Knowing that his final hour might be near, Akhenaten commissioned statues and busts of him, showing large, bizarrely slanted eyes and elongated facial characteristics. Some of these representations of Akhenaten feature clear serpentine traits that are unique in the artistic representation of the pharaohs. Images found in the Amarna art records depict the members of his royal family with distended and elongated skulls. Most scholars assume that they must all have been suffering the symptoms of Marfan syndrome, a rare genetic disorder of the connective tissues that strengthen the body's bone structure. But considering that Akhenaten's bloodline stemmed from either the Hyksos or another unknown foreign ruling influence, and was not entirely Egyptian,

Figure 8.11. Akhenaten. This rare bust was discovered in Karnak and is now at the Cairo museum. Courtesy of José-Manuel Benito.

there's a good chance that they might have inherited these elongated features from their ancient alien relatives.

It is also possible that Akhenaten was a descendent of the Shemsu Hor. After all, the circuitous manner in which he rose to the throne of

Figure 8.12. Another likeness of Akhenaten. Courtesy of Paul Mannix.

Egypt leaves open a door to speculation, as does the bold way in which he felt justified in demolishing the Brotherhood of the Snake cult. He may have descended from another form of humanoid species that survived in small numbers after the floods.

No matter where his roots lay, Akhenaten was a man out of time, born to communicate a story of good versus evil thousands of years after his revolution near the Nile. Despite his strange, alien-esque features, found throughout the artistic remains in Amarna, it's more than likely that Akhenaten, a man capable of writing deep poetry, was more human than we will ever know.

By divine chance, Akhenaten called for "living in truth"[21] and figured out things the rest of the world had either forgotten or didn't care about. This knowledge made him dangerous to the Shemsu Hor. But because he had the courage to flaunt this knowledge in their faces and abruptly attempt to put them out of business, he became a target for assassination. He managed to have an excellent family life in a fabricated society that created the world's most groundbreaking art for at least ten years—that is an absolute miracle. Seeing his family thrive in his beautiful city and knowing he defeated the Brotherhood of the Snake, if only for a brief moment in time, brought him great joy and offered hope to humanity that a better life was possible.

His palaces were raided, and his army had turned against him. With no regrets, he waited for the butchers to eventually storm Amarna and chop off his head. Akhenaten's body perished in the unknown sands of the Egyptian desert. Considering how much the people and the Shemsu Hor hated him, it's not surprising that no evidence of his body survived. This once-great pharaoh, who tried to bring back the indigenous teachings, was left for dead without a tomb or burial relics.

But Egyptology tries to teach that Akhenaten's body was found in tomb KV55 in 1907 and that he's actually Tutankhamen's father! These are the usual sleight-of-hand magic tricks with doctored-up "proof" that Egyptologists like to pass off as the truth so that we do not stumble, even by accident, across what really happened.

It makes sense that before the Shemsu Hor came to kill him, Akhenaten wanted the world to know the true face of these ancient reptilian overlords, so he had sculptures of his face carved with serpentine features. That these relics even survive is another miracle, as all of Akhenaten's images and any works pertaining to him or his family were obsessively erased from history. His temples were demolished and his throne was passed on to other pharaohs, who immediately

Figure 8.13. Interior of a tomb at Amarna. Notice the advanced architecture in a city that supposedly was constructed in only five years. From Gaston Maspero, History of Egypt, *vol. 5.*

restored the gods of the Amun priesthood and handed power back to the Brotherhood of the Snake.

His bloodline in Egypt would ultimately be destroyed as well, and his ideas of one sun god or son of god would sleep soundly for another thousand years before morphing into modern Christianity. Flinders Petrie, one of the original excavators and discoverers of Amarna and a person responsible for shedding light on Akhenaten's legacy, summed up the man beautifully:

> His affection is the truth and as the truth he proclaims it. Here is a revolution in ideas! No king of Egypt, nor in any part of the world has ever carried out his honesty of expression so openly . . . Thus in every line Akhenaten stands out as perhaps the most original thinker that ever lived in Egypt, and one of the great idealists of the world.[22]

Akhenaten lost the battle, but he won the war, for the art that he left behind is truthful and the third eye cannot be fooled because the truth is in the art. The Brotherhood of the Snake returned to power in the wake of Akhenaten's death and slowly began to steer the course of history to their projected path, minus the slight delay caused by the young rebel pharaoh.

Over time the Brotherhood split into different warring factions and eventually spawned the Knights Templars, the Freemasons, and

Figure 8.14. Akhenaten. Courtesy of Gérard Ducher.

the Knights of Malta, among other secret orders. At this point the Brotherhood of the Snake is represented through the works of the Illuminati, a collection of elite families and a committee of three hundred[23] involved in banking and corporate dominance with the goals of bringing about the New World Order ruled by a form of global government. The large number of Egyptian symbols used by these Illuminati fronts are clues to understanding just how far back these rulers go. Although they are still in control at most levels through bloodlines, it's not likely that any of the reptoid traits or features have survived.

Professor Walter Emery, an archaeologist with over forty years of field research experience found evidence that the Shemsu Hor existed in northern Egypt. Emery made a strange discovery one day while digging in Saqqara in the 1930s. After spending weeks excavating in the dry desert air, Emery cleared off the dirt and stared down at skeletons that immediately challenged everything he had been taught about ancient Egypt.

A speaker of five languages and internationally renowned, the maverick French Egyptologist Antoine Gigal writes that, by a stroke of luck, Emery

found in certain tombs the remains of people who lived in predynastic times in the north of Upper Egypt. The features of these

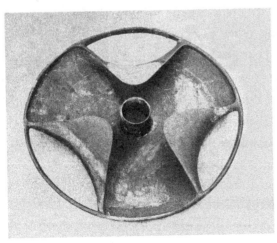

Figure 8.15. In addition to the skulls, Emery also discovered the infamous tri-lobed "schist" bowl—further evidence of highly advanced technology—near where he unearthed the skulls. From Walter B. Emery, Great Tombs of the First Dynasty, *vol. I, 1949.*

bodies and skeletons are incredible. The skulls are of abnormal size and are dolichocephalic, i.e. the cranium as seen from above is oval, and is about 25 percent longer than it is wide. Some skulls show no sign of the usual sutures. The skeletons are larger than the average for the area and especially the skeletal frame is broader and heavier. He did not hesitate to identify them with the "Followers of Horus" and found that in their lifetime they filled an important priestly role. With regard to the long-headed skulls, it seems that it is not a prehistoric lineage of evolution but rather a lineage coming from a cycle of civilization from before the Flood. It is therefore asserted that there once existed an antediluvian race that has been found here and there all over the world, a race that had a naturally elongated conical skull.[24]

More links to the mysterious Shemsu Hor were found in Iraq at an archaeological site dubbed Tell Arpachiyah, a prehistoric city situated about five miles from Nineveh. It was excavated in 1933 by Max Mallowan and his mystery novel–writing wife Agatha Christie. The pair sifted through numerous graves of the strange Halaf and Ubaid. These two ancient neolithic cultures can be dated as far back as 4600 BCE, and like Emery's discovery in Egypt, some skeletons of the Ubaid had strange, elongated skulls.[25]

The Ubaid cemetery and the surrounding archaeological area revealed other astonishing relics associated with the Shemsu Hor, including pottery with serpent-headed women and the most bizarre of all ancient statues—figurines with clear reptoid facial features and elongated skulls (see plate 23). But the mystery of these misshapen skulls isn't only peculiar to the Shemsu Hor; it also applies to Akhenaten's family, depicted in the odd images, busts, and sculptures left behind, revealing a legacy of elongated skulls (see plate 24).

9

THE ENIGMA OF
ELONGATED SKULLS

If I was educated, I'd be a damn fool.

BOB MARLEY, REGGAE ARTIST

THANKFULLY, AKHENATEN'S ENTIRE LEGACY was not destroyed after his battle with the Brotherhood of the Snake. His saga is unique in the annals of history. He left behind a remarkable collection of art and lavishly illustrated temple walls depicting the daily lives of his family. These carved and painted images are different by several orders of magnitude from all other known Egyptian art forms. Akhenaten's six daughters were shown, as they were seen in their day, with extended, elongated skulls. The adults also had elongated skulls but were usually shown with hats and headdresses that covered them. Experts believe they have uncovered at least two busts of his six offspring.

Although the experts can't agree as to which bust represents who, they do agree that, of the two busts found, one is Akhenaten's eldest daughter Meritaten. These busts have come to be known as the Princesses of Amarna and are testaments to the events that transpired during this period in Egypt's ancient past. Meritaten was certain to replace her mother Nefertiti as queen of the two lands and was

Akhenaten's favorite daughter. Before his death, he elevated her status as "chief wife"[1] in a symbolic marriage. Akhenaten was desperate for male heirs and hoped his daughters might provide his fading dynasty with them. In an interesting twist of fate, this pharaoh, who forcibly attempted to turn the cycle of ages back toward the matriarchal system, bore royal daughters, who bore still more royal daughters.

On a temple wall relief, Meritaten is shown marrying a man who is presumably Nubian Prince Smenkhkare. In appearance he has a normal human head, compared with Meritaten's elongated skull (see plate 25).

The other bust is believed to be Meketaten, best known for sitting on her mother Nefertiti's lap, basking under the rays of the sun disk's outstretched hands (see plate 26).

King Tut is the most famous member of Amarna's royal family, and he too has an elongated skull. Scholars downplay this significantly, and on television documentaries about Tut this fact is not mentioned. Another disputed topic of discussion that mainstream Egyptologists would rather not talk about is who King Tut's father actually was. They claim an obscure, tiny inscription found on a chiseled piece of granite is proof that Akhenaten was his father.[2] This even though King Tut is never shown on wall reliefs or in sculptures with Akhenaten, Nefertiti, Tiye, or the princesses. In fact, there's not even a word about him before he unceremoniously took control of the throne of Egypt.

Some scholars believe the deformities found in Akhenaten's family during the Amarna period are associated with the genetic defects of Marfan syndrome, a disorder of the connective tissues that strengthen the body's bone structure. This rare gene disorder affects the cardiovascular system, eyes, and skin but doesn't actually distend the skull to the point of elongation. Other academics relate the elongated skulls and the asexual appearance of Akhenaten to artistic exaggerations with limitless, unchecked creative license—a first of its kind. While art in the Amarna period did flourish tremendously, elongated skulls and images of strange people wearing cone-shaped hats and headdresses have been found in countries and civilizations both near and far from Egypt.[3]

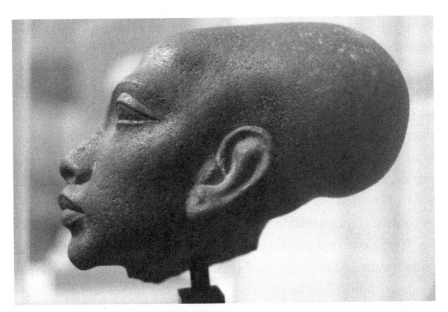

Figure 9.1. Head of the statue of a princess, one of the six daughters of Akhenaten and Nefertiti, eighteenth dynasty, c. 1350 BCE. Courtesy of Manfred Werner.

Even Hollywood screenwriter Aaron Sorkin couldn't have written a better thriller-mystery than the saga of the Starchild skull. Its circuitous plot begins in the dusty plains of the impoverished Southwest, where an American teenage girl, a native of El Paso, made an extraordinary discovery in the 1930s while visiting relatives in Mexico. After hiking during the morning hours south of Chihuahua, near Copper Canyon, the observant girl discovered the remains of two skeletons in an abandoned mine. One was normal-size and the other shaped like that of a child. We can only imagine the curiosity with which she might have examined the eerie and oddly shaped smaller skull.

While contemplating how to bring the skeletons back to El Paso, the girl hid the two skeletons in a desert ravine, intending to return for them during a more opportune moment. Later that day, an unexpected, freak flash flood swept the bones away and thwarted her plans. After days of searching for the lost skeletons, she managed to find some damaged bits of bone and both of the skulls. After the flash flood, both of the skulls were left without lower jaws and the odd-shaped Starchild skull also lost half of its upper jaw.

The girl slyly brought the skulls to her home in El Paso and kept them as a memento of her visit to Mexico. She did not attribute any particular significance to the Starchild skull, believing it to be no more than that of a poor, deformed child's head. The skulls sat anonymously until the skulls' finder died in 1997 and the skulls came into the possession of fellow El Paso natives Ray and Melanie Young. The plot thickened when Melanie Young, a neonatal nurse and deformities expert, recognized the anomalies of the Starchild skull.[4]

With newfound curiosity, the couple sought out a man capable of understanding what might possibly be an alien skull. They were referred to maverick historian Lloyd Pye, a controversial author and archaeologist with the contacts and the clout to get the job done. Best known for his classic book *Everything You Know is Wrong,* Pye became the caretaker of the Starchild skull in 1999 and has had it tested in top-notch DNA-sequencing facilities (see plate 27).

With Pye's help, the world's most eminent experts in the fields of biology, radiology, and DNA specialties have studied the nine-hundred-year-old skull vigorously. These experts have all expressed amazement at how different the skull is compared to normal human DNA sequencing; it also comprises a number of unknown DNA strains. The Starchild skull differs from the normal human cranium in many ways. The slot found on the back of a human skull contains a knot reserved for neck muscles. This is a trait found on all Earth primates. However, the Starchild had a short neck with muscles formed at the very bottom of the skull. The Starchild also had shallower eye sockets, likely resulting in far larger, bug-shaped eyes. The skull itself is much smaller, weighs less, and is more finely rounded than an average human skull.

An artist's sketch of the Starchild would look like the Hollywood grey alien—a small fellow with big eyes and a small mouth and nose. No matter how strange this sounds, there is a good chance that nine hundred years ago a traveler wandering the Mexican southlands looked exactly like that because, according to the experts, the abnormalities in the Starchild skull are not the result of deformations due to disease. If that had been the case, any learned scientist would have been able to diagnose the deformities immediately. What are not easily explainable are the anomalies found within the bone structure of the skull.

The Starchild skull is webbed with a fibrous internal element that penetrates the bone, making it lighter and more durable, a staggering characteristic, unheard of in any known specimen found currently on Earth. A bone tissue sequencing resembling something out of an X-Men comic is contained in the DNA of the Starchild skull, yet the media remains silent.[5] Why? Because reporters rarely draw attention to the subject of interventionism, the theory that at some point in the past our DNA cells were tinkered with by aliens. But this theory, which fits right into the paradigm of the ancient astronaut, somehow is more controversial than the popularly accepted school of thought known as Darwinism.

Even creationism is accorded more credence than the intervention theory. Lloyd Pye believes the Starchild skull is proof of the intervention theory, which holds that an act—that is, an intervention by alien forces—separated us from our primate cousins and thus gave us the gifts of sound, response, and vision that we're still trying to decode in the twenty-first century. Even without a physical genetic alteration, scientists are starting to discover that human and alien genes have gone hand in hand since the dawn of creation[6] and NASA has even discovered weird alien DNA in a California lake.[7] With all these DNA research–related breakthroughs, is it really that inconceivable to think the Starchild may have been an alien-human hybrid or a lost grey alien dating from nine hundred years ago?

According to DNA-test results, published as recently as October 2011, the Starchild skull unquestionably has alien genes. A team of researchers working on the skull provided fresh evidence to the scientific community that the mitochondrial DNA found in the maternal sequence was, in fact, not human at all.[8] The chains that make up DNA contain two types of sequencers—nuclear (nuDNA) and mitochondrial (mtDNA). The nuDNA comes from both parents and is found within the nucleus of the DNA cells. The mtDNA act as subcellular entities, known as mitochondria, that swim in the plasmid jelly of the DNA cell's cytoplasm. These mtDNA strains are then passed on to each generation through the maternal (that is, the mother's) line and are retained forever as long as the predecessors are female. Nuclear DNA encodes more of the genome, but its genes are continuously rearranged during the process of recombination. There is usually little to no change in mtDNA from parent to offspring. Because of this, and the fact that the mutation rate of mtDNA is higher than that of nuclear DNA and is easily measured, mtDNA is a valuable resource in tracking the ancestry of ancient humans.

Recently, the world of DNA research got even more exciting with the announcement of a whole new prehuman species. A tooth and a finger bone of the so-called Denisovans were unveiled in 2010 after being found in a cave in the frigid tundra of Siberia. Research was carried out by Dr. Svante Paabo, a pioneering geneticist at the Max Planck Institute for Evolutionary Anthropology in Liepzig, Germany. Dr. Paabo and his colleagues have become groundbreaking experts when it comes to understanding and sampling fragments of ancient DNA from fossils. He and his team are responsible for completing and publishing the definitive report on the Neanderthal genome.[9] When Dr. Paabo studied the bone fragments of the Denisovan, looking for traces of the Neanderthal lineage, he was stunned at what he discovered.

Dr. Paabo accidentally found himself in the middle of another Earth mystery when he "and his colleagues isolated a small bundle of DNA from the bone's mitochondria, the energy-generating structures within our cells. Dr. Paabo and his colleagues were surprised to discover that the Denisovan DNA was markedly different from that of either humans or Neanderthals" and later admitted that it was "a great shock"[10] to them that the DNA differed from both the human and Neanderthal groups.

Scientists' curiosity about the Denisovans was further piqued when perplexed paleo-anthropologist Bence Viola made clear statements that the tooth was in no way from either a modern human or a Neanderthal. As proof of this claim, he pointed out that the "tooth had oddly bulging sides"[11] and big flaring roots. Scientists are still looking for more fragments of the Denisovans to study; an intact skull would, of course, be ideal. Just like the Starchild, the Denisovans are more mysterious cousins of humankind in Earth's foggy ancestral history. While trying to recover nuclear DNA from the Starchild's skull to match it to the National Institutes of Health database, geneticists discovered a significant number of base pairs never seen before. The Starchild skull also has over thirty major physiological differences from that of a human skull. The Starchild skull is more than an inch and a half thicker and, upon examining photographs, it is clear that the Starchild skull's bone density is uniformly thicker and more finely shaped.

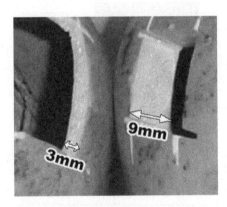

Figure 9.2. Skull thickness comparison: human skull at left; Starchild skull at right. Courtesy of Lloyd Pye, Starchildproject. com. Also see plate 28.

In the biochemistry of a typical human bone, the calcium and phosphorus levels are high while the oxygen and carbon levels are low. But in the case of the Starchild it is just the opposite: phosphorus levels are low, while carbon and oxygen levels are elevated, indicating that its biochemistry is more like that of tooth enamel than regular bone, and the calcium levels are very high. When the Starchild skull was x-rayed, five teeth were found hidden within the nasal bone structure and ready to come down. When we die, bacteria are released that scour and eat all the marrow from our bones, leaving them polished and shiny. There is no marrow left anywhere in the bone, and this occurs with all animals when they perish. Again, this normal feature of death is not replicated in the same manner with the Starchild skull.

Found within the bone tissue of the skull are sprinkles of red residue. This is not blood, at least in human form, since our blood turns black when it oxidizes. We do not know what the tiny fibrous threads or the red blotches are that dot the Starchild's bone landscape. All we really know is that, for the first time, the DNA results showing alien characteristics are indisputable and will continue to be so as further tests are carried out.

The Starchild skull is important because we can study and hold it. Unfortunately, there have been glimpses of other amazing skulls now lost to the annals of history. One of the most buzzed about on the

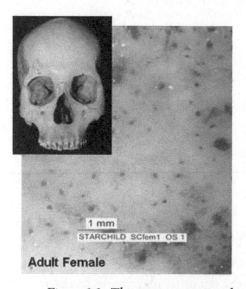 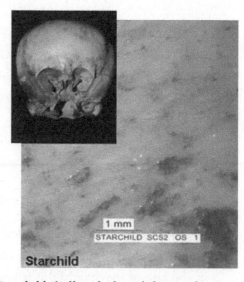

Figure 9.3. This image compares the Starchild skull with the Adult Female (AF) skull reportedly found together in Mexico circa 1930. Above left shows the exterior surface of the AF bone that is covered in porelike pits, which is normal for human bone. The Starchild skull has very little pitting, which is radically abnormal for bone. Courtesy of Lloyd Pye, Starchildproject.com. Also see plate 29a–c.

 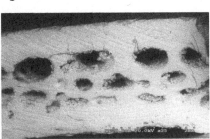

Figure 9.4. These two images show a close analysis of a fiber cluster, nicknamed the "knot." On the left is the fiber knot and on the right is the bone surface where the knot is located. Despite its appearance these fibers are not capillaries or any other tissue normally found in bone. Because nothing like this has been previously discovered, there are no established protocols to retrieve the fibers for testing, which hampers further study. Courtesy of Lloyd Pye, Starchildproject.com. Also see plate 30.

Internet is the horned skull found in Pennsylvania in the late 1800s. The skull resembles something out of a Black Sabbath video—ancient and spooky. It looks nothing like dressed-up Native American skulls with recognizable attached horns. The horns on the Pennsylvania skull are visibly distinguished as attached and are seen growing out from the bone structure of the skull. The little we know about the horned skull comes from a small article published by Reader's Digest in *Mysteries of the Unexplained* in 1992 and from a description in an obscure magazine called *Pursuit* in 1973:

> Human skulls with horns were discovered in a burial mound at Sayre, Bradford County, Pennsylvania, in the 1880's. Horny projections extended two inches above the eye-brows, and the skeletons were seven feet tall, but other than that were anatomically normal. It was estimated that the bodies had been buried around A.D. 1200. The find was made by a reputable group of antiquarians, including the Pennsylvania state historian and dignitary of the Presbyterian Church (Dr. G. P. Donehoo) and two professors, A. B. Skinner,

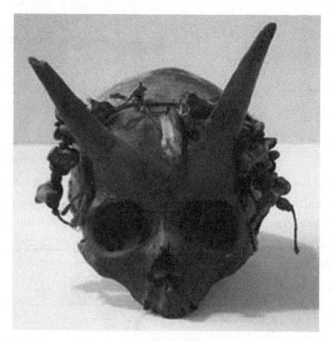

Figure 9.5. Model or real? The only photo known that shows the infamous horned human skull found in 1880s Pennsylvania. Photographer unknown. From Pursuit *6 (July 1973) and Reader's* Digest, Mysteries of the Unexplained, *1992.*

of the American Investigating Museum, and W. K. Morehead, of Phillips Academy, Andover, Massachusetts. The bones were sent to the American Investigating Museum in Philadelphia, where they were later claimed to have been stolen and have never been seen again[12]

There have been numerous accounts of human skeletons found with horns. Unfortunately, almost all of these are poorly documented and lack photographic or physical evidence. Despite this, at some level we have a deep sociogenetic memory of creatures with horns. Take, for example, the legend of the unicorn—one of our most beloved and fabled creatures, even though there is no evidence whatsoever of its existence. Most of our associations with horned figures bring to mind images of the devil and demonic entities, far removed from the fairy-tale bliss of the enchanted unicorn. Mythical giants, witch doctors, dragons, and the minotaur—all of which had horns—vastly outnumber the prancing horse forever popular with teenage girls on the scale of good versus evil.

A fascinating secondhand account even claims that master poet Lord Byron had horns:

> Lord Byron was, in a sense, a devil. Incredible as the thing may seem to the thoughtless, the handsomest man in England had a small tail, a pair of rudimentary horns, and short, squab feet divided forward from the instep into two parts, instead of being furnished with toes . . . He urged, and with considerable force, that the peculiar manner in which he wore his abundant curls effectually hid from view the rudimentary horns; and that, as he never appeared in public without his boots and trousers, none would ever suspect the existence of his other defects, with the exception of his valet, in whom he placed implicit confidence.[13]

Lord Byron isn't the only famous character from days of yore thought to have had horns. The lore of the horn has all sorts of mystical and magical ancient connotations associated with it. Throughout history, horns have been used during weddings and sacrifices, and as weapons, charms, antidotes, and decorative pieces on robes and helmets. At the corner of each masonic altar is a horn. Hindu temples built in Bombay from the seventh through the eleventh century had horn-headed guardians on their roofs and horns adorning the top of the temple spires. Chinese women in the 1300s wore horns on their foreheads indicating that they were married, and a ram's horn is used in Jewish High Holy Day services.

In volume 24 of the *Indian Antiquary*, published in 1895, a work compiled by the Royal Anthropological Institute of Great Britain and Ireland with the Archaeological Survey of India, we learn:

Figure 9.6. Coin showing the horned head of Alexander.
Courtesy of Mike Peel.

Both among the fifth century white Huns of central Asia, Persia and India and among the later Huns of Asia and East Europe the women wore horns on their heads, a practice which was the origin of the fashionable high-peaked Hunische hats of fourteen century Europe.[14]

The party god Dionysus was horned, and Alexander the Great was referred to in Arabic as the "two-horned"; he's even depicted on coins with a pronounced horn. The great sculptor Michelangelo depicted Moses with two horns. Scriptures alluding to Moses having horns are generally viewed as mistranslations from Exodus and Deuteronomy

Figure 9.7. Michelangelo's Moses *in Rome.*
Courtesy of Wknight 94.

and have been puzzled over by both Christian and Muslim scholars for thousands of years.[15]

Horns decorated the heads of the Egyptian gods, so when Moses led his people out of the wicked land of Egypt it would make sense that he was depicted with horns as a symbol of his divinely inspired deeds. The Israelites of the time believed

> that their great law-giver had become divine, that he had miraculously received the mark of divinity and of kingly power. The belief that Moses actually descended with solid horns upon his head was devoutly held, and has continued to be believed down to the middle ages.[16]

What we have discovered so far indicates that ancient people must have been accustomed to interacting with, or at least seeing, strange-looking beings—humans, hybrids, and aliens. We certainly are! Billions of people have either grown up on or been exposed to classic movies and literature like *Star Wars, Avatar,* and the *Lord of the Rings.* That's over five decades of minds conditioned to accept alien and lost worlds. Take, for instance, the legend of Frodo Baggins, a Hobbit who wandered the vast realms of Middle-Earth on a quest to destroy Sauron's ring. Frodo and the rest of the Hobbits were known as little people; they were short and smaller compared with the other inhabitants of Middle-Earth.

The Hobbits were a community of tiny people who built their own village called the Shire. This cherished slice of fictional history became real-life Earth history when small skeletons and a skull were found on the Indonesian island of Flores in 2003. Fitting in somewhere between the Denisovans, the Neanderthals, and humans, this breed of Hobbit, which once roamed the remote Flores Island, is officially known as *Homo floresiensis.* Because the ancestry of *Homo floresiensis* is unknown, it's another mystifying entry in the journal of anomalies found in human evolution.

New York Times columnist John Noble Wilford writes:

Everything about them seems incredible. They were very small, not much more than three feet tall, yet do not resemble any modern pygmies. They walked upright on short legs, but might have had a peculiar gait obviating long-distance running. The single skull that has been found is no bigger than a grapefruit, suggesting a brain less than one-third the size of a human's, yet they made stone tools similar to those produced by other hominids with larger brains. They appeared to live isolated on Flores as recently as 17,000 years ago, well after humans had made it to Australia.[17]

Announcements were made describing the skeletons and the skull as those of Hobbits. Researchers pointed out that they were a previously unknown type of hominid. This sparked a backlash among mainstream academia; the experts contended that they were merely human dwarfs suffering from genetic disorders. These beliefs were undermined after scientists at a 2009 symposium came to the conclusion that *Homo floresiensis* is indeed a distinct hominid species and that it's likely to be far older than *Homo sapiens*. They even marveled at the Hobbits' fully functioning seven-and-a-half-inch-long feet, which were out of proportion to their shorter lower limbs, and at their primitive and undefined arch bone. These were traits usually found in African apes; for the first and only time they were seen in hominids, thanks to the Hobbit-like *Homo floresiensis*.

Anthropological discoveries made over the past decade have added an amazing amount of new data in our search for the origin of humanity.

Elongated skulls have also been found on the ancient island of Malta, an area long known for curious megalithic temples. The local inhabitants don't know how these temples came to be. Found in the megalithic temples of Hal Saflieni, Tarxien, and Ggantija, these skulls seem to belong to a completely different subspecies of humans altogether. They were discovered in the 1980s, but kept hidden from the public. Our only known evidence of them comes from the photographs and writings of Maltese researchers Dr. Anton Mifsud and Dr. Charles

Savona-Ventura.[18] These findings, once obscure and ostracized, are now being validated, thanks, in part, to the recent interest in ancient and modern alien mysteries.

Perhaps the area with the most evidence of ancient alien contact, and where the most stunning discoveries have been made with regard to alien skulls, is the Peruvian highlands. The number of elongated skulls disinterred in the forests of Peru is so great that their museums are replete with astonishing examples and artifacts that provide evidence impossible to deny (see plates 31, 32, and 33). It is a well-documented fact that the Inca people were known to bind and misshape their infants' skulls on purpose to mimic the features of visitors from the sky to whom they attributed godlike qualities (see plate 34).

Some elongated skulls are in the process of being DNA-tested right now, and these skulls might be just as important in the alien grab bag as the Starchild skull. We can say without hesitation that the Starchild skull is at least half-alien, although in a March 5, 2012, interview on *Coast to Coast AM,* Lloyd Pye stated that he is convinced the skull is of a grey alien, and listed an astounding number of anomalies not found in human skulls.[19]

On November 24, 2011, an article concerning aliens and strange, elongated skulls was published by one of the world's foremost media outlets, London's *Daily Mail.* Like wildfire, this groundbreaking story quickly spread around the globe. It is rare that an article on this subject makes its way to the headlines of Yahoo!, MSN, and other mainstream media outlets without being bashed or discredited. The *Daily Mail* showcased high-quality images of an ancient, cone-headed mummy with three anthropologists agreeing, "It is not a human being."[20]

This shocking article is a huge step toward letting the alien cat out of the bag. If ever there was a case for "slow disclosure," this news article would certainly be it. But what exactly is slow disclosure, and how can we know if we're in the midst of it? We turn to this issue in the next chapter.

10

SLOW DISCLOSURE

Must a UFO land at the Super Bowl to get the world's undivided attention?"

GORDON COOPER, ASTRONAUT, PROJECT MERCURY

FOUR HUNDRED YEARS AGO, the Italian philosopher Giordano Bruno arrived at a logical conclusion that, if supported by the ruling elite of his time, would have lifted us to a reality drastically different from the barbaric human condition we seem to be trapped in. Bruno pondered this question: If Earth contained a population of intelligent beings, why couldn't there be other worlds in space inhabited by intelligent beings? The Catholic Church deemed this theory dangerous, so they promptly labeled it heretical, and Bruno was tortured and burned at the stake.[1] If anyone else thought there were intelligent beings out in space, they knew what they had coming if they voiced that opinion.

If Bruno had been alive in our times, the Internet and other wonders of the digital age—filled with daily advances in space science and UFO news—would have given his seventeenth-century mind plenty of food for thought. The flood of information provides evidence to show that, four hundred years ago, Bruno was certainly on the right track. Considering how far we have come in this area in just the last half-century, we might wonder how much more advanced we would be today

Figure 10.1. Statue of Giordano Bruno erected in Rome in 1889 at the exact spot where he was burned at the stake. Courtesy of Berthold Werner.

if Bruno's theory had been accepted four centuries ago, rather than killed on the spot.

A discussion of UFOs opens the door to a wide range of emotions and opinions—from the plain and factual to the sublime and ridiculous, and all levels in between. Society has made the topic such a hodgepodge of ideas that most serious researchers are embarrassed to talk about it. Thanks to pop culture and the invention of television, the question of UFOs has piqued the interest of hundreds of millions of people for over sixty years. Some enjoy reading about aliens or watching UFO programs; others become armchair scientists, pondering the physical possibilities of space flight. The UFO world has its own subculture, which includes a broad range of associated subtexts, such as abductions, crop circles, and animal mutilations.

While these mysterious incidents have both credible witnesses and high-level military officials looking into the matter, they continue to be ignored, ridiculed, or downplayed by various governments and mainstream media outlets. At the same time, Hollywood cranks out dozens of films showing hostile aliens threatening human extinction. Is this part of a social conditioning program, intended to make us think of aliens as evil and dangerous beings?[2] This question just adds to the puzzle of UFOs, and makes us wonder when we can expect disclosure, a word the UFO community has been begging the government to utter for years. However, what if disclosure is not imminent, but rather a slow-moving process designed to work hand in hand with a strategy established long before Bruno reached his daring conclusion? Based on the evidence emerging daily, we're entering a period of slow disclosure. This is a tricky idea to grasp, considering that the very mention of aliens can bring about as swift a death blow today as in the time of the Inquisition, albeit through annihilation of career or reputation.

In 2012 UFO news got off to an eerie start in a region of the world that might be reduced to rubble by the time this book hits store shelves. In the chaotic land of Syria, a nation currently surrounded by NATO forces, the Syrian head general claimed on national television that he saw a strange flying humanoid. This is from the report by Michael Weiss in the *Telegraph:*

A space object, that resembles a human, has entered the atmosphere of the Deir Simbel village, located about 35 kilometres from Idlib

Figure 10.2. "A Winged Ship in the Sky": headline from November 23, 1896. Courtesy of the San Francisco Call.

and halfway between Jericho and Ma'arrat Naman, where it was flying at a speed approximately 40 kmph. Syria News obtained a copy of a dispatch from Idlib Police Headquarters to the Department of Operations (Criminal Inspection). It cited witnesses who reported seeing a "space object" spinning and hovering in the village sky, coming from the atmosphere of Sarjeh and then heading towards Ahsem and from there to Kafr Nabil. They said that is [*sic*] was rising and falling above the olive and fig trees.[3]

Although the general's paranoia is justified, we can't rule out what he allegedly saw as a human-made object or secret experimental weaponry being used by either NATO or the U.S. Air Force. But a quick review of the last sixty years will show how UFO disclosure is slowly being played out.

UFO expert and disclosure advocate Richard Dolan writes,

For many years, it was hard to obtain declassified government documents about UFOs. During the 1950s and 1960s, a few documents made their way to the rest of the world, but this was rare. Then, in 1974, the U.S. government amended the Freedom of Information Act (FOIA). The result was a veritable golden age of document releases.[4]

Some of these declassified UFO documents had mysterious, blacked-out redaction lines and had been read and stamped by high-ranking military brass. Since then, we have been filling in those blacked-out lines with rapidly mounting evidence.

One of these documents was the Twining memo from 1947. Written at the beginning of the modern UFO era by Chief of Staff Nathan Twining to Air Force General George Schulgen, this two-page document shows extreme concern about "flying discs" that were definitely "real and not visionary or fictitious."[5] Twining even elaborates on the discs' amazing flying abilities and lists several now-common descriptions of UFOs, including that they were silent, fast-moving at impossible angles, shiny and metallic, and either circular or elliptical in shape with flat bottoms. These are strange descriptions, considering there were no U.S. aircraft in 1947 with these specifications or capabilities.

Figure 10.3. Grainy black-and-white image of a supposed UFO over Passaic, New Jersey (1952).

A few years later the FBI issued a memo called "Protection of Vital Installations"[6] to FBI Director J. Edgar Hoover, detailing a meeting between the Office of Naval Intelligence and the Air Force Office of Special Investigations. This memo illustrates that while the public was being told that UFOs were merely mixes of swamp gas, hoaxes, hallucinations, and weather balloons, military and government personnel were classifying and marking out anything that had to do with unidentified flying discs, balls of fire, or uncommon aerial phenomena. The report contends that the discs were flying at 2,700 mph, and that UFOs were constantly invading the airspace at Los Alamos, New Mexico. Ironically, they were doing so during the time when some of the first secret nuclear tests were being conducted there.

This bit of interesting UFO history was validated in early 2010 when former senior military officials went public about UFOs meddling with the world's nuke supplies. In 1980, near the Rendelsham Forest in Suffolk, England, a UFO allegedly tampered with the nuclear silo stationed at RAF Bentwater Base. Charles Halt, a retired senior RAF officer, witnessed the events and described in horror the odd-flying metallic triangle that shot beams of exploding lights into the sky and then teleported beings inside the RAF's buildings.[7] Halt is one of hundreds of former intelligence officials begging the British government to come clean about what it knows.

In America former Air Force Captain Robert Salas, along with six other high-ranking former officials, claim the government is lying outright. These former top U.S. Air Force officials believe that UFOs have been deactivating nuclear missiles since 1948, and the Air Force has kept this information from the public. Captain Salas says:

> The U.S. Air Force is lying about the national security implications
> of unidentified aerial objects at nuclear bases and we can prove it.
> I was on duty when an object came over and hovered directly over
> the site. The missiles shut down—ten Minuteman [nuclear] mis-
> siles. And the same thing happened at another site a week later.

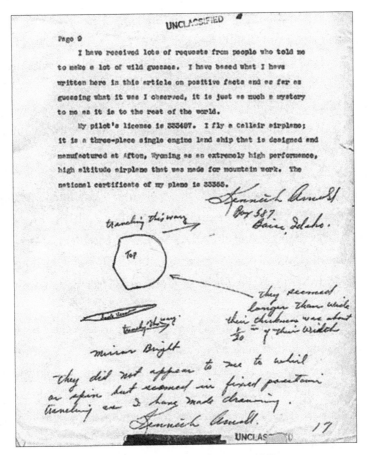

*Figure 10.4. The letter with a drawing of flying saucers
or flying disks, submitted by pilot Kenneth Arnold to
Army Air Force intelligence on July 12, 1947.*

There's a strong interest in our missiles by these objects, wherever
they come from. I personally think they're not from planet Earth.[8]

A 1951 USAF intelligence report details a harrowing encounter a
pilot had with a UFO while flying near the Lawson Air Force Base
in Georgia. Flying in an F-51 combat jet, the decorated World War II
pilot provided a no-nonsense, cut-and-dried report that dovetails perfectly with the key points discussed in the Twining memo. The report
describes an object as

flat on top and bottom and appearing from a front view to have rounded edges and slightly beveled. From view as object dived from top of plane was completely round and spinning in clockwise direction . . . No vapor trails or exhaust or visible system of propulsion. Described as traveling at tremendous speed . . . Pilot is considered by associates to be highly reliable, of mature judgment and a creditable observer.[9]

The sudden explosion of UFO sightings continued, prompting the now-famous Chadwell memo of December 2, 1952. H. Marshall Chadwell was then head of the CIA's Scientific Intelligence Branch and had an abiding curiosity when it came to UFO phenomena. The memo, which is addressed to CIA Director General Walter Bedell Smith, says:

> At this time, the reports of incidents convince us that there is something going on that must have immediate attention. . . . Sightings of unexplained objects at great altitudes and traveling at high speeds in the vicinity of major U.S. defense installations are of such nature that they are not attributable to natural phenomena or known types of aerial vehicles.[10]

The reports continued over the decades. It became apparent that the objects described were not American- or Soviet-made, or a result of natural phenomena. Rather, they were technologically sophisticated and under intelligent control. With that in mind, we might have to acknowledge what these are, and Chadwell's memo clearly understands this. Throughout the 1950s and 1960s, UFO encounters were reported, culminating in the spectacular aerial events over Tehran. With paranoia and talks of a revolution swirling in the air, an event happened on the night of September 8, 1976, that has intrigued and thrilled UFO enthusiasts all over the world. On that night, the Iranian Air Force, expecting a fight with either Russian or American jets, lost a dogfight with an unknown foe in one of the most dramatic UFO encounters of all time.

رصد كائنات ضخمة يبلغ طولها 3 أمتار وتتكلم لغة غير معروفة

سـاد الـخوف والـحذر والدهشة بين سكان منطقة مأهولة قرب الجفر فى وقت متأخر من مساء أمس.

حين حطت ثلاثة أجسام غريبة فى منطقة صحراوية قريبة من الأحياء السكنية. وجرى إغلاق المنطقة مدة ساعتين تقريبا.

ولم يتسن الدخول إليها إلا بعد انسحاب هذه الأجسام.

وقال شهود عيان من سكان المنطقة إنهم فوجئوا بهبوط هذه الأجسام الشبيهة بالأطباق الطائرة. والتى أضاء وهجها

مساحة كبيرة من الأرض. مضيفين أنهم لم يستطيعوا الاقتراب كثيرا من المكان جراء الحرارة الشديدة المنبعثة من هذه الأطباق.

Figure 10.5. Artistic rendering of the Tehran UFO,
from an Arabic newspaper. Courtesy of P199.

This unexplainable event was documented in a four-page U.S. Defense Intelligence Agency report that examined what happened, as witnessed by a control tower supervisor who saw hovering cylindrical crafts floating near the Air Force base. The stunned tower guard writes, "The two ends were pulsating with a whitish blue color. Around the mid-section was this small red light that kept going in a circle. . . . I was amazed."[11]

After dispatching the Iranian Air Force, the tower guard saw the F-4 Phantoms soar to investigate, but soon lost all communications with the fighter jets. The fighter jet pilots watched in astonishment as the unidentifiable craft glowed in different colors simultaneously before they had to break back toward base to regain their instrumentation.

Another notable UFO case from the 1970s involved the legendary Seattle guitarist and rock icon Jimi Hendrix. On July 30, 1970, Hendrix was scheduled to jam on one of Hawaii's volcanic islands as a benefit for a local Earth goddess commune. He was already in Hawaii performing on the last stop of his Cry of Love tour and decided to give a free concert for the local hippies and surfers who were able to hike up the volcano. Eager to try out the experimental sound system the commune had set up for him, Hendrix was in fine form as he warmed up his guitar. Then, suddenly, something out of this world caught his eye:

> Jimi's legendary real life encounter with a UFO during the filming of his *Rainbow Bridge* concert film in 1970 in the Halaeakala crater on the island of Maui proved Hendrix's increased desire to make contact with extraterrestrials. West Coast surf guitarist Merrell Fankhauser, who has spent considerable time living and performing on Maui, said, "The entire crew were making their trek through the crater at ten thousand feet with donkeys loaded down with cameras and other equipment when all of a sudden out of a clear blue sky a silver disc appeared hovering over a cinder cone. Jimi and some of the cast saw it first, and Jimi walked out onto the cinder field of an eight-hundred-year-old lava flow with open arms, saying, "Welcome space brothers!" Dozens of phone calls came into the local radio station about the sighting.[12]

Hendrix claimed the sighting reenergized him and gave him a fresher, more positive outlook on the future. A few months later he would be dead and *Rainbow Bridge* would be shelved and banished to bootleg status without an official release.

UFO incidents continued in the 1980s and '90s, but obtaining declassified documents has become increasingly difficult. This doesn't mean disclosure isn't happening, however.

On February 27, 1995, Disney premiered a one-hour television special, hosted by Hollywood movie mogul Michael Eisner, called *Alien Encounters from New Tomorrowland*. Even though this program had a huge budget and the backing of Disney, it aired only once in five states. Apparently, this TV special might have been a little ahead of its time.

Plate 1. Masonry in hallways toward the Great Sphinx of Giza. Was this high-level stone work completed in around 2,500 BCE as speculated by Egyptologists or was it completed much, much earlier? Courtesy of Ad Meskens.

Plate 2. Kharga Oasis in the Libyan Desert is the largest oasis known to exist in western Egypt. It is located about two hundred kilometers west of the Nile Valley. Kharga Oasis is also well known for featuring the well-preserved Temple of Hibis, which was first built by Pharaoh Psamtik II of the twenty-sixth Saite dynasty (664–525 BCE). Courtesy of Hanne Siegmeier.

Plate 3. Sunset over the salt lake at Fatnis in Siwa Egypt. Courtesy of Thom Chandler.

Plate 4. *The Subsiding of the Waters of the Deluge* by Thomas Cole (oil on canvas, 1829).

Plate 5. The shaft cut into Djedefre's pyramid, viewed from the top of the remains of the pyramid. Courtesy of Jon Bodsworth.

Plate 6. Abu Rawash Burial Pit. Courtesy of Ahly Man.

Plate 7. Laser cut marking in the side of the Abu Garab crystal compass. Courtesy of Soundofallthings.com.

Plate 8. Alfred Watkins's front door, 5 Harley Court, in Herefordshire, England. Although the plaque describes him, correctly, as a photographer and antiquarian, his name has come to be associated preeminently with the theory of ley lines, those invisible connective pathways supposedly linking ancient features, such as mounds, moats, hill forts, standing stones, wayside crosses, and churches. Courtesy of ceridwen.

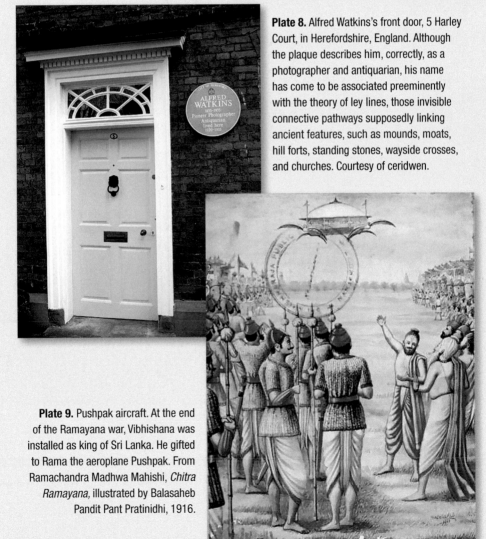

Plate 9. Pushpak aircraft. At the end of the Ramayana war, Vibhishana was installed as king of Sri Lanka. He gifted to Rama the aeroplane Pushpak. From Ramachandra Madhwa Mahishi, *Chitra Ramayana,* illustrated by Balasaheb Pandit Pant Pratinidhi, 1916.

Plate 10. Praying to Ra. Courtesy of Guillaume Blanchard.

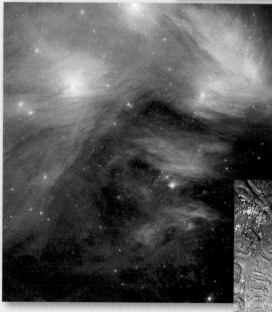

Plate 11. The Pleiades (or Seven Sisters) open cluster: infrared image from NASA's Spitzer Space Telescope. Courtesy of John Stauffer.

Plate 12. Dendera zodiac. Courtesy of Olaf Tausch.

Plate 13. Location of Abydos on a map of ancient Egypt. Courtesy of Lanternix.

Plate 14. Temple of the Osirian with water. Courtesy of Steve F.-E. Cameron.

Plate 15. Preparation of ayahuasca, Province of Pastaza, Ecuador. Courtesy of Terpsichore.

Plate 16. Thulsa Doom Snake Head. Screenshot. Courtesy of Universal.

Plate 17. Diana in *V.* Screenshot. Courtesy of Universal.

Plates 18. Serpentor. Courtesy of Hasbro.

Plate 19. Serpentor's action figure by Hasbro.

Plate 20. A giant Thutmose III smiting enemies on the seventh pylon at Karnak. Courtesy of Markh.

Plate 22. Nefertiti.

Plate 21. Thutmose III before the god Ra with Sunship hanging above them. 1455 BCE. Catalogue number 1634. Image taken at the Altes Museum, Berlin. Courtesy of Keith Schengili-Roberts.

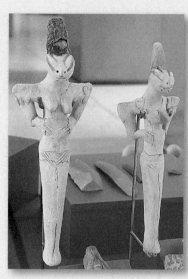

Plate 23. Serpentine figures of the Ubaid. Courtesy of Mary Harrsch, Flickr.com.

Plate 24. Akhenaten's daughters, from an Amarna wall painting. Courtesy of Jon Bodsworth.

Plate 25. A relief of a royal couple in the Armana style. The figures have variously been identified as Akhenaten and Nefertiti, Smenkhkare and Meritaten, and Tutankhamen and Ankhesenamun. The relief dates to after the former king's death. Courtesy of Andreas Praefcke.

Plate 26. Relief of Queen Nefertiti kissing one of her daughters. Courtesy of luluinnyc.

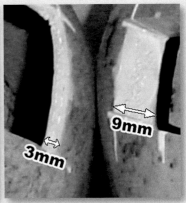

Plate 27. Lloyd Pye with the Starchild skull, right, compared to a human skull. Courtesy of Lloyd Pye, Starchildproject.com.

Plate 28. Skull thickness comparison: human skull at left; Starchild skull at right. Courtesy of Lloyd Pye, Starchildproject.com.

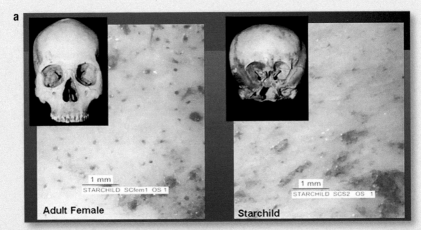

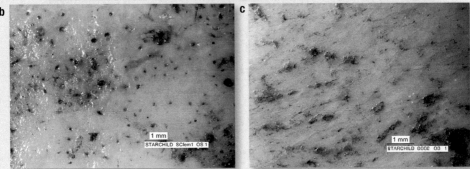

Plate 29a–c. Plate 29a compares the Starchild skull (right) with the Adult Female (AF) skull reportedly found together in Mexico circa 1930. Above left in 29a shows the exterior surface of the AF bone that is covered in porelike pits, which is normal for human bone. The Starchild skull has very little pitting, which is radically abnormal for bone. The two details, 29b and 29c, show a closer view of the two skulls, with the human skull on the left and the Starchild skull fragment on the right. Courtesy of Lloyd Pye, Starchildproject.com.

Plate 30. Another view of the mysterious "knot" fibers and their location in the bone fragment of the Starchild skull. Courtesy of Lloyd Pye, Starchildproject.com.

Plate 31. Paracas skulls of Peru. Courtesy of Brien Foerster, Hiddenincatours.com, www.hiddenincavideos.com.

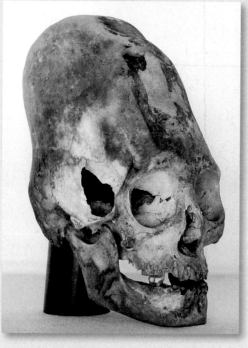

Plate 32. A closer view of one of the Paracas skulls of Peru. Courtesy of Brien Foerster, Hiddenincatours.com, www.hiddenincavideos.com.

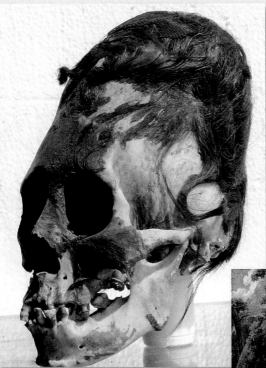

Plate 33. Elongated skull with hair from the Paracas History Museum, www.paracasculture.com. Courtesy of Brien Foerster, Hiddenincatours.com, www.hiddenincavideos.com.

Plate 34. Flathead woman with a child, from between 1848 and 1853. Courtesy of Paul Kane.

Plate 35. Tomorrowland at Walt Disney World, Orlando, Florida. Courtesy of Joe Penniston, Flickr.com.

Plate 36. NASA Space Launch System (SLS) graphic. Courtesy of NASA.

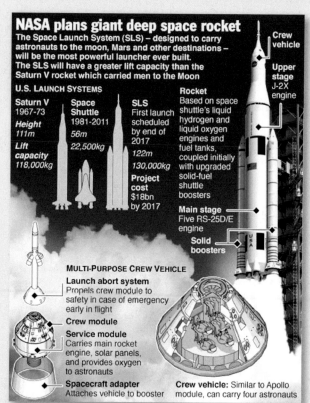

NASA plans giant deep space rocket

The Space Launch System (SLS) – designed to carry astronauts to the moon, Mars and other destinations – will be the most powerful launcher ever built. The SLS will have a greater lift capacity than the Saturn V rocket which carried men to the Moon

U.S. LAUNCH SYSTEMS

Saturn V
1967-73
Height
111m
Lift capacity
118,000kg

Space Shuttle
1981-2011
56m
22,500kg

SLS
First launch scheduled by end of 2017
122m
130,000kg
Project cost
$18bn by 2017

Rocket
Based on space shuttle's liquid hydrogen and liquid oxygen engines and fuel tanks, coupled initially with upgraded solid-fuel shuttle boosters

Crew vehicle

Upper stage J-2X engine

Main stage
Five RS-25D/E engine

Solid boosters

MULTI-PURPOSE CREW VEHICLE

Launch abort system
Propels crew module to safety in case of emergency early in flight

Crew module

Service module
Carries main rocket engine, solar panels, and provides oxygen to astronauts

Spacecraft adapter
Attaches vehicle to booster

Crew vehicle: Similar to Apollo module, can carry four astronauts

Plate 37. The first successful launch of the *Minotaur IV* lite launch vehicle occurred at 4 p.m. on April 22, 2010, from Space Launch Complex-8 at Vandenberg Air Force Base in California. The rocket launched the Defense Advanced Research Projects Agency's Falcon Hypersonic Technology Vehicle 2. Courtesy of Andrew Lee.

Plate 38. NASA's Mars exploration rover *Spirit* has found a patch of bright-toned soil so rich in silica that scientists posit that water must have been involved in concentrating it. Courtesy of NASA.

Plate 39. The DARPA–U.S. Army telerobot Solon, exploring Devo Rock Canyon on Devon Island on July 26, 2001. Courtesy of the Mars Society.

Plate 40. *Total Recall* Mars view. Screenshot. Courtesy of Universal.

Plate 41a and 41b. Plate 41a: U.S. Air Force Space Command patch; courtesy of USAF. Plate 41b: Black triangle captured over Belgium; courtesy of J. S. Henrardi. Notice the triangular shape reflected in both the patch and the aircraft—naval and air force branches of these Space Commands are likely flying and maintaining the back-engineered UFO spaceships, like the commonly seen TR3 black manta triangular crafts.

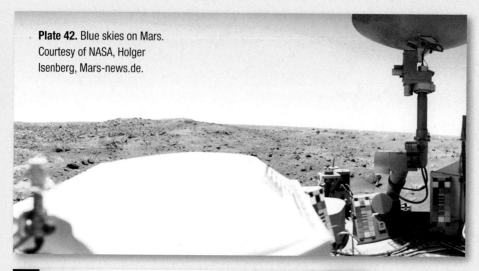

Plate 42. Blue skies on Mars. Courtesy of NASA, Holger Isenberg, Mars-news.de.

Plate 43. Blue sky on Mars caught during Nasa's live Jet Propulsion Laboratory (JPL) press conference (2004). Courtesy of Rense.com.

Plate 44. This color photo of the surface of Mars was taken by *Viking Lander 2* at its Utopia Planitia landing site on May 18, 1979, and relayed to Earth by *Orbiter 1* on June 7, 1979. It shows a thin coating of ice on the rocks and soil. NASA. Courtesy of Roel van der Hoorn.

Plate 45. Landslide on Mars, showing possible streams of water. Courtesy of NASA.

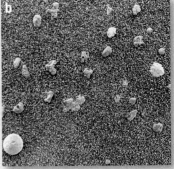

Plate 46a and 46b. This artist depiction of an astronaut finding ancient life on Mars (left) doesn't seem so far-fetched in light of the NASA image from the rover *Opportunity* that shows spherules on Mars resembling seashells. Right: Martian spherules on the ground, as seen by the rover *Opportunity*. Plate 46a courtesy of D. Mitriy and plate 46b courtesy of NASA.

Plate 47. Anubis, supervisor of the mummification process. Courtesy of André from Amsterdam.

Plate 48. The djed pillar. Courtesy of Olaf Tausch.

Plate 49. Mummified bull at the National Museum of Natural History, Washington, D.C. Courtesy of Pccromeo.

a

b

c

Plate 50. Hybrid creatures? Narmer Palette, Egypt, ca. 3100 BCE. Royal Ontario Museum in Toronto. Courtesy of Daderot.

Plates 51a–c. Plate 51a shows a serpent patch representing their control of the world, plate 51b is an NWO patch depicting its control over space, and plate 51c is another grey alien patch, which defies explanation as to what it really represents. Courtesy of Vigilantcitizen.com.

Broadcast on the independent network UPN without advance promotion or marketing, this unusual documentary presents a clear case that our planet has been visited at numerous times by UFOs and alien visitors in the distant past and the present day.

It is possible that this documentary was slipped in quickly and quietly as a disclosure tactic or that it was sneaked in mischievously without the approval of the Pentagon. This latter explanation seems more plausible, since it was revealed in the aftermath of 9/11 that the Pentagon is ultimately responsible for giving the green light to most of the productions coming out of Hollywood—especially big-budget films intended to reach a mass audience—and has been for quite some time. This was learned when the Pentagon blocked the release of a scene in one of the *Spider-Man* movies that showed airplanes flying into the Twin Towers.[13] Later it was reported to have been a helicopter. Just the same, the scene was deleted. All of this proves that higher approval is needed before the public sees the final product.

The Disney UFO documentary might have been a case of a "slip-by," later recalled for good. Although the film is listed in the archives of the Internet Movie Database (IMDB), it has never been officially released, nor are there plans to make this rare documentary available for purchase. However, thanks to someone who recorded the program on a VCR and uploaded it on YouTube, we have proof that Disney staged an elaborate psyops program, disguised as a promo for an alien encounters ride set to open at Disney World.[14]

This new attraction, released in the Tomorrowland section of the Magic Kingdom theme park at Walt Disney World in Orlando, was a dark, sci-fi experience that used state-of-the-art sound techniques and stunning visual effects unfit for children under the age of twelve (see plate 35). Maybe the ride served a purpose far beyond offering a thrilling and entertaining family moment. Perhaps the ride was a probe to measure the public's reaction and acceptance of aliens. Considering the limited audience and time that it was open, the ride remains a riddle, as does the documentary that wouldn't be available if not for the wonders of the Internet. Some of the key excerpts from retired military officers filmed in *Alien Encounters from New Tomorrowland* are quoted below:

Capt. Kevin Randle:

There's beings from another planet. We do not know where they come from. We do not know what they're doing here. There's nothing we can do about it. Any time a technologically superior civilization comes in contact with a technologically inferior civilization, the technologically inferior civilization ceases to exist—not necessarily through conquest, not necessarily through invasion, but because the technology changes the underlying social structures of that civilization, and it disintegrates.[15]

Clifford Stone:

The hotline between Moscow and Washington was set up so that they could go ahead and make last-minute pleas, that "We're not attacking you, and you're not attacking us." The purpose of this was to ensure that a UFO appearing on the scopes and being mistaken for enemy aircraft would not touch off a nuclear war. In November of 1975, essentially every SAC [Strategic Air Command] base in the United States was visited by UFOs. We have reason to believe that the UFOs went ahead and had some effect on changing the codes within the missiles, within the launch control facility, to change where the missiles would hit. Planet Earth has always been a laboratory for alien life-forms, which can drop in from space or slowly mutate into bizarre fleshy organisms at our feet [holding a large mushroom]. Understanding the nature of these strange creatures from above, and below, is the greatest challenge of our age. We now know that our future, indeed the future of Earth itself, rests in the balance of the solid and the ethereal, of common sense and the irrational, in our relationship with alien life as grotesque as a fungus, or as glorious as the heavens.[16]

In April 2011 the National Security Agency (NSA) leaked vital and relevant documents in regard to the alien question and admitted the slow-disclosure news that we had made contact. Even though this was blockbuster news, it wasn't broadcast on prime time. A report by mathematician and cryptographer Dr. Howard Campaigne concerns alien messages received from outer space. The Soviet *Sputnik* satellite also picked up these messages, but linguists on both sides of the Atlantic didn't understand what they meant.[17]

On June 19, 2011, a team of Swedish treasure hunters made a remarkable find when they accidentally discovered a massive disc-shaped UFO that had crashed on the ocean floor. By examining the sonar images, showing what appear to be impact skid marks trailing a downed saucer about nine hundred feet, team leader Peter Lindberg thinks that

> the tracks show the object has moved, either on or since settling to the ocean floor. Six of the nine-member team were asleep in their bunks on-board the Ocean Explorer's ship at the time of the discovery, but the three watching the sonar 'couldn't believe' what they were seeing.[18]

Lindberg acquired funds from a private investor and investigated further, sending a team of divers down to intensify the analysis of the remarkable find. They were shocked to discover that all their electronic equipment failed when they came within two hundred meters of the supposed UFO, but when they backed off their equipment began working again.[19] Whatever is there is active or still emits some sort of energy. Photographic images taken of the site on the ocean floor only compound the questions surrounding this vehicle because they show evidence of stone circle formations and what appear to be steps. Is it possible that a temple was built around a fallen alien saucer in an era before the last Great Flood? And is it also possible that for hundreds, if not thousands, of years, ancient humans worshipped at and made pilgrimages to the ancient downed saucer? Even master filmmaker and Illuminati whistle-blower Stanley Kubrick might have leaked info about the Baltic Sea UFO during a brief scene in his movie *2001*.[20] The Baltic UFO is an intriguing mystery that the mainstream media has shot down as nothing more than the hoax of the century.[21]

Meanwhile, in Canada, Paul Hellyer, former deputy prime minister and Canadian minister of national defense, responsible for unifying the Royal Canadian Army into the Canadian Armed Forces, is one of the highest-level whistle-blowers in the world. Never shy or soft-spoken, he's blatantly open about his feelings toward disclosure and the subject of UFOs.

Hellyer blames the U.S. government for keeping the existence of aliens secret, and for suppressing vital information for purposes of control and greed:

> Oh, I'm absolutely convinced of it. These things were not invented here. And I think people have to get accustomed to this new reality. We lived too long in a sense of isolation, thinking that Earth was the center of the cosmos and that we were the only species and, therefore, probably the most advanced. And when we come to the realization that we're not any of those things then I think we should be aware of it, learn to live with it and certainly try to take advantage of anything that we can learn from visitors from anywhere. Basically, I'm a full-disclosure person. People keep talking about transparency and still not telling the truth, and this applies in various other areas as well as UFOs, and it is just about time that we started getting open with each other and trying to get along and live together.[22]

More controversial UFO news came out in 2011, this time reaching the absolute top of the pyramid when it comes to modern-era conspiracy theories. John F. Kennedy, one of the most popular and beloved presidents in American history, asked to know everything about UFOs and aliens and even wanted to get together with the Soviets on the matter. Two letters that Kennedy wrote are today known as Kennedy's Secret Memos. One is a letter written by JFK on November 12, 1963, asking the director of the CIA for information concerning the paranormal. The other was sent to the NASA administrator, expressing a wish for space exploration to be carried out together with the Soviet Union.

The CIA released these documents for the first time to author William Lester under the Freedom of Information Act. But according to the *Daily Mail:*

> Conspiracy theorists said the documents add interest to a disputed file, nicknamed the "burned memo," which a UFO investigator claims he received in the 1990s. The document, which has scorch marks, is claimed to have been posted to UFO hunter Timothy Cooper in 1999 by an unknown CIA leak, but has never been verified. In a note sent with the document, the apparent leaker said he worked for CIA between 1960 and 1974 and pulled the memo from a fire when the agency was burning some of its most sensitive files. The undated memo contains a reference to "Lancer," which was JFK's Secret Service code name. On the first page, the director of Central Intelligence wrote: "As you must know, Lancer has made some inquiries regarding our activities, which we cannot allow. Please submit your views no later than October. Your action to this matter is critical to the continuance of the group." The current owner of the "burned memo," who bought it from Timothy Cooper in 2001, told AOL News that it shows that when JFK asked questions about UFOs the CIA "bumped him off."[23]

Ten days after sending the secret memo to the CIA, Kennedy was assassinated in front of a large viewing audience watching on national television.

This begs the question: How many more people need to be killed, persecuted, ignored, or ridiculed before the government admits to

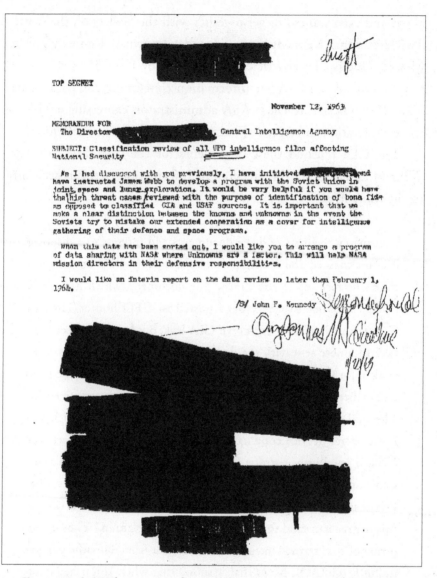

*Figure 10.6. JFK's memo to the CIA director, asking for the UFO files
(November 12, 1963). This image is the work of an employee of
the Executive Office of the President of the United States, taken or made
during the course of the person's official duties.*

what's been known for decades? Ben Rich, former CEO of weapons developer Lockheed and the father of the Stealth bomber, admitted on his deathbed in 1995 that aliens were real.

In May 2010 the *Mufon UFO Journal* published an article writ-ten by aerospace engineer Tom Keller in which Ben Rich is quoted as saying:

> We already have the means to travel among the stars, but these tech-nologies are locked up in black projects, and it would take an act of God to ever get them out to benefit humanity. Anything you can imagine, we already know how to do. We now have the technol-ogy to take ET home. No, it won't take someone's lifetime to do it. There is an error in the equations. We know what it is. We now have the capability to travel to the stars. First, you have to understand that we will not get to the stars using chemical propulsion. Second, we have to devise a new propulsion technology. What we have to do is find out where Einstein went wrong.[24]

Prominent UFO researcher Nick Cook admitted in his book, *The Hunt for Zero Point,* that Rich told him "of a virtual warehouse where ideas that were too dangerous to transpose into hardware were locked away forever, like the Ark of the Covenant in the final scene of *Raiders of the Lost Ark.*"[25]

Boyd Bushman is another senior Lockheed scientist who claimed UFOs were real and that extraterrestrials left us technology that has enabled us to back-engineer rockets and other spaceships. Bushman was the inventor of the Stinger missile, and a pioneer in laser and infrared technology, holding over twenty-six U.S. patents and numerous more classified patents. In a video presented by David Sereda, Bushman explains how magnets are used in the UFO's antigravity propulsion system and demonstrates how to build a mini-UFO with copper and aluminum. Then he tells a strange story about a translucent UFO once held at Area 51.[26]

Dr. Edgar Mitchell, a former NASA astronaut, the sixth man to ever walk on the moon, and a veteran of Apollo 14, not only claims that aliens exist but that the government has been hiding the facts for over sixty years. Mitchell shocked the listening audience of Britain's *Kerrang!* radio show on July 23, 2008, when he said that our current technology was weak compared to theirs and

> had they been hostile, we would have been gone by now. I happen to have been privileged enough to be in on the fact that we've been visited on this planet and the UFO phenomenon is real. I've been in military and intelligence circles who know that beneath the surface of what has been public knowledge, yes—we have been visited. Reading the papers recently, it's been happening quite a bit. This is really starting to open up. I think we're headed for real disclosure.[27]

Mitchell reiterated these claims on "The NASA Connection" episode of *Ancient Aliens,* saying, "This is not unknown knowledge. There are people that know and there appear to be perhaps several different species of aliens visiting here and [it] looks like they have been for a long, long time."[28]

Examining the latest findings in the field of astronomy, we can also make a case for slow disclosure. Although going largely unnoticed by the mainstream media, the space news that has emerged within the last few years is remarkable and exciting. The prospect of traveling among the stars, in search of civilizations similar to ours, is slowly etching itself into the consciousness of future generations.

Space is full of mysteries, one of which is the strange landscape of Saturn's moon, Titan. This gigantic moon is bigger than the planet Mercury and is shrouded in a fog of nitrogen. Its environments range from icy mountains to vast deserts and creepy lakes of dark, bubbly gases. All these sights went unseen for millions of years, covered by thick layers of heavy clouds, until NASA's *Cassini* arrived in 2004 and managed to peek beneath the clouds with its advanced radar.

Michael Hanlon writes about the possible future importance of Titan:

Figure 10.7. Astronaut Edgar D. Mitchell, Apollo 14 *lunar module pilot, moves across the lunar surface as he looks over a traverse map during extravehicular activity (EVA). Lunar dust can be seen clinging to the boots and legs of his spacesuit. Courtesy of Alan Shepard.*

Many scientists believe that Titan is the most Earth-like place in the solar system and could even be home to some sort of weird and exotic life. Sure, it is cold (–180°C, so you'd have to wrap up warm), but the pressure will not kill you, and extreme cold is much easier to deal with than extreme heat. Indeed, with heated clothing covering every square millimeter of skin there is a chance that Titan could be the only place in the solar system where a human could walk unencumbered by a full-on pressure suit, merely a supply of oxygen. And not just walk; the combination of low gravity (about a seventh of

Earth's) plus the thick air means a fit human could strap on a pair of wings and fly by muscle power alone.[29]

Titan is one of the moons that could yield valuable insights into the evolution of planetary systems unlike our own. It is also an example of how a moon can maintain environments hospitable for life, despite orbiting planets that do not. Titan became a major player in the future of space travel when, on June 29, 2012, it was announced that a massive watery ocean lies buried under a thick crust of ice. Scientists believe that the discovery of this ocean means there's a good chance that some form of microbial life might exist on Titan.[30]

NASA astronomers can now see into the farthest reaches of the known universe using the Hubble Space Telescope. By watching a distant explosion of a supernova nine billion years in the making, scientists believe this event might help them in their quest to understand the mystery of dark energy. Dark energy is what drives the acceleration of the universe, and stretches and pulls it apart. So far its origin has been unknown to scientists and physicists. Named SN Primo, the supernova that exploded is rare and distinct. The project leader, Dr. Steven Rodney of John Hopkins, says:

> Type Ia supernovae likely arise when white dwarf stars, the burned-out cores of normal stars, siphon too much material from their companion stars and explode. If we look into the early universe and measure a drop in the number of supernovae, then it could be that it takes a long time to make a Type Ia supernova. Like corn kernels in a pan waiting for the oil to heat up, the stars haven't had enough time at that epoch to evolve to the point of explosion. However, if supernovae form very quickly, like microwave popcorn, then they will be immediately visible, and we'll find many of them, even when the universe was very young. Each supernova is unique, so it is possible that there are multiple ways to make a supernova.[31]

More discoveries concerning dark energy are being made by the world's grandest machine of science—the Large Hadron Collider. The European Organization for Nuclear Research (CERN) built this $10 billion atom smasher in hopes of re-creating the big bang, and uncovering subatomic particles, supernovas, and other mysteries associated with our universe. On July 4, 2012, scientists at CERN claimed to have discovered a previously unknown subatomic particle.[32]

The universe is bursting with hundreds of billions of stars. In the Milky Way alone, researchers have suggested that there may be over 100 million stars pulsating with planets similar to those found in our solar system and over 10 billion stars possibly thriving with habitable planets.[33] Scientists at the European Southern Observatory (ESO) recently announced the discovery of a Super-Earth, which they believe is the first alien planet capable of supporting life. Astronomers associated with the discovery revealed that the Super-Earth is one of sixteen other planets double the size of Earth discovered by HARPS, the agency's high-tech telescope. Astronomers believe planet HD 85512 has water and oceans similar to ours because the planet is located just far enough from its star, on the outer, warmer edges of the habitable zone, ideal for supporting life. Lisa Kaltenegger of the Max Planck Institute for Astronomy in Heidelberg, Germany, says, "We are building up a target list of Super-Earths in the habitable zone,"[34] and, once the new supertelescope currently being assembled by the ESO is finished next year, humankind will finally be technically capable of finding and studying more of these Earth-like planets, moons, and exoplanets in distant galaxies.

A scene familiar to most readers of this book is the iconic shot of Luke Skywalker staring into a horizon with two suns, stargazing with ambitions of joining the rebellion while stuck on the lonely desert planet of Tatooine. George Lucas, who wrote and directed *Star Wars,* studied ancient mythology, ancient Earth mysteries, and Frank Herbert's *Dune* for years while researching and writing the *Star Wars* saga. Conspiracy theorists have long contended that Lucas had insider knowledge from NASA and used *Star Wars* as a clever way to out some of these hidden space secrets, held by the elite. One secret was the existence of habitable Earth-like planets coexisting with two suns. It is a secret no more.

Early in 2012, William Welsh of San Diego State University, who led a study into the possibility of extraterrestrial life, said:

> Nasa's Kepler telescope detected two new planet systems with two suns—named Kepler-34 and Kepler-35—leading Nasa astronomers to say that planets like the fictional Tatooine are common. . . . this work further establishes that such "two sun" planets are not rare exceptions, but may in fact be common, with many millions existing in our galaxy. This discovery broadens the hunting ground for systems that could support life.[35]

Another secret that Lucas subliminally slipped to the masses was the notion of the "Death Star"—a floating space weapon or large military space command center orbiting in space. Iapetus is a moon of Saturn that eerily resembles a faded and destroyed version of the Death Star and actually doesn't look like moons as we know them at all. Amazingly, the image of Iapetus as the Death Star also appears

Figure 10.8. Luke Skywalker staring at twin suns in Star Wars.
Screenshot. Courtesy of Lucasfilm Ltd.

preserved in three-billion-year-old, sphere-shaped artifacts found deep below the Earth in the Wonderstone Silver Mine in South Africa. Some two hundred Death Star balls, averaging one to four inches in diameter and composed of an unnatural nickel-steel alloy, were pulled from the precambrian rock stratus by South African miners in the late 1970s. To this day these tiny Death Star–like souvenir spheres remain one of Earth's most baffling mysteries. Some of them can be seen at the Museum of Klerksdorp, in South Africa.[36] Sustaining prolonged manned sojourns deep into the cosmos has been a dream of humans, but the odds of this flight being achieved are enormous, considering all the factors required for such a fantastic voyage. Journeys to distant planets in our own solar system can take months, leaving a large window open for challenges relating to life support, oxygen, and various mechanical or computer system failures. According to NASA, there's a good chance that if we make it to the planet Mars with traditional rocket technology, that won't occur until the 2030s. By that time, privately funded probes might already beat them to the punch, thanks to the emerging boom in commercialized space travel.

After canceling the Space Shuttle missions and the *Constellation* program, NASA created the Space Launch System, or SLS, a new heavy launch crew and cargo flight vehicle and futuristic version of the dated Space Shuttle. Unveiled during a press conference on Capitol Hill, the proposed $10 billion SLS rocket system uses a fuel mix of liquid hydrogen and oxygen in order to help cut costs. The official National Advisory Council's Concept of Operations (NAC Con Ops) report published and presented by NASA states:

> The SLS is a feasible option to launch demanding missions to explore the solar system. The SLS capabilities provide three main advantages to science payloads: higher energy, larger diameters, and larger mass. . . . The SLS can fly large or medium class payloads to higher energy orbits. This potentially enables direct missions to the outer planets that are currently only achievable using indirect flights

with gravity-assist trajectories. An SLS could enable these missions using direct flights with shorter interplanetary transfer times, which enables extensive in situ investigations and potentially sample return options. The SLS also provides 8.4 m and 10.0 m fairings to launch payloads with larger diameter apertures. This capability allows Earth observing, astronomical missions (e.g., planet finders), etc., with the ability to launch large single mirrors and lenses without the expense, complexity, and mass of segmented optics. . . . The SLS provides a heavy-lift capacity, allowing complex spacecraft to be launched with much higher masses. The large payload capacity of the SLS permits the addition of extra fuel for propulsive maneuvers, shielding to protect from harsh radiation, drill strings and casings for drilling, and redundancy. The SLS could potentially enable sample return from Jupiter's moon Europa, because it would have the payload capacity to provide shielding for a lander on the surface, and sufficient fuel for propulsive maneuvers out of the gravitational well of Jupiter.[37] (See plates 36 and 37.)

Criticism of the SLS mostly centers on NASA's failure to create new technologies that do not require rockets. Congressional mandates force NASA to use older Space Shuttle components for the SLS, thus eliminating any alternative, privately built technology. Technically, this makes NASA another branch of the federal government. Using billions more of the taxpayers' money, NASA officials are hedging their bets that the advancements made with SLS rocket technology will get them to the curious Martian moon Phobos, where they plan on setting up a space station as a good leeway point for the exploration and landings on Mars.[38] But is the money NASA spends on rocket research just another magician's trick to continue fooling the public, which it has successfully done for the past six decades? Are there other ways we can get to the stars and walk on distant moons without noisy rockets? Can the recent developments in teleportation and wormhole physics provide the answers we've been looking for in order to really get humans to Mars? And if so, has NASA been secretly doing this already?

Using wormholes to travel to various points of the galaxy has been a popular theory for scientists and sci-fi writers since the 1970s, when the *Millennium Falcon* in *Star Wars* jumped through hyperspace to evade the Imperial fleet. Wormholes are an anomalous feature in the theory of general relativity. Scientists imagine them to be shortcuts between two points in time, which connect regions of empty space, creating an encased road for objects to travel through. NASA officials announced proof that wormholes exist in space on July 4, 2012, when they reported the discovery of hidden portals or electric diffusion-folding regions in the magnetic fields between the Earth and the Sun's atmosphere.[39]

Scientists at the Eurasian National University in Kazakhstan believe they have finally uncovered how to make this transition possible by studying neutron stars. Vladimir Dzhunushaliev and his coauthors posted their investigational theories in a recent report that can be found in the archives of Cornell University.[40]

Dzhunushaliev's scientific team began

investigating the idea of wormholes between stars when they were researching what kinds of astrophysical objects could serve as entrances to wormholes. According to previous models, some of these objects could look similar to stars. This idea led the scientists to wonder if wormholes might exist in otherwise ordinary stars and neutron stars[.] To investigate these differences, the researchers developed a model of an ordinary star with a tunnel at the star's center, through which matter could move. Two stars that share a wormhole would have a unique connection, since they are associated with the two mouths of the wormhole. Because exotic matter in the wormhole could flow like a fluid between the stars, both stars would likely pulse in an unusual way. This pulsing could lead to the release of various kinds of energy, such as ultrahigh-energy cosmic rays. Instead of being empty tunnels, these wormholes would contain a perfect fluid that flows back and forth between the two stars, possibly giving them a detectable signature.[41]

Recently, scientists at the Department of Physics at Ben-Gurion University of the Negev in Israel published a report claiming that fully traversable wormholes now exist:

> From the demand that no surfaces of infinite coordinate time redshift appear in the problem we are led now to a completely traversable wormhole space, according to not only the traveler that goes through the wormhole (as was the case for the LLB [lightlike brane]), but also to a static external observer, this requires negative surface energy density for the shell sitting at the throat of the wormhole. We study a gauge field subsystem which is of a special non-linear form containing a square-root of the Maxwell term and which previously has been shown to produce a QCD-like confining gauge field dynamics in flat space-time. The condition of finite energy of the system or asymptotic flatness on one side of the wormhole implies that the charged object sitting at the wormhole throat expels all the flux it produces into the other side of the wormhole, which turns out to be of compactified ("tube-like") nature. An outside observer in the asymptotically flat non-compactified universe detects, therefore, apparently neutral object. The hiding of the electric flux behind the wormhole is the only possible way that a truly charged particle can still be of finite energy, which points to the physical relevance of such solutions, even though there is the need of negative energy density at the throat of the wormhole, which can be of quantum mechanical origin.[42]

We can't talk about the possibility of traversing wormholes without mentioning the other popular theory of space and time travel—teleportation. Other than a flying Ferrari, teleportation has been the dreamiest way of travel in the mass consciousness of recent pop-culture fantasy. The matter-shifting moments seen during *Star Trek* are still a long way off, but progress has been made in moving entangled quantum particles and photons. By isolating two entangled photon ions, they become webbed in an invisible thread, creating a mirrorlike response mechanism. Therefore, whatever is done to one photon is immediately repeated in the other.

The National Laboratory in Hefei conducted these quantum teleportation experiments in China for the Physical Sciences Department at Microscale and the Department of Modern Physics. A remarkable breakthrough was made during their research:

> Scientists in China have broken the record for quantum teleportation, achieving a distance of about 10 miles, according to a new study in Nature Photonics. That's a giant leap from previous achievements. In the latest experiment, researchers entangled two photons and zapped the higher-energy one through a special 10-mile-long free-space tunnel, instead of a fiber one. The distant photon was still able to respond to the changes in state of the photon left behind, an unprecedented achievement.[43]

In Australia, physicists at the University of Queensland have discovered how to travel to the future without the need for Doc Brown's DeLorean. Using a combination of time-based teleportation and quantum entanglement physics, scientists Jay Olson and Timothy Ralph explain how to make a shortcut to the future, and that time traveling is possible without having to go through the time in between. Trying to imagine this tricky act of science is a hard one, and so is explaining it to the general public. An example that scientists Ralph and Olson use is the teleportation of a qubit sent into the future:

> The idea is that a detector acts on a qubit and then generates a classical message describing how this particle can be detected. Then, at some point in the future, another detector at the same position in

Figure 10.9. DeLorean time machine (from Back to the Future) *at the Historic Auto Attractions Museum in Roscoe, Illinois. Courtesy of Lautenbach.*

space, receives this message and carries out the required measurement, thereby reconstructing the qubit. But there's a twist. Olson and Ralph show that the detection of the qubit in the future must be symmetric in time with its creation in the past. "If the past detector was active at a quarter to 12:00, then the future detector must wait to become active at precisely a quarter past 12:00 in order to achieve entanglement." . . . They call this process "teleportation in time."[44]

This news comes on the heels of research by a team of Japanese scientists at the University of Tokyo, who claim to have transported light particles from one place to another by using a mixture of Schrödinger's cat theory and quantum entanglement physics. A team, led by Noriyuki Lee,

> linked a light packet to one half of a pair of entangled particles, and then destroyed the light and the particle it had been linked to. But because the remaining particle of the formerly entangled pair

maintains a link to its partner—which had been linked with the light packet—the light can be reassembled elsewhere. Though the technology is one small step on the road to teleporting a human, it echoes the particular destruction and reassembly of the teleporting deck used in *Star Trek*.[45]

These complex aspects of quantum mechanics were just theories a few years ago, but as the technological progress accelerates, these once-theoretical ideas are turning into full-blown realities. Universities are not the only ones experimenting with and researching wormholes, teleportation, and time travel. For a long time now, the military-industrial complex has been dumping black-budget dollars into this research as well. Mostly locked up in covert operations and classified government projects, it is extremely hard to say just how far they have advanced behind the scenes and outside of public view.

In the teleportation physics study done by Eric Davis of Warp Drive Metrics, and funded by the USAF, an inquiry was made into collecting information about teleporting material objects through space and time. They even looked into the possibilities of psychic teleportation, related to remote viewing or what the report refers to as *p-teleportation*. They also studied the geometry of space-time vacuums, quantum entanglement, and the groundbreaking realms of exotic teleportation, or *e-teleportation*. This can be described as the science of sending people or inanimate objects through a stargate with the help of layered space dimensions or parallel universes. A stargate is a variation of a wormhole that uses a flat entry point instead of the more familiar spherical-shaped Lorentzian sculpted space-time geometry.

The author of the report presented lots of theories, math, and equations but seemed to be most excited by the time-traveling possibilities made in the psychic realm:

P-teleportation, if verified, would represent a phenomenon that could offer potential high-payoff military, intelligence and commercial applications. This phenomenon could generate a dramatic revolution in technology, which would result from a dramatic paradigm shift in science. Anomalies are the key to all paradigm shifts![46]

Cosmic thinker and world-renowned physicist Paul Davies has no problem believing that we can travel into the future and says, "In the case of time travel, we've known for 100 years that it is possible to travel into the future. In fact, it has actually been demonstrated but most people's fascination is going back in time, not forward."[47] However, going back in time is where the real challenge lies. Davies, a regents professor at Arizona State University, wrote the best-selling book *How to Build a Time Machine* to educate the public about the reality of actually being able to zoom to the past. Davies maintains that spaceships will be able to fly through black holes created from complex exotic matter with antigravitational properties.[48]

The Defense Advanced Research Projects Agency (DARPA) is another branch of the military-industrial complex interested in teleportation and quantum entanglement physics. DARPA created a project called QuEST (Quantum Entanglement Science and Technology) in hopes of inventing supercomputers that mimic the human brain, stargates, and teleportation transponder stations.[49] DARPA officials claim that they are still seeking the funding for the project, and so far they have outsourced their efforts to independent researchers.

There's a good chance that DARPA officials, who don't have to go through the peer review process and have been funding most of the major universities' research projects since the 1960s, already knows how to travel through wormholes and safely teleport objects through space, whether physical or psychic. Perhaps this public announcement—at a time when news of teleportation and quantum entanglement physics is starting to leak into reputable online news sources and high-level, peer-reviewed university studies—is DARPA officials' way of covering their tracks.

One year after the Soviets started the space race by launching the satellite *Sputnik 1,* President Dwight D. Eisenhower and MIT president

James R. Killian created the Advanced Research Projects Agency (ARPA) to counter any missiles being fired from space and to boost U.S. technology programs. ARPA was formed by Department of Defense Directive 5105.15 in February 1958[50] and was the first step toward research and development projects that could ultimately fall into classified categories.

ARPA officials produced their first satellite within eighteen months of forming and would go on to invent and develop an astonishing number of new technologies over the next fifty years. The most famous and important was the Internet, which started as a computer program known as ARPANET, created in the early 1970s. Also in the 1970s, ARPA added the letter *D,* representing the word *Defense,* which allowed even more flexibility when it came to secret classification, and continued to develop technological staples of our modern world with a list—that we know of—that includes GPS (Global Positioning System) navigation, stealth flight capability, electronic speech translators, and unmanned aerial vehicles, commonly known as drones. DARPA also has an interest in developing bionic limbs, exoskeletal armor, cloaking devices, biometric cognitive passwords,[51] cars that can be driven with the mind,[52] and Transformer-like robotic cheetahs that can run faster than we can.[53] (See plate 39.)

What DARPA has been involved with that hasn't been disclosed yet is probably much more shocking, considering that in 2009 alone, DARPA's budget was a staggering "$651 billion"[54]—more than the combined budgets of Europe, China, and Russia put together. With the recent announcement of a super planet found in the Goldilocks Zone that has more water than Earth,[55] the rush for manned missions in space is at a fevered pitch. Recently, DARPA put out a call to launch a hundred-year mission to Mars and began funding private start-up space companies, like SpaceX, looking for new rocket and spaceship designs capable of such a long journey.[56] All this newfound interest in getting to Mars has fanned the flames of conspiratorial fires, raging across the Internet, that claim DARPA has already been to Mars in a secret space program known as Project Pegasus.

11

GET YOUR ASS TO MARS!

Dr. Lull: "Hi, I'm Dr. Lull."

Douglas Quaid: "Nice to meet you."

Dr. Lull: "Ernie, patch in matrix-B. Would you like us to integrate some alien stuff?"

Douglas Quaid: "Sure. Why not?"

Dr. Lull: "Two-headed monsters? Don't you watch the news? We're doing alien artifacts now. It's wild. Yeah, they date back a million years."

Ernie: "Wow. That's a new one. Blue skies on Mars."

Dr. Lull: "Been married long?"

Douglas Quaid: "Eight years."

Dr. Lull: "Oh, I see. Slipping away for a little hanky-panky."

Douglas Quaid: "No. I'm fascinated with Mars."

DAN O'BANNON AND RONALD SHUSETT,
FROM THE MOVIE *TOTAL RECALL*

THE SECRET PROJECT PEGASUS has sparked an infamous controversy: basically, conspiracy theorists believe that we have already been to Mars and established a colony there (see plate 40). We owe knowledge of this covert project to self-proclaimed whistle-blower Andrew Basiago, an environmental lawyer from Washington State, with a BA in history from UCLA and a master's degree in philosophy from the University of Cambridge. He is a member of the Mensa high-IQ society and is an accomplished editor, journalist, and author. Basiago's source of information is firsthand.

He claims that his father worked with DARPA in a secret time-based physics experiment and that as a child he was involved in a study for the programs being developed for space's new frontier—Mars. According to Basiago, with the use of quantum access technology, he was able to physically teleport to various locations in the space-time continuum. Basiago claims to have been present at Lincoln's 1863 Gettysburg speech and describes what happened when he arrived in Pennsylvania:

> My shoes were lost in the transit through the quantum plenum that took me from the plasma confinement chamber at the time lab in East Hanover, NJ in 1972 to Gettysburg, PA on the day that Abraham Lincoln gave his famous address there in 1863. When I walked into downtown Gettysburg, where the shops were, after walking into town along the north-south [artery] that led into Gettysburg, a cobbler by the name of John Lawrence Burns accosted me and took me inside a millinery shop and furnished me with a pair of men's street shoes and a Union winter parka that he took from a stack of military clothing in a storeroom at the back of the shop. In this image [not shown here], one can see how over-sized the shoes were. I can confirm that this image was taken right after President Lincoln arrived on the dais, because when I walked over to this location and stood in this manner to detract attention from my shoes, I had been standing over by the dais, and Lincoln had not yet arrived, and I only stood in this position for several minutes before the quantum field effect produced by the plasma confinement chamber ended and I found myself back in the time lab in New Jersey.[1]

Basiago also states that Donald Rumsfeld was a team leader at Project Pegasus and even brought back footage of the events on 9/11 three decades before they happened. The eerily accurate trick of folding a $20 bill to reveal an astonishingly clear image of the Twin Towers minutes before their destruction may have been an insider leak, a clue that there is something sinister going on behind the scenes. As proof of his Gettysburg visit, Basiago claims a Civil War picture, spotted by a fan while researching historic Gettysburg documents, shows him in the image. The photo is of a teenager with a big coat and shoes. Basiago claims he was nineteen years old when he made his first jump to the planet Mars in 1981. He maintains that there has been a secret space program run by DARPA for a long time and a colony has already been established on Mars. According to Basiago, this colony is a result of the advancements made through Project Pegasus.

Secret programs are labeled so for obvious reasons. They are almost impossible to prove. Basiago claims that, since its inception in the late 1960s, Project Pegasus has thrived using "off-the-books" black-budget dollars. This trend continues today, when newspaper headlines claim trillions of unaccounted-for dollars lost by federal agencies. While this secret space program progressed, its philosophy evolved to include a colony on Mars with underground cities as a safeguard for protecting certain human bloodlines in the event that nuclear war, or some other cataclysmic, apocalyptic event destroyed the Earth.

From 1981 to 1983, Basiago claims to have visited this colony and even walked the Martian surface after teleporting from CIA facilities near El Segundo, California. According to Basiago, he even witnessed the teleportation of then CIA trainee Barack Obama to Mars.[2] This announcement, made on the popular late-night radio program *Coast to Coast AM,* put Andrew Basiago's infamous popularity over the top. The "Obama on Mars" news lit up the Internet and even forced an official denial from the White House.[3]

Basiago received an unexpected challenge when famed remote viewer Major Ed Dames called in to the show via the wild card line.

Earlier in the program, Basiago said Major Dames had instructed them at a clandestine Mars seminar for time travel. Dames refuted all of Basiago and his guests' claims about DARPA and physical teleportation.[4] Basiago responded that Dames was lying about what he knew. Basiago pointed out that everything in the military is compartmentalized and some projects are so secret they are on a need-to-know basis. In Basiago's defense, we know this to be true.

For example, during the testing of the first atomic bomb, there were people working on the project who did not know what the project would ultimately be. A great true-life documentary that proves this is standard procedure with secret projects is *Atomic Mom,* about Pauline Silvia, a Navy biologist conducting radiation test experiments at the Nevada atomic testing range.

Basiago's backup whistle-blower is Laura Magdalene Eisenhower, the great-granddaughter of DARPA's founder. Eisenhower says she was recruited for the Mars colony when she was thirty-three,[5] but turned it down. Eisenhower and Basiago want the people to be aware of secret technologies and the occult history of the elite. Her theories about a secret space program took on a whole new level of curiosity when the London *Daily Mail* reported that Eisenhower's great-grandfather, Ike, had three secret meetings with aliens in the 1950s![6]

A search on YouTube will turn up clips of Laura Magdalene Eisenhower's various interviews in which she speaks about conspiracies such as the Martian-Aryan bloodlines, past lives, the Archons, 9/11, and reptilian shape-shifters.[7] That she was recruited at the curious age of thirty-three is interesting. Why so old? The number *thirty-three* is known to be a highly regarded occult number with many layers of symbolism. In this case it may indicate something more sinister than the conspiracies Laura Magdalene Eisenhower speaks about. This number may be a key to understanding that Basiago, Laura Eisenhower, and coconspirators, including the journalist Alfred Webre, the man responsible for publishing Basiago's initial claims in the *Examiner,* are part of an elaborate psychological operation.

Andrew Basiago's statements are so out of the ordinary that we can assume several scenarios: he may be a storyteller with a vivid imagination, on par with Isaac Asimov's; he might be the subject of a mind-control experiment, whose mind was seeded with false memories; he might be an elaborate disinformation plant, instructed to muddy the waters of the disclosure movement; or, perhaps, Andrew Basiago really went to Mars and met Obama there! To be fair, it has not just been Basiago who has brought up the ideas of an underground Mars colony and a secret space war. This terrain has been a heated topic of debate for the past twenty years, thanks to the theories of Richard C. Hoagland.

Richard Hoagland is no stranger in the scientific community. His fascination with outer space goes back to childhood, and by the age of nineteen he had achieved the type of recognition most of his elders in the field could only dream of. The evening of *Mariner 4*'s first orbit around the planet Mars, Richard Hoagland broadcast an all-night, transcontinental radio show in Springfield, Massachusetts, that linked to NASA's Jet Propulsion Laboratory (JPL) control center in Pasadena, California. The young Hoagland and WTIC-Radio, in Hartford, Connecticut, coproduced this event, which was subsequently nominated for the top award in journalism: a Peabody. A look at Hoagland's impressive resume shows positions such as former NASA consultant; Space Museum science curator; researcher; author; and, during the historic Apollo missions to the Moon, science advisor to Walter Cronkite and CBS News. Because of his impressive credentials, his opinion is valued and he has numerous followers and fans who trust his knowledge and judgment.

Hoagland's book, *The Monuments on Mars,* introduced us to the famous images of the face on Mars and the five-sided pyramid. The geometry used in the construction of this pyramid is known, if at all, as sacred. Nothing has been the same ever since. These theories have sparked the imagination of stargazers, thinkers, truth seekers, and astronomers (amateur and seasoned professionals alike) and have fueled Hoagland's growing popularity among conspiracy theorists.

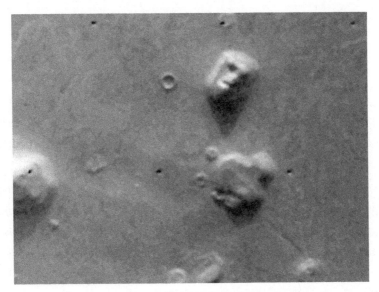

Figure 11.1. Face on Mars. Courtesy of NASA.

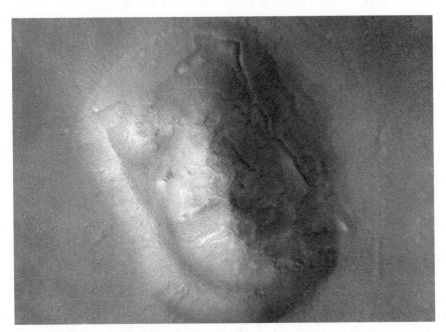

Figure 11.2. Updated image of the "face" on Mars, which later appeared to have been destroyed intentionally.
Captured by the HiRISE telescope camera on Mars Reconnaissance Orbiter. The image is slightly rotated from the original 1976 image. This version is not map-projected and has been cropped, and the curves were adjusted slightly to bring out detail in the shadowed areas. Courtesy of NASA.

The official NASA denial of Hoagland's Martian face theory is that "it's a trick of light and shadow," something that sounds like more of a dismissal than proof, since the statement is not conclusive and the pyramid, according to NASA, is an eroded rock formation. Even though they could end the controversy once and for all, NASA officials refuse to discuss this subject further. The idea of alien intelligence is a subject notable scientific minds of our time accept not simply as a possibility, but as a likelihood. NASA is at the core of the space science community. It would be ludicrous, considering the scientific process, not to look further into Hoagland's claims. This lends credence to the conspiracy that NASA has indeed conducted investigations outside the public's view.

Hoagland hasn't exactly rushed to clear his name, either. Ralph Greenberg, a professor of mathematics at the University of Washington, critiqued Hoagland's work and challenged him to a public debate.[8] The encounter has not taken place, and it is unlikely it will. Hoagland also refused to release a series of images from an early 1990s television show, called *UFO Diaries,* that appear to show him holding photos of a detailed face on Mars and a crater showing a five-sided pyramid.[9] Hoagland did not remember doing this and says these were paid actors, and the sensational photos were merely props. He has also refused to respond to researcher and filmmaker Jay Weidner's documentary *Kubrick's Odyssey,* which exposes how Stanley Kubrick filmed the Moon landing that was broadcast to millions of homes. Weidner demonstrates how Kubrick used a technique known as front-screen projection to project images on a "green screen" made with scotchlite tapings.[10] The tiny glass beads that made up the scotchlite screen contain bright speckles that can be seen in the lunar backdrop of the Moon landing. This cinematic trick was also used in the landmark film *2001: A Space Odyssey,* that coincidentally (or not) was filmed at the same time as the Apollo Moon landing. Weidner points out that Hoagland's claim of crystal and glass Moon bases are nothing more than the scotchlite imperfections of the ancient (by today's standards) green screen used during filming. The spectrum of debate puts Richard Hoagland in a unique category, where he stands as the lone authority.

Unperturbed by his critics' comments, Richard Hoagland continues to promote his theory, defending his position by saying the critics do not understand the complexity of torsion field physics, a theory of energy in which the quantum spin of particles can be used to cause emanations without mass and energy in order to carry information through a vacuum at one billion times the speed of light. This theory was conceived by a group of Soviet scientists in the 1980s, who since then have disbanded amid shouts of fraud and embezzlement of government funds.[11] Interestingly, the Russian Ministry of Science and the Ministry of Defense continued to fund the study of torsion physics from 1992 to 1995 and 1996 to 1997, respectively, through a private enterprise called the International Institute for Theoretical and Applied Physics (later called UVITOR).[12] The theory has been used to prove the existence of faster-than-light travel (FTL), extra-sensory perception (ESP), homeopathy, and levitation, as well as providing a rationale for the supposed functioning of miracle cures and other yet-to-be-explained phenomena.

This field of physics may not be fully understood by anyone. There have been no attempts to properly explain torsion physics and how it correlates to the more obscure areas of physics. Since Richard Hoagland has not been proven as either an authority or a fraud, the best way to verify his claims is to listen to what he has to say. As a popular guest on many alternative news programs, Hoagland has become the grandfather of the Truth Movement, and the opinions based on Hoagland's theories have cemented his role as current Mars and space news guru. Hoagland is extremely well respected, despite some accusations that he merely rose through the ranks of the Freemasons' invisible college and is actually working under NASA's direction, leaking controlled information or, as it is more popularly known—disinformation. Disinformation is a label strongly associated with anything that has to do with Mars.

New studies have shown that our DNA holds the collective

memory of our ancestors.[13] This might explain the strange fascination the planet Mars has held in our genetic memory since the beginning of written history. If NASA officials have assembled a private space fleet using suppressed technologies, it makes sense that they would target a place similar to Earth for exploration. Mars fits the bill. Buzz Aldrin disclosed information concerning a monolith on the Martian moon Phobos during an interview in 2009 on C-SPAN.[14] Aldrin confirmed that this monolith, like the one seen in Kubrick's *2001,* is alien-made and is a sign that we should begin taking steps toward the habitation of Mars by building a space station on Phobos as a jumping-off point. Maybe what Aldrin is really saying is that it's already been done. Phobos is an ideal halfway point for exploring Mars, mostly because it has no atmosphere and it requires less fuel to get there.[15]

NASA and the European Space Agency (ESA) have plans to conduct a joint expedition to Phobos in hopes of acquiring planetary samples that can be brought back to Earth and studied. This at a cost to the taxpayers of $8.5 billion.[16] Suspicions of what NASA has really been

Figure 11.3. Mars Monolith? Courtesy of Mars Global Surveyor.

up to rose again when the Russian space agency sent the $160 million probe *Phobos Grunt* to Phobos in hopes of obtaining soil samples and investigating the mysterious monolith. Strangely, the advanced probe never made it past Earth's orbit and came crashing down into the Pacific Ocean near Chile. The Russians vociferously blamed NASA for shooting down the probe by using scalar radar waves, a claim that was denied by the Pentagon.[17]

This battle for the rights to view Mars would be justified if NASA astronauts had been going to the red planet secretly for the past two or three decades. Even if they hadn't, with the advancements made in telescopes and HD-infrared imaging, NASA officials know that Mars was once home to alien civilizations. NASA no longer appears to be interested in searching for extraterrestrial life. Proof of this can be found by examining the SETI (Search for Extraterrestrial Intelligence) program, which was initially funded by NASA, only to be canceled despite SETI's accounting for only 0.001 percent of NASA's budget.

SETI fell into nonprofit hands in the 1980s and has been kept afloat thanks to the rescue efforts of billionaire philanthropist Paul Allen. SETI hasn't found any signals and most likely never will, considering their outdated and obsolete scanning technology. It's likely that NASA canceled the program because it already knows the truth about life in outer space.

The alien fantasy has been embedded in our pop culture for more than half a century, and Hollywood has done its part, leading us to believe that NASA has a desire to make contact with extraterrestrial life-forms. Evidence suggests they already have, and despite the programming from blockbuster movies and the vast amount of military insiders–turned–whistle-blowers who have gone public with this claim, NASA continues to deny it.

Antigravity propulsion system units alone would single-handedly end our dependency on oil. Few Americans are aware that a U.S. Space Command was created in the 1980s.[18] Those working with the Naval and Air Force branches of these Space Commands are likely flying and maintaining the back-engineered UFO spaceships, like the commonly seen TR3 black manta triangular crafts (see plates 41a and 41b).[19]

We've been living under the illusion that we are all alone in the universe and that no life-forms other than us have ever lived in the solar system. We're supposed to believe that humans are unique to the cosmos, and so far every "official"[20] report issued by NASA and the White House supports this notion, which is directly contradicted by the scientific process they adhere to. We're also supposed to believe that the skies on Mars are red, and according to every photo released, they are. But what if NASA had discovered that the skies on Mars aren't red at all, but blue?

When we think of Mars, the first image that comes to mind is that of an ancient, red planet. Even to the naked eye, Mars appears red. This is because Mars lacks oceans, and its landscape is generally reddish-brown. If we looked at Earth from Mars, the overpowering blue tints of the oceans, and the Sun's reflective light mixed with Earth's atmosphere, would drown out the shades of colors of most of the landscape. If we reversed this and removed all the water from Earth, over time Earth would take on the same color and appearance as Mars. Earth's sky glows blue because of an atmospheric phenomenon known as Rayleigh scattering. Discovered by British physicist Lord Rayleigh in 1871, our blue sky is the result of the scattering of light, and electromagnetic radiation particles infinitely smaller than the light's wavelength. Once this is mixed with Earth's oxygen-laced atmosphere, it creates blue skies.[21]

Scientists at NASA tell us that Mars has red skies because of the constant scattering of brown dust flying around in the Martian atmosphere, creating an array of red colors like the ones we see during sunset. But for this to be true, it must mean that there's a constant barrage of dust storms on Mars, polluting the atmosphere. The problem with this theory—and NASA has to realize it—is that vast amounts of dust would not survive in an atmosphere that is also host to ice caps, fog, clouds, and early-morning ground frost. Dew and other water-related moisture would eventually wash away and rid the atmosphere of this red Martian dust, leaving blue skies on Mars most days, if not every day.

In 1997 the Hubble Space Telescope was used to monitor a massive dust storm on Mars that could affect the landing of the *Pathfinder*. Hubble provided amazing photos that show thick clouds made of icy water particles, similar to cirrus clouds. Quoting from an official NASA report, University of Toledo scientist Philip James says, "If dust diffuses to the landing site, the sky could turn out to be pink like that seen by *Viking*. Otherwise, *Pathfinder* will likely show blue sky with bright clouds."[22] This is an admission rarely made and unknown to the average Mars enthusiast.

They say a picture is worth a thousand words, and the pictures of Mars are all tinted with a red hue. But what if those pictures have been digitally altered to make them appear that way? And if so, why is it so important for Mars to remain red as far as the general public is concerned? In 1976 NASA spent millions of dollars on the exploratory probe *Viking Lander I* to Mars. The curious scientists bit their nails in anticipation for a chance to see the first color images of another planet, and when the first pictures of Mars streamed to the lab at JPL they could hardly believe their eyes. The first dispatched image of Mars showed with astonishing clarity, a reddish-brown landscape similar to deserts in Arizona, rocks covered in green mossy patches, and a blanketing blue sky (see plates 42 and 43).[23]

Until it was leaked a few years ago, these Earth-like images were never shown to the public, whose tax dollars fund all of NASA's ventures. This, and every image since, have been deliberately altered, reddened, and recalibrated to maintain the false impression that Mars has no green algae, lichen, water, or oxygen in its atmosphere, all of which are basic building blocks for life.[24]

Why NASA would continually deny or hide this wonderful discovery about Mars is unknown. However, whatever their reasons, it can't be good for the billions of people trapped on a dying Earth that slowly appears to be turning into a giant prison planet. Maybe the elites know the Earth is doomed and want Mars for themselves in order to preserve their bloodlines, as Basiago and Laura Magdalene Eisenhower claim.

Since the first images streamed into the Jet Propulsion Laboratory in the 1970s, it has been known that Mars has blue skies, and later in 2004 the ESA captured images of rivers running through Martian canyons. Jurrie van der Woude, a veteran image coordinator at JPL, says, "Both Ron Wichelman and I were responsible for the color quality control of the *Viking Lander* photographs, and Dr. Tomas Mutch, the Viking imaging team leader told us he got a call from the NASA administrator asking that we destroy the Mars blue sky negative created from the digital data."[25]

At a live NASA press conference at the JPL press center in Pasadena, California, on January 10, 2004, an image appeared that has launched more speculation about the space agency's secretive endeavors. When members of the Mars *Rover* scientific team—Chris Voorhees, Joy Crisp, and Matt Golombek—were discussing mineral testing being done by NASA, an unaltered picture of Mars briefly appeared in the slide show projected behind their news conference table. This panoramic image, captured by NASA's probe *Spirit,* showed Mars with a clear blue sky (see plate 43).[26] This revealed a vastly different reality from all the other shots of Mars released with red skies. This slight mistake, or quick-witted whistle-blowing, has been captured and preserved for us to see.

Thanks to the advancements made in digital photography, it's now easier than ever to compare and analyze official NASA and JPL images of Mars. If we take the image of the unfiltered true picture of Mars and use a simple image-processing program, we can raise the blue-green color spectrums to 50 percent and the red to 25 percent and instantly we'll come upon the red Martian landscape we are all familiar with. Why is this important?

A blue sky means that oxygen and nitrogen are in the atmosphere, and this can provide a sustainable environment for life and allow humans to breathe. In the book *Mars: The Living Planet,* Barry E. DiGregorio with Gilbert V. Levin and Patricia Ann Straat explains how tests done on soil from Mars were sabotaged, rigged, and eventually ignored to disprove any evidence of life discovered by head scientist Dr. Gilbert V. Levin. Even thirty-five years after finding this evidence, NASA officials are still staging press conferences announcing that they are "seeking signs of life,"[27] while ignoring Dr. Levin's findings and the results of the *Viking Lander* experiments. Microbiological evidence of life has been discovered on Mars, but NASA insists that the instrumentation and data collected had to be faulty, and officially claimed that life on Mars wasn't possible, due to the lack of water.[28] When scientists began pointing out images showing signs of water that NASA had desperately tried to hide for decades, space agency officials started to backpedal, slowly disclosing what they claim are "new findings" that reveal the possibility that NASA has known since 1976 that there is water on Mars and the planet has a blue sky like Earth's (see plate 44).

Before he died, the astronomer and mathematician Sir Fred Hoyle visited Dr. Levin and warned him that there was "deep political motivation behind government efforts to suppress information about life on Mars." Hoyle would go on to tell Dr. Levin to take personal safety precautions and even explained that "not only had the *Viking* detected life on Mars, but that, in a clandestine return sample mission to Mars, the U.S. government had obtained living microorganisms which were now under cultivation for potential applications mandated secret for now."[29]

These once-hidden secrets about Mars are slowly starting to emerge. Dr. Michael Meyer, lead scientist for NASA's Mars Exploration Program, made an announcement concerning photographs taken from the Mars Global Surveyor, saying, "We have followed the water and we have found repeated and predictable evidence suggesting water flowing on Mars. These observations give the strongest evidence to date that water still flows occasionally on the surface of Mars."[30] This public statement, clearly admitting that water has been located on Mars, was hardly reported in the mainstream media. This should come as no surprise, since our awareness has been molded to repress any interest whatsoever in the future and in the possibility of space travel and extra-terrestrial colonization. The ones with advanced information obviously have the best opportunities.

We need only look back at the colonization of the United States to see how this works. The notion of inhabiting another planet is not a far-fetched idea; indeed, our purpose may be to do so. As in all conquests in the history of our civilization, the most powerful individuals, the ones leading the way, are the ones who reap the greatest benefits, including glory, honors, titles, lands, legacies, and the ability to write history from a perspective that casts them in the best light. It is not inconceivable that religious and corporate empires have already set their sights on what appears to be the next big move for humankind. This would require the kind of order and discipline that indisputably cannot be left to the ever-wavering opinion of the present-day average human. What better way to achieve one's goals than to do so unencumbered by regulations, with the most sophisticated methods and advanced tech-nology, under the auspices of deeply rooted, reputable universities, and all the while manage to nudge the public to look away by promulgating false information, aimed appear both uninteresting and threatening?

Making absolutely no attempt to disguise their dark side by symboli-cally naming their most costly endeavor *Lucifer*, the Vatican, of all entities, holds the distinct honor of having the most far-reaching telescope created and then installed at a facility in Arizona. The giant Church of Rome has invested an enormous amount of money on a device that reason indicates must have many more practical applications than simply a desire for a bet-ter connection with God by peering deep into the cosmos. The Vatican is clearly interested in deep space. If the powerful Catholic Church doesn't rely on firsthand information from the Lord, or on secondhand informa-tion from the government, why should we? NASA's insistence that the weather on Mars is too cold for flowing water to be possible appears to be a lie, crumbling at such a fast rate that recent science news articles show that NASA is quickly changing their tune.

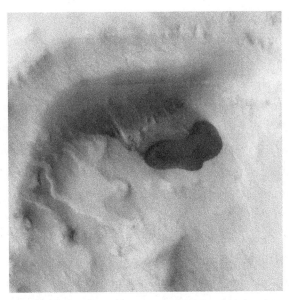

Figure 11.4. A structure that resembles a lake located in the center of this crater of the southern hemisphere of Mars. Courtesy of P. R. Christensen, N. S. Gorelick, G. L. Mehall, and K. C. Murray.

Steve Squyres, lead researcher for NASA's *Spirit and Opportunity* Mars rover, claims that a rock has been found containing gypsum and other elements required to prove that at one time water was present on Mars (see plate 38). He is convinced that this finding is "the single most bulletproof observation that I can think of that we've made this entire mission."[31] Dr. Charles Liu, an astrophysicist at the American Museum of Natural History, also believes the discovery proves there was water on Mars. Usually, where there's water there is also life. Since landing on Mars in August 2012, the *Curiosity* rover has found evidence of water, and it appears the necessary building block for life is indeed present in Mars' ancient history (see plate 45).[32]

The *Curiosity* rover is a futuristic spacecraft about the size of a MINI Cooper equipped with the most advanced radiation detectors and the most sophisticated scientific instruments ever used.[33] *Curiosity* has analyzed the largest solar flare event in the solar system since 2005, providing riveting information and data heretofor unknown about the breadth and scope of solar storms and flares. *Curiosity* was specifically designed to measure the amount of radiation exposure the human body might face during future manned missions to Mars. NASA is obviously investigating the effects of the Van Allen radiation belt. *Curiosity's* objective is to seek and study traceable parts of fundamental building blocks of life, like methane, within the Martian atmosphere.[34]

One specific study indicates that NASA officials have particular interest in the gas methane, but downplayed their curiosity. Barry Evans writes in the *North Coast Journal* that

> the rover is not designed to look for life. However, one of Curiosity's many instruments is designed to probe the puzzle of methane in Mars' atmosphere, which, perhaps significantly, waxes and wanes with the Martian seasons. One explanation is that the methane comes from the metabolism of microscopic organisms. Within a month or so after landing, Curiosity's Tunable Laser Spectrometer should be able to determine if the gas is geochemical or biological (life!) in origin.[35]

Circumstances indicate that NASA knows, and has known for some time, that there was or there is life on Mars. The information from the *Curiosity* rover will add to what must already be an astonishing amount of data and information that has been kept from everyone outside the tight NASA brotherhood. Astrobiologist Charley Lineweaver and his team of scientists from the Australian National University recently published a paper in the scientific journal *Astrobiology* that claims at least 3 percent of Mars is habitable. Lineweaver told the global French news agency AFP, "What we tried to do, simply, was take almost all of the information we could and put it together and say 'is the big picture consistent with there being life on Mars?' And the simple answer is yes. There are large regions of Mars that are compatible with terrestrial life."[36]

Through comparisons between core temperatures and atmospheric

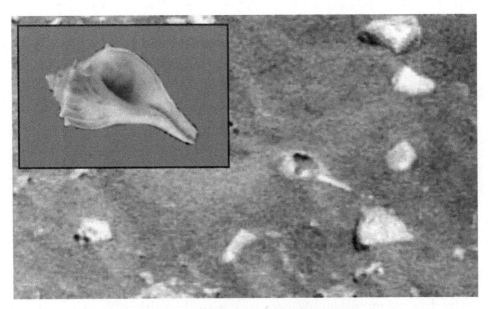

Figure 11.5. Martian seashells? NASA.
Courtesy of Sir Charles W. Shults III.

Figure 11.6. Martian seashells spread out. NASA. Courtesy of Sir Charles
W. Shults III. Also see plates 46a and 46b.

pressure, Lineweaver concluded that there are livable areas on Mars, and that areas with Earth-like conditions were underground. This is a theory long held by alternative secret space program researchers that claim NASA has already established underground colonies and bases on the red planet. This is consistent with footage in which researchers have pointed out strange dome-formation buildings and glasslike tunnels on the surface of Mars.[37]

If NASA scientists have indeed explored Mars, imagine their shock at discovering a planet similar to ours with ancient monuments, oxygen, blue skies, life, fossils, forests, and oceans. You can see clear evidence of Mars surface water, forests, and bio-organisms by checking out the invaluable research done by Joseph P. Skipper at Marsanomalyresearch. com.[38] The only real difference is that the lands of Mars have seen better days and more than likely resemble what the Earth will look like in the future. If an advanced, alien civilization truly lived on Mars, how did they get there? Where did they come from? How were their bodies able to survive prolonged journeys in space? Perhaps the mummies of ancient Egypt hold a key to this complex riddle of space travel.

12

ETERNAL CLONES, MUMMIES, AND HYBRIDS

You know and I know my clone sleeps alone,
She's out on her own forever
She's programmed to work hard, she's never profane,
She won't go insane, not ever
No V.D., no cancer, on TV's the answer
No father, no mother, she's just like the other
And you know and I know my clone sleeps alone

PAT BENATAR, ROCK ARTIST

THE EGYPTIANS BELIEVED the body was a manifestation of physical harmony formed by the divine complexities of the soul. The closest translation to English of their word for *death*—which they don't have a word for—is a term referred to as "westing,"[1] because it is associated with the Sun's disappearance on the western horizon each night. Similar to other ancient cultures, the Egyptians believed in reincarnation. Just as the Sun sets each day in the west and rises each day in the east, thus was death and rebirth. The ancient Egyptians elaborated on their beliefs about the afterlife by preparing earthly bodies with specific ceremonial procedures and mummification. They surrounded the deceased with their personal material goods, including furniture, wine, and food. Included were the mummified remains of their physical bodies and internal soft organs. Following the prescribed funerary rites, the organs were soaked in perfume and kept in vases called canopic jars.

When discussing these practices, traditional Egyptologists claim that the Egyptians were obsessed with death. It seems unlikely that the Egyptians would be obsessed with an idea they didn't even conceptualize, per se. Instead, the obsession is more with resurrection and rebirth. The ancients believed that if the physical body had met all its earthly needs, the soul would be free to move into the realms of the afterlife. More importantly, the ties to the earthly world would be severed, leaving the essence of the soul a choice to reincarnate or not without being tethered to the former life. However, there may be more to the genius of ancient Egyptian funerary practices than what we assume.

Ancient Egyptians taught the populace the importance of living a good and just life by instilling in their minds the parable known as the Weighing of the Heart ceremony. When our soul leaves our body at the point of death, Anubis, the jackal-headed god, met that soul. Anubis would announce to the one who had passed that he had dropped his earthly garment. The deceased then stood before the gates of the underworld and had his heart weighed against the goddess Maat's feather of Truth. The soul itself would judge its own accomplishments in life, and if any remembrance brought heaviness to the heart, the scales would tip. Fair witnesses, or objective onlookers, would observe the evaluation. Had the life been lived well and in a moral fashion, the heart would be "light as a feather" and the soul would proceed to the next realm of the underworld.[2]

Judaism and Christianity would distort this scene thousands of years later, calling it Judgment Day. In the Christian version, Peter meets the soul at Heaven's Gate. A life review would ensue, and external adjudicators would harshly judge the person. Religious fables instilled the fear of God and of eternal damnation to Hell if the deceased had not followed the commandments. This revision of the collective cultural myth

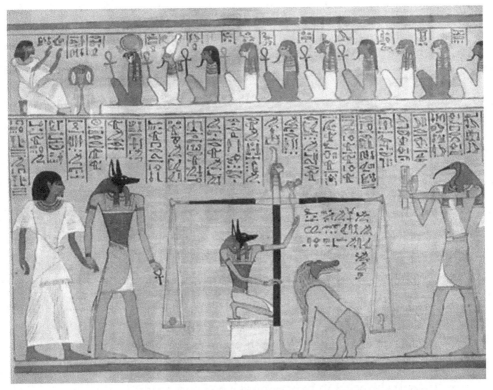

Figure 12.1. Weighing of the Heart. Courtesy of Jon Bodsworth.

significantly changed not only visions of what happens when people die; it also changed how people live. But the church did not stop there. The idea of reincarnation was a widely accepted notion in the religious beliefs of most ancient cultures. Even early Christianity appears to accept this natural cyclical progression. Nature recycles everything! It is how new life is fostered from death. The foundation of reincarnation is the idea that our souls cannot learn every lesson in one life. Dramatically, in 325 CE, at the Council of Nicaea, reincarnation was outlawed after Constantine declared Christianity to be the state religion of Rome.[3] There were dire consequences for anyone who continued to believe in reincarnation, and offenders would be tortured and killed.

Over time, all things Egyptian were raided, stolen, eroded, destroyed, removed, mistranslated, and eventually forgotten by later Christian scholars and writers.[4] The Council of Nicaea decided which books would be included and excluded from the official Bible. Under the threat of punishment by death, some brave souls rescued scrolls in earthenware jars and hid them in caves. In 1945 some of these scrolls were found in a small village in Egypt near the Temple of Dendera.[5] While all these sacred texts held a plethora of secrets, they were damaged fragments that were translated by Christian zealots and kept from public view for decades. Today new revelations are being made as these scrolls are interpreted in a larger context without the dogma of church doctrine or the threat of death keeping their secrets from the light of day.

One of these discoveries is that early Christians believed in mummification. The Torah notes that Joseph's family was mummified and given a huge funerary celebration and that "Joseph died at the age of 110 years; and he was embalmed and placed in a coffin in Egypt."[6] In other words, the practice of mummification was widespread before the Christians annihilated it. The thoroughness with which the practice was demonized, ridiculed, and obliterated raises a number of questions. Where did the belief in preserving the body originate?

Our advances in the field of biology and genetic composition grow by leaps and bounds, and scientists now recognize the value in conserving tissue and preserving organs. Advanced instruments can ascertain differences between our DNA today and the DNA of Egyptians 3,500 years ago, offering clues to our growing understanding of the evolution and devolution of DNA.

Time and time again, we misinterpret what the ancient Egyptians left for us because our science has lagged behind theirs. As we gain greater scientific knowledge of biology, physics, and cosmology, we can reexamine Egyptian artifacts, hieroglyphic writing, and symbolism to grasp what the ancients already understood. We were not able to properly decipher those symbols because we had not reached the level of technology required to do so. With a parade of examples of this phenomenon, we can safely assume the Egyptians had mastery of mysteries we have not yet even considered. As we stand at the crossroads of scientific discovery in the field of stem cell science, there is a movement to preserve body tissue. Recently, scientists have learned that they can preserve the greatest number of stem cells by cryopreserving the entire placenta in combination with umbilical cord blood banking.[7] If newborns or their blood relatives are in need of stem cells in the future, they can be generated from that cord blood. The ancient Egyptians understood this.

The ruling practice of dynastic Egypt was based on the tradition that each dynasty was a continuous bloodline of one extended family. Each successive pharaoh had to marry the daughter of the pharaoh before him. In the last ten years, science has gained considerable insight

Figure 12.2. The Mummy film poster (1932).
Courtesy of Universal.

into mitochondrial DNA, or mtDNA—which seems to be the underlying factor in the dynastic rule of Egypt. Even though dynastic Egypt was increasingly patriarchal, past matriarchal and matrilineal practices were still depended on. When the bloodline came to an end, a new dynasty started. This kept the mtDNA intact, carried through the mother's bloodline, and ensured the matrilineal descent through the X-chromosome. The father line carries the Y-chromosome, which is inconsequential in matrilineal descent.

For example, if we were to examine the mtDNA of a family circle composed of five related individuals and a friend, the first thing we would see is that there is one person outside the bloodline. Next we would see that, like rings on a tree that increase one per year, the marks of mtDNA can show the oldest, the middle, and the youngest of the related individuals.[8] If we were allowed to examine samples of mtDNA of Egyptian mummy tissue, we would be able to conclusively point out who is related to whom and who is in a different bloodline, and who is older and who is younger. This process is essential in tracing the bloodlines through the remaining royal mummies of dynastic Egypt. During the 1800s and the 1900s, large caches of Egyptian royal mummies were found, unwrapped, and shipped all over the world, and some were put back into different sarcophagi than they were found in. Tomb raiders and rogue explorers were in search of treasure and had little reverence for the ancient beings they were robbing. As a consequence, there is a muddle in the family trees of almost all the dynasties, that of King Tutankhamen being the most notorious. However, modern Egyptology carries its own agenda when it comes to the DNA testing of mummy tissue with a long history of sabotage, especially in the case of King Tut.[9]

We have been told that the ancient Egyptians designed their burial methods with spiritual reincarnation in mind; however, it is much more likely that they were actually planning a physical reincarnation as well. Considering that they had their organs separated and sealed in different containers, we can posit that they were also intending a return to Earth

Figure 12.3. Howard Carter opens the innermost shrine of King Tutankhamen's tomb near Luxor, Egypt. One of Carter's water boys found the steps down to the shrine. The New York Times *Photo Archive (1923).*

in a physical form (see plate 47). They just didn't realize how long it would take!

One of the mysteries of nature is the life of the caterpillar. It is a small creature that lives long enough to wrap itself in a cocoon for a few days while generating internal energy that miraculously produces a metamorphosis. When the process is finished, the cocoon drops away and from it a beautiful butterfly appears. This mystical progression cannot be duplicated in a lab, but scientists have created butterfly hybrids.[10] By combining two different-colored butterflies native to Central America, researchers at the Smithsonian Tropical Research Institute in Panama have created unique, laboratory-born butterflies. This experiment, and many like it, offer an abundance of new knowledge about creating and preserving hybrid species in labs. The results reveal a significant amount of information as to what the ancients might have actually had in mind during the process of mummification and organ preservation.

The ancient pharaohs themselves might have lost track of the initial concept of mummification's links to cloning. In the *Eyes of the Sphinx,* Erich von Däniken writes, "The original purpose, the hopes of a physical resurrection was quickly forgotten. Promoted by the priesthood, which made a large profit from the business of mummification,"[11] the resulting industry proved far more lucrative than its initial purpose.

With the advancements in DNA research, it is now possible to extract data from the cells of ancient mummies. Mummified DNA can preserve for eternity the genetic message contained within cells. With proper preservation of these elements, a mummified body can theoretically provide genetic information to generations far into the future. Perhaps the ancient Egyptians were recounting stories of procedures their distant ancestors witnessed thousands of years before. Nevertheless, it seems clear that they understood the preservation of body tissue and soft organs as well as the science behind cloning.

In the crypts of Hathor's Temple at Dendera, there are frescoes of "lightbulbs" depicted high on the front and back walls, but what these devices are depicting remains a topic of much debate. The most popular theory is that these tubes represent a form of lighting or an ancient form of battery conducting electricity. Considering that no soot has ever been found near walls adorned with hieroglyphs, scientists have always wondered what source of light was used while composing and chiseling these intricate, perfectly aligned symbols. Another theory about the lightbulbs is that they represent an incubator or test tube, which clearly shows a serpent wiggling its way through the bulb. One may very well consider this an ancient illustration of the Shemsu Hor's knowledge of advanced DNA and cloning techniques. In both the crypt and the room off the hypostyle hall, there are males holding the enormous devices. The bulbs themselves are as long as the men are tall. The base of each bulb has a large lotus flower as an exterior container of sorts. Inside the bulb is a serpentlike specimen undulating upward.

Figure 12.4. The so-called Dendera light in one of the crypts of Hathor Temple at the Dendera Temple complex. Courtesy of Lasse Jensen.

Figure 12.5. Another view of the Dendera light in one of the crypts of Hathor Temple at the Dendera Temple complex. Courtesy of Lasse Jensen.

Figure 12.6. Serpent and Horus reliefs, situated on the next panel of the "lightbulbs." Courtesy of Olaf Tausch.

Figure 12.7. Dendera light relief sketch: travels in upper and lower Egypt, 1802. Courtesy of Vivant Denon.

Figure 12.8. A scene on the west wall of the Osiris Hall that is situated beyond the seven chapels and entered via the Osiris Chapel. It shows the raising of the djed pillar. Courtesy of Jon Bodsworth.

These tubes representing the Shemsu Hor and DNA contain images of serpents that are connected to and grow out of the blue lotus flower, a symbol of the sacred feminine that gives life. Over time, these images would be misinterpreted and eventually morph into myths and speculation. A djed pillar, often referred to as the spinal cord of Osiris, is another out-of-place hieroglyph found near the lightbulbs, which clearly depict some sort of machine. It can be seen covering an entire wall, being propped up by men almost half the size of the device (see plate 48).

Other strange glyphs and symbols can be found accompanying the djed. The entire scene may be communicating to us the secrets of cloning and DNA. Why else would the Egyptians go to all the trouble of mummification if they never expected the preserved DNA to have a function in the distant future? This is a possibility that E. A. Wallis Budge argues:

Egyptians firmly believed that besides the soul there was some other element of the [person] that could rise again. The preservation of the corruptible body too was in some way connected with the life in the world to come, and its preservation was necessary to ensure eternal life; otherwise the prayers recited to this end would have been futile, and the time honoured custom of mummifying the dead would have had no meaning.[12]

It turns out that humans were not the only beings that the Egyptians mummified. The original purpose of mummifying animals may have been to preserve DNA from a variety of species. However, the sheer number of similar specimens may have turned into a business for the priesthood because archaeologists have been shocked to discover that almost every living thing in Egypt was, at some point, mummified. Scorpions, weasels, fish, eels, rats, and cats were all preserved and wrapped in cotton. Mummies of mammals, amphibians, and reptiles were all found in abundance in ancient Egypt (see plate 49).

In archaeological excavations carried out since the 1920s, it is estimated that over four million jugs filled with mummified ibis birds, and 200,000 mummified crocodiles have been discovered near the Fayyum Oasis. The ancient cult of mummification stretches back into the mysterious predynastic era of Egyptian history. It seems that the preservation of DNA was so powerful that it remained in the consciousness of Egyptians for thousands of years after the initial experiments.

Creation myths from ancient Babylon introduce us to a list of rulers associated with a time before the Flood. After the floodwaters receded, these rulers went to work maintaining and experimenting with the creatures that had survived.

Ancient historian Eusebius gives an account of this epoch in the history of the Chaldean culture:

In the first year appeared a monster endowed with human reason named Oannes, who rose from out of the Erythraean Sea, at the point where it borders Babylonia. He had the whole body of a fish, but above his fish's head he had another head which was that of a man, and human feet emerged from beneath his fish's tail; he had a human voice, and his image is preserved to this day. He passed the day in the midst of men without taking any food; he taught them the use of letters, sciences and arts of all kinds, the rules for the founding of cities, and the construction of temples, the principles of law and of surveying; he showed them how to sow and reap; he gave them all that contributes to the comforts of life. Since that time nothing excellent has been invented. At sunset this monster Oannes plunged back into the sea, and remained all night beneath the waves, for he was amphibious. He wrote a book on the origin of things and of civilization, which he gave to men.[13]

Figure 12.9. A fish-headed god, a hybrid of early Babylonian mythology. From Gaston Maspero.

Following the Babylonian creation myth, a variety of strange creatures were born out of these dark waters. Some could reproduce themselves asexually, others procreated sexually, and some were hermaphroditic, carrying characteristics of both male and female natures simultaneously. Some beings bore humans with two wings, others with four wings and two faces, and still others with one body and two heads. There were horned humans who had the legs of goats and human-horse creatures with hybrid bull features.[14] These cross-cultural tales speak of diverse sorts of dragon-shaped beings, hybrid fish, reptiles, snakes, and many types of astonishing creatures of differing appearances.

According to legend, the records of these creatures were preserved at the Temple of Belus, built after the deluge. The Greek historian Herodotus, "describes in detail the spectacular and multitiered temple of Zeus Belus at Babylon. He never gives the god's Babylonian title Bel or name Marduk, but he marks him by the foreign epitaph Belus."[15] The likelihood that the Temple of Belus will be found are slim.

Prominent biblical scholar Matthew George Easton describes the ruins as follows:

> An immense mass of broken and fire-blasted fragments, of about 2,300 feet in circumference, rising suddenly to the height of 235 feet above the desert-plain, and is with probability regarded as the ruins of the tower of Babel. This is 'one of the most imposing ruins in the country.' Others think it to be the ruins of the Temple of Belus."[16]

Corroborating the creation myth recounted by Eusebius is the newly revealed ancient Egyptian art from the Temple of Dendera that depicts the very creatures of which Eusebius speaks. These illustrations are little known, since they were hidden behind a thick layer of dark fungus until 2010 when the massive expanse of the ceiling of the temple, towering forty feet above ground level, was laboriously cleaned. It may be reassuring to consider that records of such creatures are left in fire-blasted ruins in a lost temple. That way, they can be

Figure 12.10. Scorpion-men of mashu underneath a winged ship.
From Gaston Maspero.

Figure 12.11. Eagle-headed god, a hybrid of early Babylonian mythology. From Gaston Maspero.

Figure 12.12. Cylinder seal with human-headed winged lions.
Courtesy of Henry Walters.

Figure 12.13. Cylinder seal with griffins and a winged disk.
Courtesy of Henry Walters.

SOME FABULOUS BEASTS OF THE EGYPTIAN DESERT.[2]

Figure 12.14. Fabulous beasts of the Egyptian desert.
From Gaston Maspero.

easily dismissed as a fanciful Babylonian myth. When these creatures are visibly depicted one after another as bas-reliefs across an enormous area, we need pause and attempt to comprehend what is being portrayed. What did the Egyptians know, and how did they learn about these things? There are plenty of strange beasts and hybrid creatures found throughout ancient Egyptian art (see plate 50), and some of these bizarre biological anomalies can be verified by science today.

Recent discoveries in biotechnology are redefining the realm of the possible.[17] As new data is integrated into our own developmental research, we see that what was once considered science fiction is now sprouting firm roots in modern technology. Fusing scientific discoveries in bioengineering, cell regeneration, and stem cell research, scientists have opened the gateway to the controversial science of cloning. Scientists in Britain have discreetly "created more than 150 human-animal hybrid embryos in British laboratories"[18] and are on track to redefine what we know about stem cell therapy.

There are even plans to clone a wooly mammoth from the well-preserved bone marrow found in a pristine femur bone discovered by Russian scientists in Siberia.[19] Mainstream academia has admitted that the ability to clone ancient species is only three to five years away, which means that DARPA has most likely already done it. It would not be far-fetched to imagine a future where our grandchildren will be taking their children to the zoo to see fully cloned dinosaurs.[20]

Dr. Robert Lanza, chief scientific officer of Advanced Cell Technology (ACT), has conducted stem cell and regenerative medicine research for more than twenty-five years. He has successfully created clones of kidneys that could single-handedly end the need for donors. James Chapman writes for the London *Daily Mail:*

> Scientists have created the world's first test-tube organs in a break-through that could revolutionise transplant medicine. The American experts are claiming to have used cloning technology to transform cells taken from a cow's ear into functioning kidneys. The "spare-part" kidneys were genetically identical to the cell donor and so were not rejected when they were transplanted into the animal. The scientists are confident that the same technique will work in humans within the next few years. Using just a few skin cells, doctors would be able to grow perfectly matched organs with none of the problems of rejection associated with donor tissue. They have already started trying to produce other tissues, including heart cells. The team of scientists at Advanced Cell Technologies in Massachusetts, a private firm, attracted international controversy when they announced the creation of the world's first human embryo clones late [in 2011].[21]

Clones of rhesus monkeys[22] have been created at Oregon Health and Sciences University. This is nothing compared to the news of a 300-million-year-old forest recently discovered underneath volcanic ash in China. This uniquely preserved forest even predates the dinosaurs and again throws all the geological facts we assumed were true right out the window.[23]

The scientists responsible for cloning the first mammal, Dolly the sheep, in Edinburgh recently announced the cloning of the world's first human brain cells.[24] The advances made in cloning in the past twenty years have been incredible and beg the question: How far have we gone? In 1985 Dr. Svante Paabo, then director of the Department of Cell

Figure 12.15. Wooly mammoths near the Somme River.
Courtesy of Charles R. Knight.

Research at the University of Uppsala, Sweden, reported that the preserved state of some Egyptian mummies was so perfect that they would have no problems cloning these ancient Egyptians:

> To elucidate whether this unique source of ancient human remains can be used for molecular genetic analyses, 23 mummies were investigated for DNA content. One 2,400-year-old mummy of a child was found to contain DNA that could be molecularly cloned in a plasmid vector. I report here that one such clone contains two members of the Alu family of human repetitive DNA sequences, as detected by DNA hybridizations and nucleotide sequencing. These analyses show that substantial pieces of mummy DNA . . . can be cloned and that the DNA fragments seem to contain little or no modifications introduced postmortem.[25]

All these DNA mysteries may not be confined to the Earth. Recently, NASA has admitted that our own solar system contains the building blocks required for DNA to be made in space.[26] It may be astonishing to some that humankind is currently capable of bioengineering, yet it is much more astonishing to consider that the ancient Egyptians were also cognizant of these techniques. The prospect of creating clones and rebuilding tissue with stem cells is now a scientific fact. The knowledge of this new, biotechnological conquest has shed light on previously indecipherable glyphs of ancient Egypt, revealing that cloning could have been in use tens of thousands of years ago during the last Golden Age.

The iconography pointing to the knowledge that the Nile civilization has provided for us is found all over NASA, DARPA, and other corporate and military tentacles belonging to the shadow government. It seems that at the highest levels of these clandestine organizations, ancient Egypt's past connections with aliens is indeed known and has been used to develop an entire secret space program to explore and honor this mystery.

13

SECRET SPACE ODYSSEY

The most terrifying fact about the universe is not that it is hostile but that it is indifferent, but if we can come to terms with this indifference, then our existence as a species can have genuine meaning. However vast the darkness, we must supply our own light.

STANLEY KUBRICK, FILMMAKER

IT IS COMMON KNOWLEDGE that most if not all of NASA's high-level personnel are Masons. This close-knit and powerful corps of NASA officials may even have had their own private Masonic Moon landing, which Richard Hoagland boasted about when he described it in his best-selling book *Dark Mission*. If Hoagland is a NASA plant, then it's likely he's also a Mason. Indeed, his attitude that "Masons are the good guys" suggests that his questionable roots may stretch back to the brainwashing techniques perfected by the brotherhood of NASA. In his book *Dark Mission*, Hoagland writes that when the astronauts returned from the *Apollo 11* mission, they had their memories "deliberately altered"[1] and wiped clean. Memory manipulation is more than a theme for science-fiction books and movies. In this case it would explain the bizarre footage of the Apollo astronauts showing them struggling to remember in detail what they actually saw on the Moon

229

and out in space. The three weeks the astronauts spent in quarantine would have given NASA plenty of time to break down, wipe clean, and reprogram their memories in time for their inevitable press conference. Lastly, a curious fact about Masons, especially the branch of Rosicrucian Masons, is that they conceal the initials *RC* somewhere in their name. This leaves us with the possibility that Richard C. Hoagland is still employed to disseminate certain information that will assist in the continued manipulation of humanity. Whether true or not, his words can be dissected for other purposes that have nothing to do with any occult allegiances.

Looking back at the Moon landing through existing film footage, biographies, and histories, we find some strange anomalies. These cast doubt on the validity of the event generally acknowledged as the touchstone of the high-tech society we know today. One in particular involves astronaut Buzz Aldrin. Prior to the *Apollo 11* mission, Buzz Aldrin's mother committed suicide. He was depressed and even turned to alcohol. A person suffering from psychological trauma could not possibly be considered a healthy and fit specimen for such a mission, especially considering the talent pool NASA had at its disposal. If the mission was a covert operation that required easily programmable psyches, however, the choice of Buzz Aldrin would make perfect sense. His emotional state at the time would have made him much more susceptible and responsive to a program of manipulated mind control. If this was a deciding factor in choosing Aldrin as one of the three crew members of *Apollo 11,* the three weeks spent in mind-altering quarantine did not help the astronauts get their stories straight.

During the press conference on August 12, 1969, in Houston, the faces of the *Apollo 11* heroes—Buzz Aldrin, Neil Armstrong, and Michael Collins—speak volumes. None of their physical behavior or body language suggests the obvious enthusiasm of conquering heroes who have been to the Moon and back. What they do reveal is the odd behavior of confused, sullen, shocked men, unaware of what's going on around them.[2] They can barely answer the questions coherently, and none can agree on whether they saw stars from space or not. This awkward press conference can be viewed today in its entirety on YouTube, despite NASA's rather suspicious claim to have "lost" all the original *Apollo 11* footage. NASA's claim accounts for this footage never having been shown to the public again since it originally aired in 1969. The footage was miraculously discovered forty years later when it was digitally "restored," providing a touched-up version to be cherished by all humankind.[3]

Figure 13.1. Masonic Moon medals from 1979.
Courtesy of Conspiracyarchive.com.

The mysteries surrounding the Apollo mission footage and the bizarre behavior of the astronauts should raise a red flag to any serious researcher of NASA and the space program. The act of creating false or synthetic memories, or planting ideas like those seen in the film *Inception*, has already been achieved with experiments done on mice by scientists at the Scripps Research Institute and MIT.[4] It's even speculated that the *Apollo 11* astronauts were drugged, implanted with false memories, and made to act out an elaborately filmed production of the landing in order to make them believe they had been to the Moon all along.

The main problem with accepting that a Moon landing actually took place when NASA said it did, is that space atmosphere is dangerous once you leave Earth's orbit and begin to pass through the Van Allen belt, a radiation belt so deadly some scientists believe it would kill any human being, not to mention frying any film or camera equipment. Now that this deadly obstacle is familiar to a wider range of scientists, we reluctantly suspend our disbelief in favor of *Apollo 11* overcoming being radiated to a crisp, but it is a downright impossibility that the camera equipment they carried on the mission could have possibly survived unscathed to provide the image Earth viewers were treated to.

Assuming the *Apollo 11* astronauts did make it past the Van Allen belt, then Buzz Aldrin's admission to having witnessed a UFO should be given more attention. Buzz Aldrin is the most outspoken, beloved, and publicly available astronaut of the Apollo era. He has even made an appearance on the popular TV show *Dancing with the Stars*. But decades of living under the weight of what might be the world's biggest hoax could be wearing on him. During a taped interview with filmmaker Bart Sibrel, Buzz lost his cool when Sibrel suggested that a transparent Earth decal in the command module's window gave the appearance that the astronauts were adrift in lunar orbit. Before storming out of the interview, Aldrin threatened to sue if the footage was ever released.[5]

The aggressive Sibrel has made a career stalking and ambushing Apollo astronauts and confronting them about walking on the Moon, even going as far as pulling out a Bible for them to swear on. His guerrilla filmmaking tactics are perceived as disrespectful and distasteful, and after questioning Buzz Aldrin for a second time, the old West Point graduate and Korean War veteran punched Sibrel in the face with a solid right cross that made national headlines.

What about the Moon rocks? If we didn't go to the Moon, where did all those Moon rocks the astronauts and rovers brought back with them come from? It may surprise many to know we don't have to go to space to find alien rocks. On January 18, 2012, it was announced that a Mars meteor shower left behind fifteen pounds of rocks in the Moroccan Desert.[6] It's believed in the conspiracy circles that NASA has been manufacturing Moon rocks with basalt and meteorites local to Antarctica since the 1960s and juicing them up with a little added radiation. Over the years hundreds of Moon rocks have gone missing[7] and one even turned out not to be a rock at all. Such was the bizarre discovery made by Dutch scientists after examining a Moon rock given to the Netherlands by the Apollo astronauts during a goodwill mission in the 1970s. The supposed Moon rock turned out to be nothing more than a piece of petrified wood.[8]

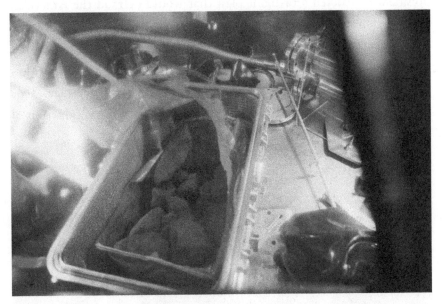

Figure 13.2. Apollo 11 *Moon rocks. Courtesy of NASA.*

Thanks to a classification order by Lyndon B. Johnson, any other mysteries to be revealed about the Apollo missions will have to wait until 2026, when the files become declassified. The controversial documents will then be used to point fingers at people long since dead. The Moon landings and the subsequent NASA space program that Kennedy had so proudly wished for would turn out to be a long way off. Even Kennedy doubted that any of it was possible.[9] Sadly, after his murder, the future of the program was left to Lyndon B. Johnson, who was likely informed by the world's best rocket scientists that they needed at least twenty more years to be able to send a man to the Moon and return him safely back to Earth.

The U.S. rivalry with the Soviets in the space race were at a dead heat, so members of the Johnson administration couldn't afford to sit back and twiddle their thumbs, no matter how far along the rocket scientists claimed to be. Is it really that much of a stretch to think they wouldn't have gone as far as to fake the Moon landing?

The shadow elite who ruled the country during Johnson's tenure as president concocted a brilliant plan that would defraud the American taxpayers out of billions of dollars over the course of five decades. If they couldn't actually send a man to the Moon and return him safely at that point, then they would fake the whole project, hire one of the world's greatest directors to film it, and essentially end the space race. This would give NASA ample time and cover to focus on the production of

Figure 13.3. Buzz Aldrin with Luther A. Smith, the Sovereign Grand Commander, and the Masonic flag he took to the Moon. Courtesy of Conspiracyarchive.com.

the real space program that would eventually put a man on the Moon when it was technologically possible. The money would come from tax-payers and be funneled through black budgets.

Using the NASA rocket programs as a front, DARPA developed a separate space program behind the scenes. The information housed under this secret program can provide the real answers to the questions of space travel and whether or not we have gone to the Moon or Mars. Now that China, Russia, and India have each independently achieved the required technology to go to the Moon, NASA's recent announcement declaring certain areas of the Moon to be no-fly zones is suspicious and questionable.[10] What does NASA have to hide?

In 2011 the Indian probe *Chandrayaan-1* spacecraft detected water[11] and ice on the Moon and found evidence of a giant underground chamber large enough to maintain a small lunar base protected from radiation and extreme weather.[12] In 1985 the Canadian singer Corey Hart prophetically declared that we can get "water from the Moon,"[13] a conspiracy NASA may have known and long denied until the Indian probe proved otherwise. It wouldn't take long for NASA officials to come clean about this in typical flamboyant American style, claiming they dropped a few bombs on the Moon, which resulted in over a billion gallons of water being released from the ice once trapped under the Moon's south pole.[14] The findings of the Indian probe contradict the information supposedly gathered by the Apollo missions, once again tipping the scales in favor of theories that claim there was no lunar landing in 1969.

If NASA officials had been going to the Moon and Mars via a secret space program for the past two or three decades, it makes sense they would be in a bit of a panic and would attempt to prevent other countries from finding out about that. They're even considering building a joint base with Russia to keep an eye on developments and prevent things from getting out of hand. China also hopes to establish a space station by 2020. This sudden burst of competition has made NASA officials nervous because there appears to be evidence that there has been a secret space program going on all along. NASA has slashed its space budget, to the shock and outrage of fellow scientists and employees, and literally made a 180-degree turn to the point of abandoning funding for further missions to Mars altogether.[15] It seems as if they are more desperate than ever to keep their secret space program a secret!

Independent research seems to indicate that the higher-ups at NASA and the USAF have lots to explain to the general public. Such are the claims by UFO researcher Ed Grimsley, who, equipped with a pair of third-generation night-vision goggles, says he's been seeing delta- and saucer-shaped UFOs flying over New Mexico for years. He's even watched advanced aerial battles performing unheard-of maneuvers while shooting what appeared to be lasers. He challenges any skeptic to come on a UFO-watching tour with him and use the night-vision goggles. George Noory took Grimsley up on the offer and was astonished by the UFOs he watched through the night-vision glasses in the skies above San Jose, California.[16]

There have been numerous videos assembled from the various space missions conducted by NASA, Russia, China, and the European space agency, all supporting the existence of either a clandestine space program or alien UFOs. The footage on these videos was recorded, compiled, and made public by UFO researcher Jeff Challender before his untimely and suspicious death in 2007 and can be viewed in the astounding documentary *Secret Space: What Is NASA Hiding?*[17] This documentary clearly shows strange activity taking place in Earth's orbit.

British UFO researcher Timothy Good is a titan in his field, with over forty years of worldwide research and countless hours spent interviewing astronauts, pilots, scientists, military intelligence officials, and NASA specialists. A prolific lecturer, Good was the first Western UFO researcher interviewed on Russian television following the fall of the Soviet Union. He has also spoken at the Pentagon and at French Air Force headquarters. He's served as a consultant on several congressional UFO investigations and has written classic bestsellers like the recent

Need to Know: UFOs, the Military and Intelligence, which goes into detail about UFO theories, ranging from the secret space program to the holographic motherships cited in Project Bluebook.

Good discusses briefings of U.S. presidents about alien encounters, writing:

> A number of former presidents, such as Truman and Eisenhower, gained access as a matter of course. Others have been briefed, in varying degrees, and some have even been exposed either to alien craft and/or the aliens themselves—dead or alive. President Richard Nixon, for example, is reported to have arranged for his friend Jackie Gleason, the comedian and musician, to view alien bodies at Homestead Air Force Base, Florida, in 1973.[18]

Paul A. LaViolette, who has numerous science degrees and a Ph.D. in physics, also shares Timothy Good's views on the secret space program. LaViolette believes that our understanding of Einstein's theory of general relativity is wrong and that UFOs use antigravity craft, flown with the knowledge of electrogravitic physics.[19] His belief that NASA has known about and been experimenting with antigravity propulsion systems supports the claims of hacker Gary McKinnon, a young computer whiz who says that while poking around NASA's top-secret webspace he discovered evidence of a massive space fleet being commanded by an unknown branch of the USAF.

These allegations sparked an immediate response from the American military. McKinnon was extradited from the UK to Washington, D.C., and charged with hacking crimes that might result in his being locked up in prison for the rest of his life. McKinnon could disappear forever without a trial because of the indefinite detainment clause attached to the National Defense Authorization Act, which Congress passed and President Obama signed into law on December 31, 2011.[20]

This is a bold step, considering that McKinnon is a British citizen who committed a crime on British soil and, after being arrested by the

British Tech task force, shouldn't have to face charges in the United States. But, again, due to laws passed in Britain following the 7/7 terrorist attacks (the British counterpart of 9/11), the pro-American Extradition Act gives American military officials the authority to block or dismiss any court rulings they disagree with. Despite McKinnon's claims that he will kill himself if he's extradited, and against the orders of doctors who have diagnosed him with Asperger's syndrome, the United States hasn't stopped aggressively taking steps to remove McKinnon from his home in England and tossing him into an undisclosed location in indefinite detainment without a trial.

McKinnon is facing a hellish ordeal, and it begs the question: Why go to all that trouble if McKinnon didn't actually see what he claims to have seen? In his own words, this is how he described it:

> A NASA photographic expert said that there was a Building 8 at Johnson Space Center where they regularly airbrushed out images of UFOs from the high-resolution satellite imaging. I logged on to NASA and was able to access this department. They had huge, high-resolution images stored in their picture files. They had filtered and unfiltered, or processed and unprocessed, files . . . I was able to briefly see one of these pictures. It was a silvery, cigar-shaped object with geodesic spheres on either side. There were no visible seams or riveting nor reference to the size of the object, and a satellite looking down on it presumably took the picture. The object didn't look man-made or anything like what we have created. Because I was using a Java application, I could only get a screenshot of the picture—it did not go into my Temporary Internet Files. At my crowning moment, someone at NASA discovered what I was doing and I was disconnected. I also got access to Excel spreadsheets. One was titled "Non-Terrestrial Officers." It contained names and ranks of U.S. Air Force personnel who are not registered anywhere else. It also contained information about ship-to-ship transfers, but I've never seen the names of these ships noted anywhere else.[21]

Strengthening McKinnon's claim, we turn to an obvious yet never publicly considered method of verification: the Pentagon's mission patches. Evidence of secret space fleets and clandestine space operations can be found by studying the various mission patches of the Pentagon. These patches are common because everything in the military is branded. Whether you're a private first class or a captain it doesn't matter: essentially, everyone in uniform can be boiled down to a symbol. Traditionally, military symbols are images of heroic figures rooted in history, and bold designs based on contemporary pop culture. NASA started using patches in 1965 and since then every black operation involving the space race has followed suit with the CIA, the DOD, and the recently declassified secret organization known as the National Reconnaissance Office.[22] These mission patches issued by the Pentagon are meant to identify, symbolize, and explain to the crew who receive them the objectives of their assigned black ops program.

Figure 13.4. Grey alien patch. Courtesy of Vigilantcitizen.com.

Most of these patches can't be associated at all with the typical bars, stars, and ribbon iconography of the mainstream U.S. military. Attention to this hidden slice of fascinating military history is due in part to the trailblazing research of Trevor Paglen. He compiled and published his book, *I Could Tell You But Then You Would Have to Be Destroyed by Me: Emblems from the Pentagon's Black World*, in 2008, after spending years sending hundreds of Freedom of Information Act (FOIA) requests to the State Department. Paglen eventually obtained over sixty black ops mission patches, and since his book's initial publication, dozens more of these cryptic and bizarre symbols have been released.

Never before seen by the public, these patches are assigned to classified and secret operations. Their symbols provide clues directly related to the Pentagon and NASA's penchant for occult principles, secret societies, aliens, UFOs, mythical creatures, space rockets, and Latin lingo (see plates 51a, 51b, and 51c). The public had never before seen these patches, and the reason is quite clear. People were not ready to confront and accept evidence of this magnitude.[23] We can only speculate as to what secret mission each patch represents, since Bob Mehal, the head spokesmen for the Department of Defense, refuses to elaborate, telling *Newsweek* it "would not be prudent to comment on what patches did or did not represent of classified units."[24] *Prudent* probably meaning his life would be at stake. It's likely that, beyond educated guesses, NASA will not voluntarily come clean.

The bizarre imagery found on these patches should be enough to convince anyone that there's a lot more to the space race that we have never been told. Consider that any technology made public has already been used by the military for at least the past twenty years, and the claims of UFO experts that the military-industrial complex has back-engineered and developed alien technology that's hundreds of years more advanced than what we can imagine. One such example was DARPA's announcement (on Twitter!) that they supposedly lost another hypersonic HTV-2 experimental aircraft that launches from an advanced *Minotaur IV* rocket. This advanced drone has the desired aim of reaching any spot on the planet within minutes![25]

NASA scientists and independent researchers have concluded that it snows on Mars and its North and South Poles are buried under massive, frozen ice caps. Both science and science fiction have fantasized about freeing this ice through nuclear detonation, and NASA officials actually had plans to nuke the Moon in 1959.[26] Science has established that the universe is shrinking; at one point the Sun was bigger and Mars was closer to it. This means that Mars had Earth-like conditions capable of creating and sustaining life sometime in the past.

Photographic evidence appears to confirm that there are far-reaching plains of petrified forests and fossilized timber, strange fossils, and skulls on Mars. It is not clear whether the skulls are robotic, mechanical, or animal.[27] But perhaps the most intriguing discoveries made on Mars are the massive blocks and megalithic stones found scattered throughout the cold and dry landscape. Similar to those found in Egypt, these large Martian blocks showcase intricate, right-angle curves and drilled holes.[28] Back on Earth, a startling discovery made by an ostracized and suppressed French archaeologist just might provide the most stunning clues yet concerning ancient Egypt and the planet Mars. What's even more shocking is that on the Giza Plateau we can find physical evidence of advanced alien contact deep in Egypt's past, and it has been hiding in plain sight all this time.

14

POLYMER SCIENCE,
THE GIZA PLATEAU, AND
THE BUILDING BLOCKS
FROM MARS

The truth will set you free. But first, it will piss you off.
GLORIA STEINEM, NOTED FEMINIST

ONE CAN BECOME QUICKLY OVERWHELMED while staring at the blocks that make up the Great Pyramid. Some are massive and finely cut, while others are more crude and added during later periods. Some of the stone blocks composing the pyramid are fused together so precisely they appear to have been poured into place, instead of being cut and then arranged. Were these massive limestone blocks once used in a manner similar to cement-making techniques? Were the blocks once a liquefied sludge that was re-formed and molded back into stone?

The chemical process involved in cement making has become a staple of everyday society, thanks to concrete sidewalks and the roads we drive on. But was concrete also prevalent in ancient Egypt? Internationally renowned French scientist Joseph Davidovits believes so, and his theories have irritated Egyptologists, who have mostly ignored him for the past thirty-five years. Considering that Davidovits has a stellar academic profile, we can see why mainstream Egyptologists have chosen to quietly dismiss him instead of criticizing his work head-on. Davidovits's impressive resume includes a French degree in chemical engineering, a German PhD in chemistry, and extensive tours as a guest professor at distinguished universities around the world. Since 1979 he's been the director of the Geopolymer Institute in Saint-Quentin, France, and is considered the world's leading expert on all things related to cement.

Davidovits has had the pyramid blocks expertly analyzed and studied. He has used his firsthand knowledge of cement to conduct thorough geopolymer experiments, both in the laboratory and on the Giza Plateau, all studies convincing him that the limestone blocks found in the Great Pyramid were not transported there after being rigorously hewn from quarries by crude slave labor. Rather, the rough blocks were assembled in some sort of container and then transformed into a liquid state with other materials added to the "cement" mix.

Philip Coppens, the late investigative journalist and author of *The Ancient Alien Question*, has made sure that his compatriot Davidovits's theories aren't forgotten. Coppens writes:

> From an engineering perspective, this technique would make the construction of the Great Pyramid much easier: there were no immense limestone blocks to be moved; there is no real need for a ramp and the transport of the stone material could be done faster, as less care was required in moving the limestone—the limestone was merely an ingredient and if it broke, no-one cared. Furthermore, the technique could also explain how the tremendous accuracy in the construction of the pyramid was achieved: the famous "no cigarette paper is able to be fitted between two stones." Rather than figuring out how two hewn stones were perfectly fitted into each other on site, instead, we would have wooden moulds that were placed next

to a completed "block," upon which "cement" was poured into the mould, then left to dry, before the next stone was made. This guaranteed that each one fitted perfectly to the next. It also fits in with the evidence on the ground. Some of the blocks that are allegedly hewn have large lumps trapped within the mass; others have wavy strata; others have differences in density between the stones of the pyramids and the natural stones located in the quarries; and there is a general absence of any horizontal orientation of the shells in the pyramid blocks, when normal sedimentation would be expected to result in shells lying flat. All of this is telltale signs for an expert like Davidovits that claims the stones were cast, not hewn.[1]

This theory of a "geopolymer" technique used in the building of the Great Pyramid hadn't even been considered until Davidovits first proposed it in 1974. Egyptologists ignored Davidovits's claims, and his works, published in France to great popularity, were delayed fourteen years before they were published in English. Davidovits's works have long been out of print and made available only by self-publication, adding intrigue to the seeming cover-up by Western academia. Davidovits confirmed these out-of-place "geopolymers" in a sample from the Great Pyramid in 1982, and further chemical analysis proved the pyramid stones are vastly different from the local limestone found in the quarries.

This undermines everything that traditional Egyptology teaches us about how the pyramids were built. Davidovits writes:

> The results were compared with pyramid casing stones of Cheops, Teti, and Sneferu. The quarry samples are pure limestone consisting of 96–99 percent calcite, 0.5–2.5 percent quartz, and very small amounts of dolomite, gypsum and iron-alumino-silicate. On the other hand the Cheops and Teti casing stones are limestone consisting of: calcite 85–90 percent and a high amount of special minerals such as opal CT, hydroxy-apatite, a silico-aluminate, which are not found in the quarries. The pyramid casing stones are light in density

and contain numerous trapped air bubbles, unlike the quarry samples which are uniformly dense. If the casing stones were natural limestone, quarries different from those traditionally associated with the pyramid sites must be found, but where?[2]

In 2006 a joint American-French study by Professors Gilles Hug and Michel Barsoum, used x-rays, plasma torches, and electron microscopes to study stone fragments from the Toura and Maadi quarries near Giza. While comparing their findings with the stones from the Great Pyramid, they concluded that the chemistry of the stones was not the same and that at some point the quarry rocks had been chemically altered. Egyptology's former gatekeeper, Zahi Hawass—a close friend of ex–Prime Minister Hosni Mubarak and essentially the number-two man in Egypt's government before it was overthrown during the 2011 revolution—immediately denounced this finding and, by way of the *New York Times,* called the theory "highly stupid."[3] Despite receiving wide-ranging praise for their work from distinguished scientists, such as Guy Demortier of the Namur University in Belgium and Linn Hobbs, professor of nuclear science and engineering at MIT, Professors Hug and Barsoum were unprepared for the onslaught of name calling and character-assassination tactics directed at them by mainstream academia. Even if we close our eyes to reason and wholeheartedly believe mainstream Egyptology's claim that the pyramids were built 4,500 years ago and designed by Imhotep, the discovery made by Hug and Barsoum is still amazing because it means the ancient Egyptians had developed a form of concrete.

It is traditionally accepted that the Romans improved upon the concrete first developed by the Greeks. But since we now know that most, if not all of Greek philosophy stems from Egypt, it would follow that the Greeks also learned this water-based, concrete-making technique from the Egyptians at some point. Last seen in vases around 4500 BCE, this complex geopolymer concrete-making procedure was outside the scope of modern thinking until a few decades ago. Why would Egyptians forget this procedure, if the pyramids were built by their ancestors?

The pyramids are not from the era of Cheops, but were constructed at an unknown time during the Golden Age, when the process of concrete making was a common practice, perhaps learned from the hero in Eusebius's accounts. Remarkably, we can find evidence of aliens' intervention during this Golden Age in the geopolymers of the pyramid stones themselves. More shocking still, the remains of such stones come from the enigmatic red planet Mars.

Baffling as it must have seemed at first, it is now indisputable, based on scientific evidence, that the geopolymer concrete composite comprising ancient Egypt's pyramid stones contains a mixture of water with natron, broken bits of limestone and shells, plus a silica substance that is found prolifically in Martian rocks. The striking chemical composition of the Great Pyramid stones reveals that the silica polymorphs in the stones are filled with opal-A and opal-CT, synthetic elements not abundant in the silicon found on Earth but common in silica rocks from Mars. There's a good chance that the synthetic polymers found in the Giza pyramids and in other Egyptian megalithic buildings were also made with Martian minerals.

Figure 14.1. Original casing stones at the base of the northern face of the Great Pyramid. Courtesy of Jon Bodsworth.

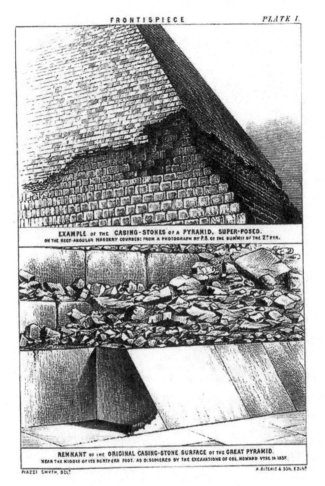

Figure 14.2. Plate I from Charles Piazzi Smyth, Our Inheritance in the Great Pyramid, *3rd ed. (London, 1877), further shows the casing stones of the Great Pyramid.*

The Martian silica seems to provide the extra element needed for creating the geopolymer concrete mix found in ancient Egypt's megalithic stones. This alien silica is also the same as the one identified by NASA scientists using thermal emission spectrometer (TES) data from the Mars rovers (see plate 38).[4]

The knowledge of these Martian-based mineral elements will finally crush the absurd mainstream theories about the Giza pyramids and their builders and corroborate the ancient astronaut theory of the Golden

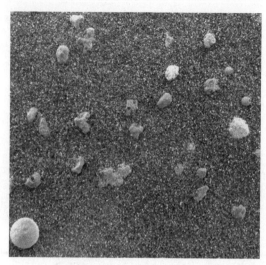

Figure 14.3. Martian spherules on the ground, as seen by the rover
Opportunity. *This magnified look at the Martian soil, near the Mars*
exploration rover Opportunity's *landing site, Meridiani Planum, shows*
coarse grains sprinkled over a fine layer of sand. The image was captured on
the tenth day, or sol, of the rover's mission by its microscopic imager, located
on the instrument deployment device, or "arm." Scientists are intrigued by
the spherical rocks, which can be formed by a variety of geological processes,
including cooling of molten lava droplets and accretion of concentric layers
of material around a particle or "seed." The examined patch of soil is 3
centimeters (1.2 inches) across. The circular grain in the lower left corner
is approximately 3 millimeters (0.12 inches) across, or about the size of
a sunflower seed. A color composite (see color plate 46b) was obtained by
merging images acquired with the orange-tinted dust cover in both its open
and closed positions. The varying hints of orange suggest differences in mineral
composition. The blue tint at the lower right corner is a tag used by scientists
to indicate that the dust cover is closed. Courtesy of NASA.

Age sky gods. This is a sentiment shared by the prophet Jeremiah, who
famously declared, "You performed miraculous signs and wonders in
the land of Egypt—things still remembered to this day!" (Jeremiah
32:20), and by first-century Roman-Jewish historian Josephus, who, in
The Antiquities of the Jews, also wrote about the mysterious Golden Age
gods of ancient Egypt:

They also were the inventors of that peculiar sort of wisdom, which is concerned with the heavenly bodies and their order. And that their inventions might not be lost before they were sufficiently known, upon Adam's prediction that the world was to be destroyed at one time by the force of fire, and at another time by the violence and quantity of water, they made two pillars; the one of brick, the other of stone: they inscribed their discoveries on them both, that in case the pillar of brick should be destroyed by the flood, the pillar of stone might remain, and exhibit those discoveries to mankind; and also inform them that there was another pillar of brick erected by them. Now this remains in the land of Siriad (Egypt) to this day.[5]

Another long-overlooked clue to identifying Egypt's ancient connection with Mars are the three Martian volcanoes Ascraeus, Pavonis, and Arsia Mons (see figure 14.4). These three volcanoes are in the same disposition as and line up with the three main pyramids of the Giza belt. The most famous volcano on Mars, and the biggest one in the solar system, also geometrically corresponds with the alignment of the Egyptian mountain Al-Wajit, found west of the Giza Plateau and transformed to resemble Olympus Mons.[6] The theories of alignment of the Great Pyramids, first with Orion's belt, and now with the three Martian volcanoes Ascraeus, Pavonis, and Arsia Mons, appear to be credible and eerily similar. When comparing images of the two theories side by side, they may both be clues to understanding how long-ago construction of the pyramids took place.

Horus was associated with Mars and is even depicted with a giant red circle over his head (see figure 14.5). The name of the ancient city of Cairo, when translated from the Arabic *Al-Kahira,* actually means Mars.[7] Ares, the Greek god of war, was associated in ancient history with both Mars and the giants.[8] Ancient literature even states that either the Golden Age gods or their offspring were giants. Numerous frescoes of the gods in ancient Egypt do indeed show these deities as double the size of the human inhabitants.

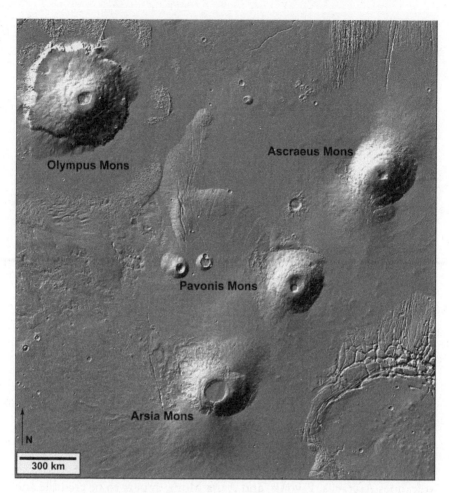

Figure 14.4. The volcano fields of Olympus Mons are represented by the main three pyramids of the Giza Plateau. Courtesy of NASA.

Controversial pictures proving mummified evidence of ancient giants have been kept hidden since 1988. These mesmerizing pictures, taken in Egypt by Swiss nightclub owner Gregor Spörri, were exclusively revealed on March 9, 2012, by Germany's biggest newspaper, *Bild*. Seen for the first time in public, the pictures show a giant, thirteen-inch, mummified finger.[9] If this picture reflects reality, as it appears to, since the article received no official rebuff, it means the person the finger belonged to was well over ten feet tall.

Adding more intrigue to the role ancient giants played in Earth's

Figure 14.5. Horus with Mars over his head. Courtesy of Jon Bodsworth.

history is the massive footprint found embedded in rock on the side of a cliff in South Africa.[10] Maybe these giants were around at the time when the Göbekli Tepe complex was in use. This megalithic stone conundrum, discovered by a Kurdish shepherd in 1994 in southeastern Turkey, has been dubbed "the world's oldest religious center." Mainstream academia, as seen by publication of this find in *National Geographic,* has even accepted and reported that the Göbekli Tepe is over twelve thousand years old![11] More secrets of the Göbekli Tepe can be found while studying the complex from above. It spreads out like a star map, pointing out clues and symbols to understanding where we come from by reflecting Taurus the Bull, Orion, and the much-loved homeland of Hathor, the Pleiades (see figures 14.6 and 14.7).[12]

A team of scientists studying the Chinese pyramids has reached the conclusion that an advanced race of aliens built them over twelve thousand years ago. They developed this theory by cross-referencing local myths, strange artifacts, and a series of red-hued pipes that run underneath the Chinese pyramid complex. This vast expanse of private

Figure 14.6. Göbekli Tepe. Courtesy of Teomancimit.

Figure 14.7. A three-dimensional stone carving of a lizard at Göbekli Tepe. Courtesy of Teomancimit.

land, guarded by the Chinese military, "stretches out much farther than what is visible and evidence suggests a highly technological network of pressurized pipes supplying water and possibly fuels."[13] When scientists analyzed these pipes, they were shocked to discover that 8 percent of the metal was from an unknown origin and couldn't be identified.

The fact that these ancient mysteries were unveiled in 2012 is both remarkable and extremely promising. Revelation of these ancient secrets could mean that we are experiencing an era of expanding consciousness, or perhaps we have progressed to a point when we can finally decipher what the ancient symbols mean. Will the Old World Order finally crumble and allow us to write history anew, based on the fresh discoveries of the twenty-first century?

There's a new wave of progress occurring in Egypt. With the military taking over after the revolution, it was anybody's guess what the future of archaeology would be like in Egypt, but the change was immediate, and apparently for the better, since Hawass was thrown out of power. Fear-based propaganda by Western media, following the revolution, prompted a sharp decline in tourism in Egypt, but while Westerners stayed away, folks from Asia, Europe, and South America continued to enjoy the now–less crowded sites of Egypt. The Muslim Brotherhood's presidential victory has cast some doubt on how this will play out. Egypt's military rulers are being confronted by pressing socioeconomic problems, putting a dent in the exceptional amount of cleaning and restoration the military has done to the Egyptian temples up to this point.

Most of this work is concentrated around the ancient city of Abydos, where, shortly after the revolution, the military marched in with tractors and armed guards. They began digging and searching for something in the lands behind the ancient megalithic Osirian Temple. They also smashed in the walls of prominent Egyptologist Howard Carter's house, looking for objects that had long been rumored to be hidden between the walls by Carter himself.[14] It has been speculated that the hunt is for the ancient head of Osiris, which is believed to be a helmetlike machine.

The Golden Age lands of Abydos compose a wide swath of desert that encompasses thousands of miles of real estate behind the Seti Temple and the Osirian complex. This endless stretch of wide-open desert, where the military is focusing its excavations, is known as the "gap." It hides many secrets, still completely buried underneath the sand. By using satellite imagery, we can see all kinds of strange and unnatural designs here. Some of these designs suggest a type of archaeology meant to be seen from above, like the cliffside images of the Nazca lines in Peru. Deep in the Egyptian desert, behind Abydos, are strange markings and imagery that spark the imagination when seen from above. These shapes and signs may turn out to be nothing more than freakishly odd land formations, tricks of the eye, military bombing ranges, or hidden human enclaves. Or they might be clues worth investigating further. High-tech satellites are turning up more and more evidence of lost cities and pyramids than ever before. And with the recent announcement that the United States military is giving away (through the secret space program) two satellites more powerful than Hubble to NASA—it makes one wonder: What do they really know?

A cross-referenced review of Golden Age myths will lead one to the conclusion that the inhabitants of Earth, in the time called Zep Tepi in the early Golden Ages, traveled to and from, at least, the planet Mars. This conclusion is based on known facts about ancient Egypt's dynastic past, a study of the hieroglyph illustrations in ancient monuments, the Martian silica found within the geopolymer stones of the pyramids, and the applicable modus operandi of modern space and archaeological systems. All this points to alien engineering in the ancient realms of Egypt's mysterious past.

NOTES

CHAPTER 1.
THE GOLDEN AGE

1. "Popular Experts Biography: John Anthony West," www.world-mysteries .com/pex_12.htm (accessed June 25, 2013); "The Mystery of the Sphinx," www.youtube.com/watch?v=qQ-xh3kedW4&feature=related (accessed June 25, 2013).

2. Geraint Hughes, "John Anthony West in Ibiza," http://ibizatimes.blogspot .com/2006_09_10_archive.html (accessed June 19, 2013).

3. Nigel Strudwick, *Texts from the Pyramid Age* (Leiden, The Netherlands: Brill Academic Publishers, 2005), 65.

4. Robert Bauval, "The Age of the Sphinx," *AA&ES* magazine (August 1996), http://ds.dial.pipex.com/town/parade/henryr/quest/sphinx/ (accessed June 25, 2013).

5. Stephen S. Mehler, *The Land of Osiris* (Kempton, Ill.: Adventures Unlimited Press, 2002), 180.

6. "Platonic Year," http://dictionary.reference.com/browse/platonic+year (accessed June 25, 2013).

7. Helen Mary Tirard, *The Archaeological Journal,* vol. 47 (London: Oxford, 1896), 35.

8. Walter Cruttenden, "History and Celestial Time," www.binaryresearchinsti tute.org/bri/research/papers/history_and_time.shtml (accessed June 25, 2013).

9. "Isaac Newton's Occult Studies" http://en.wikipedia.org/wiki/Isaac_ Newton's_occult_studies (accessed June 19, 2013).

10. Ralph Ellis, *Mary Magdalene: Princess of Provence and the House of Orange (Egyptian Testament)* (Coventry, U.K.: Edfu Books, 2011), 114.

11. "72," www.seedtheseries.com/blog/72.html (accessed June 25, 2013); Robert Schoch, "The Great Sphinx," www.robertschoch.com/sphinxcontent.html (accessed June 25, 2013).

12. "Travel Cairo," MobileReference, Amazon Digital service (2011).

13. Michele R. Buzona, Antonio Simonettib, and Robert A. Creaser, "Migration in the Nile Valley during the New Kingdom Period: A Preliminary Strontium Isotope Study," *Journal of Archaeological Science* 34, no. 9 (September 2007): 1391–1401.

14. Dan Eden, "Tiahuanaco: Gateway to the Gods," www.viewzone.com/tiax.html (accessed June 25, 2013).

15. Owen Jarus, "'Huge' Structure Discovered near Snefru's Bent Pyramid in Egypt May Be an Ancient Harbour," *Heritage Key*, August 25, 2010, www.bibliotecapleyades.net/egipto/esp_egipto05.htm (accessed June 25, 2013).

16. Frederick Converse Beach and George Edwin Rines, *The Americana: A Universal Reference Library, Comprising the Arts*, vol. 8 (New York: Scientific American, 1908), 245.

17. Sanchuniathon, Richard Cumberland, Squier Payne, Eusebius (of Caesarea, Bishop of Caesarea), and Eratosthenes, *Sanchoniatho's Phoenician History* (London: R. Wilkin, 1879), 97.

18. "Ethnic Origin, Language and Literature of the Phoenicians," http://phoenicia.org/ethnlang.html (accessed June 25, 2013).

19. Rob Waugh, "'Britain's Atlantis' Found at Bottom of North Sea," *Daily Mail* (July 2, 2012).

CHAPTER 2.
PYRAMIDS OF THE BAND OF PEACE

1. Maxim Yakovenko, "The Key to Understanding the Pyramid: A Scientific Report into the Meaning of the Word and Term Pyramid," www.world-pyramids.com/pyramid.html (accessed June 25, 2013).

2. C. Edward Sachau and Muhammad ibn Ahmad Biruni, *The Chronology of Ancient Nations* (London: William H. Allen & Co., 1879), 25–29.

3. Ibid.

4. Jennifer Viegas, "Pyramids Packed with Fossil Shells," Discovery News, April 25, 2008, www.abc.net.au/science/articles/2008/04/28/2229383 .htm#.UZvgYJUalY8 (accessed June 19, 2013).

5. Joseph Jochmans, "How Old Are the Pyramids?" *Atlantis Rising* 8 (Fall 1996): 23–25, 52, 54–56.

6. Ibid.

7. Charles Piazzi Smyth, *Life and Work at the Great Pyramid During the Months of January, February, March, and April, A.D. 1865,* vol. 3 (Edinburgh: Edmonston and Douglas, 1867), 95.

8. "William Wilde," Royal Irish Academy, June 3, 2010, www.ria.ie/news-(1)/ william-wilde-seminar-and-public-lecture.aspx (accessed June 25, 2013).

9. Charles Piazzi Smyth, *Life and Work at the Great Pyramid,* 96

10. David Wilcock, *The Source Field Investigations: The Hidden Science and Lost Civilizations behind the 2012 Prophecies* (New York: Dutton, Penguin, 2011).

11. James R. Coffey, "Abu Rawash: An Egyptian Pyramid Like No Other," February 19, 2011, http://archaeology.knoji.com/abu-rowash-an-egyptian -pyramid-like-no-other (accessed June 19, 2013).

12. Edward F. Malkowski, *Ancient Egypt 39,000 BCE* (Rochester, Vt.: Bear & Co., 2010), 225.

13. "The Pyramid of Djedefre at Abu Rawash by Jimmy Dunn Writing as Alan Winston," TourEgypt.net, June 13, 2011, www.touregypt.net/featurestories/ djedefre.htm (accessed June 19, 2013).

14. "Pyramid Secrets" Divinecosmos.com, http://divinecosmos.com/start-here/ books-free-online/26-the-end-of-our-century/142-chapter-09-the-secret-of -the-great-pyramid (accessed June 19, 2013).

15. D. Davidson and H. Aldersmith, *Great Pyramid: Its Divine Message* (London: Kessinger, 1992), 52.

16. William Henry, "Place of the Gods: The Stargate at Abu Ghurab, Egypt," www.bibliotecapleyades.net/stargate/stargate10.htm (accessed June 19, 2013).

17. "The Pyramid Code—Episode 2: High Level Technology," Youtube www .youtube.com/watch?v=HwajptlULl4 (accessed June 19, 2013).

18. Blair Jackson, *Grateful Dead Gear: The Band's Instruments, Sound Systems, and Recording* (London: Backbeat Books, 2006), 186; "Grateful Dead Vacation Tapes of Egypt," www.youtube.com/watch?v=vUk46KcVtIw (accessed June 19, 2013).

19. "Abusir Black Granite Floor," www.ancient-egypt.co.uk/abusir/index.htm (accessed June 19, 2013).

20. Wayne Herschel, ""Star Map Egypt," TheHiddenRecords.com, http://thehiddenrecords.com/egypt.htm (accessed June 19, 2013).

21. Jimmy Dunn, "The Pyramid Field of Dahshur," www.touregypt.net/dhashur.htm (accessed June 25, 2013).

22. "Dr. Royal Rife," www.rife.org/ (accessed June 25, 2013).

23. "The Bent Pyramid," www.guardians.net/egypt/cyberjourney/dahshur/bentpyramid/bent1.htm (accessed June 25, 2013).

24. "The Pyramid Code: Episode 2: High Level Technology," www.youtube.com/watch?v=HwajptlULl4 (accessed June 19, 2013).

25. Ibid.

26. "The Pyramid of Maidum," Nefertum.com, January 11, 2008, www.nefertum.com/egypt/11f_maidum_pyramid.html (accessed June 25, 2013).

27. "Crack inside Red Pyramid," www.flickr.com/photos/vasenka/4688183208 (accessed June 25, 2013).

28. Stephen S. Mehler, "Was There an Explosion in the Great Pyramid in Antiquity?" www.gizapyramid.com/stephen%20mehler%20research%20article.htm (accessed June 25, 2013).

29. "Herodotus: An Account of Egypt," Athenaeum Library of Philosophy, http://evans-experientialism.freewebspace.com/herodotus_egypt02.htm (accessed June 25, 2013).

30. Frances Cronin, "Egyptian Pyramids Found by Infra-Red Satellite Images," BBC, May 24, 2011, www.bbc.co.uk/news/world-13522957 (accessed June 25, 2013).

31. "Baghdad Battery," www.world-mysteries.com/sar_11.htm (accessed June 25, 2013).

32. Jeff Peckman, "Physicist's Breakthrough Book on Subtle Energy and Healing Released," *Gadgets & Tech,* May 19, 2010, www.examiner.com/ufo-in-denver/physicist-s-breakthrough-book-on-subtle-energy-and-healing-released (accessed June 25, 2013).

33. Alfred Watkins, *Early British Trackways: Moats, Mounds, Camps and Sites* (New York: Cosimo Classics, 2005), 16–34.

34. Chris Dunn, "Evidence of Ancient Electrical Devices Found in the Great Pyramid?" Gizapower.com, June 2, 2011, www.gizapower.com/Anotherrobot.htm (accessed June 25, 2013).

35. Margaret Cheney, *Tesla: Man Out of Time* (New York: Simon & Schuster, 2001), 245.

36. "Victor Schauberger: The Path of Natural Energy (Implosion)," 1985, Avaxhome.ws, http://avaxhome.ws/ebooks/engeneering_technology/pathofnaturalenergy.html (accessed June 25, 2013).

CHAPTER 3.
ASTRONAUTS IN
ANTIQUITY

1. Michael Lieb, *Children of Ezekiel* (Durham, N.C.: Duke University Press, 1998), 52.

2. "*Playboy* interview: Erich von Däniken," 1974, http://wutwouldyoudo .proboards.com/index.cgi?board=general&action=display&thread=244 (accessed June 25, 2013).

3. Zecharia Sitchin, *The 12th Planet,* audiobook, www.youtube.com/ watch?v=mYmkophY2Pk (accessed June 25, 2013).

4. Marie Louis-Thomsen, "Sumerian Language," www.scribd.com/doc/ 49440363/Thomsen-The-Sumerian-Language (accessed June 25, 2013).

5. "The Electronic Text Corpus of Sumerian Literature," University of Oxford, http://etcsl.orinst.ox.ac.uk/ (accessed June 25, 2013).

6. Donald MacDonald, *Introduction to the Pentateuch: An Inquiry, Critical and Doctrinal, into the Genuineness, Authority, and Design of the Mosaic Writings,* vol. 1 (Edinburgh: T. & T. Clark, 1861), 163–69.

7. John Noble Wilford, "After 90 Years, a Dictionary of an Ancient World," *New York Times,* June 6, 2011, www.nytimes.com/2011/06/07/ science/07dictionary.html (accessed June 25, 2013).

8. "Greek-Hebrew Definitions," www.bibletools.org/index.cfm/fuseaction/ Lexicon.show/ID/H6051/`anan.htm (accessed June 25, 2013).

9. Joseph Blumrich, *The Spaceships of Ezekiel* (New York: Bantam, 1974).

10. "Hindu Cosmology," www.hinduwisdom.info/Hindu_Cosmology.htm (accessed June 25, 2013).

11. W. Raymond Drake, *Gods and Spacemen in the Ancient East* (London: Sphere, 1973), 49.

CHAPTER 4.
CLOSE ENCOUNTERS OF
THE SUN DISKS AND SKY CULTS

1. Peter M. Worsley, "50 Years Ago: Cargo Cults of Melanesia," *Scientific American,* April 24, 2009, www.scientificamerican.com/article .cfm?id=1959-cargo-cults-melanesia (accessed June 25, 2013).

2. "A Noble Cause: The Life and Work of Nikolai Miklouho-Maclay (1846–1888)," University of Sydney Online, http://sydney.edu.au/museums/ events_exhibitions/macleay_past/miklouho_maclay.shtml (accessed June 25, 2013).

3. Gary Matlack, "John Frum and the Cargo Cults," Damninteresting.com, February 9, 2007, www.damninteresting.com/john-frum-and-the-cargo -cults (accessed June 25, 2013).

4. Paul Raffaele, "In John They Trust," Smithsonian.com, February 2006, www.smithsonianmag.com/people-places/john.html (accessed June 25, 2013).

5. E. A. Wallis Budge, *Egyptian Literature Comprising Egyptian Tales, Hymns, Litanies, Invocations, the Book of the Dead and Cuneiform Writings* (London: Colonial Press, 1901).

6. Edouard Naville, *Records of the Past: Being English Translations of the Assyrian and Egyptian Monuments* (London: Samuel Bagster and Sons, 1875), 103–12.

CHAPTER 5.
HATHOR OF THE PLEIADES

1. E. A. Wallis Budge, *The Gods of the Egyptians or Studies in Egyptian Mythology,* vol. 1 (London: Methuen & Co., 1904), 430.

2. Kate Freeman, "NASA's World-Beating Supercomputer Gets 14 Percent Faster," Mashable.com, June 21, 2012, http://mashable.com/2012/06/21/ nasas-world-beating-supercomputer-gets-14-faster/ (accessed June 25, 2013).

3. Gaston Maspero, *The Dawn of Civilization: Egypt and Chaldea* (London: Society for Promoting Christian Knowledge, 1894), 119.

4. E. A. Wallis Budge, *The Egyptian Book of the Dead* (London: Kegan Paul, Trench, Trubner and Co. Ltd., 1898), 123.

CHAPTER 6.
REPTOIDS AND THE SHEMSU HOR

1. Tim Radford, "Rock Art Clue to Nomad Ancestors of Egyptian Pyramid Builders," *The Guardian,* April 5, 2003, www.guardian.co.uk/uk/2003/apr/05/arts.science (accessed June 25, 2013).

2. Andrew Collins, "What Leading Egyptologist Dr. Alaaeldin Shaheen Did Not Say to Ignite a Debate That Will Run and Run," www.andrewcollins.com/page/articles/shaheen.htm (accessed June 25, 2013).

3. Antoine Gigal, "Egypt before the Pharaohs," Gigalresearch.com, 2010, www.gigalresearch.com/uk/publications-pharaohs.php (accessed June 25, 2013).

4. Dr. Sameh M. Arab, "The Ancient Library of Alexandria and the Re-Built of the Modern One," www.arabworldbooks.com/bibliothecaAlexandrina.htm (accessed June 25, 2013).

5. Paul A. LaViolette, *Earth under Fire: Humanity's Survival of the Ice Age* (Rochester, Vt.: Bear & Co., 2005), 76.

6. Cynewulf, *The Old English Elene, Phœnix, and Physiologus* (London: Oxford University Press, 1817), xlii.

7. Auguste Mariette, *The Monuments of Upper Egypt* (Boston: J. H. Mansfied & J. W. Dearborn, 1890), 88.

8. Stefan Lovgren, "Giant Ancient Egyptian Sun Temple Discovered in Cairo," *National Geographic* (March 1, 2006), http://news.nationalgeographic.com/news/2006/03/0301_060301_egypt.html (accessed June 25, 2013).

9. Margaret Alice Murray, *The Osireion at Abydos* (London: Bernard Quaritch, 1904), 14.

10. "Ophiuchus," www.graveworm.com/occult/precess/ophiuchus.html (accessed June 25, 2013).

11. Gerald L. Berry, *Religions of the World: From Primitive Times to the 20th Century* (New York: Barnes & Noble, 1954), 9.

12. E. A. Wallis Budge, *Osiris and the Egyptian Resurrection,* vol. 2 (New York: G. Putnam's Sons, 1911), 1.

13. "Ancient Egyptians Used Helicopters and Airplanes for Battles?" Pravda, November 11, 2005, http://english.pravda.ru/history/11-11-2005/9213-egypt-0 (accessed June 25, 2013).

14. M. Don Schorn, *Elder Gods of Antiquity: First Journal of the Ancient Ones* (Huntsville, Ark.: Ozark Mountain Publishing, 2008), 221.

15. "Reptilian Agenda: Archives," www.davidicke.com/articles/reptilian -agenda-mainmenu-43 (accessed June 25, 2013).

16. "Thuban: Alpha Draconis," http://domeofthesky.com/clicks/thuban.html (accessed June 25, 2013).

17. Tonya Reiman, "The Reptilian Brain: A Prehistoric Hold-Over, Hiding Out in the Human Head," www.bodylanguageuniversity.com/public/238 .cfm (accessed June 25, 2013).

18. Bruce T. Lahn, "Human Brain Evolution Was a 'Special Event,'" Howard Hughes Medical Institute, December 29, 2004, www.hhmi.org/news/ lahn3.html (accessed June 25, 2013).

19. "Paleoworld: Troodon Dinosaur Genius," www.youtube.com/ watch?v=u9nsMt02j4o (accessed June 25, 2013).

20. Jeff Hecht, "Smartasaurus," *Cosmos*, June 2007, www.cosmosmagazine .com/node/1444 (accessed June 25, 2013).

21. Rob Waugh, "Welcome to Our New Lizard Overlords," *Daily Mail*, April 12, 2012, www.dailymail.co.uk/sciencetech/article-2128650/Welcome -new-lizard-overlords-New-study-suggests-alien-worlds-super-intelligent -dinosaurs.html (accessed June 25, 2013).

22. Yngve Vogt, "World's Oldest Ritual Discovered; Worshipped the Python 70,000 Years Ago," *Apollon*, November 30, 2006, www.apollon.uio.no/ english/articles/2006/python-english.html (accessed June 25, 2013).

23. Balaji Mundkur, *The Cult of the Serpent: An Interdisciplinary Survey of Its Manifestations* (New York: State University of New York Press, 1983), 252.

24. Paul Schellhas, *Representation of Deities of the Maya Manuscripts,* vol. 4 (Cambridge, Mass.: Harvard University Press, 1904), 18.

25. "Hopi Snake Dance," http://encyclopedia2.thefreedictionary.com/ Hopi+Snake+Dance (accessed June 25, 2013).

26. Sir Reginald Fleming Johnston, *Lion and Dragon in Northern China* (New York: E. Dutton and Company, 1910), 386.

27. John Bell, *"Bell's New Pantheon; or, Historical Dictionary of the Gods, Demi-Gods* (London: J. Bell, 1897), 162.

28. "Pergamum Serpent," www.google.com/search?q=Pergamum%20 serpent&hl=en&safe=off&prmdo=1&prmd=imvns&biw=1020&bih=55 6&um=1&ie=UTF-8&tbm=isch&source=og&sa=N&tab=pi&ei=7jhDT 8u8NaSZiALku9W6AQ (accessed June 25, 2013).

29. Pausânias, *Mythology & Monuments of Ancient Athens* (New York: Macmillan and Co., 1890), lxxvi.

30. *Journal of the Royal Asiatic Society of Great Britain and Ireland* (London: The Society, 1897), 220.

31. Henry D'Oyley Torrens, *Travels in Ladâk, Tartary, and Kashmir* (London: Saunders, Otley, and Co., 1862), 87.

32. *Asiatic Society of Bengal* (Calcutta, India: Asiatic Society, 1879), 81.

33. *The English Illustrated Magazine* 18 (New York: MacMillan and Co., 1898), 568.

34. Viggo Fausbøll, "Indian Mythology According to the Mahābhārata" (London: Luzac and Co., 1902), 28.

35. Louis Ginzberg, *The Legends of the Jews: Bible Times and Characters from the Creation to Jacob* (Philadelphia: Jewish Publication Society of America, 1913), 71.

36. James Robinson, *The Nag Hammadi Library in English* (Leiden, the Netherlands: E. J. Brill, 1984), 172–79.

37. Jennifer Viegas, "World's Oldest Marijuana Stash Totally Busted" *NBCNews.com,* December 3, 2008, www.nbcnews.com/id/28034925/ns/ technology_and_science-science/t/worlds-oldest-marijuana-stash-totally -busted/#.UZ4tmJUalY8 (accessed June 20, 2013).

38. "Seshat," http://en.wikipedia.org/wiki/Seshat (accessed June 25, 2013).

39. "Rick Strassman," www.rickstrassman.com/ (accessed June 25, 2013).

40. Andy Isaacson, "Amazon Awakening," *New York Times,* October 13, 2010, http://travel.nytimes.com/2010/10/17/travel/17Ecuador.html (accessed June 25, 2013).

41. Richard M. Dolan, "Book Review: The High Strangeness of Dimensions, Densities, and the Process of Alien Abduction," Sott.net, September 10, 2008, www.sott.net/articles/show/165468-Book-Review-The-High -Strangeness-of-Dimensions-Densities-and-the-Process-of-alien-Abduction (accessed June 25, 2013).

42. Chris Wilson, "The Real Mystery Lurking in the Chapel Where Dan Brown Set *The Da Vinci Code,*" Slate.com, May 17, 2011, www.slate.com/ articles/life/the_rosslyn_code/2011/05/the_rosslyn_code_5.html (accessed June 25, 2013).

43. "St Clair Research," www.stclairresearch.com/content/storiesNorse.html (accessed June 25, 2013).

44. Liz Allick, "Disney Buys Jim Henson's Muppets," *The Vista,* November 10, 2011, www.theusdvista.com/business/disney-buys-jim-henson-s-muppets-1.2694455.

45. Ryan Rigley, "Five Things You Didn't Know about the Lizard," July 3, 2012, http://splashpage.mtv.com/2012/07/03/amazing-spider-man-lizard-facts (accessed June 25, 2013); "Spiderman: Lizards, Lizards, Everywhere," www.youtube.com/watch?v=f6GyH6tRwAo (accessed June 25, 2013).

46. "Conan the Adventurer: Night of the Fiery Tears," www.youtube.com/watch?v=osFuH_W_8tU (accessed June 20, 2013).

47. "How the Animated Series G.I. Joe Predicted Today's Illuminati Agenda," Vigilantcitizen.com, December 9, 2010, http://vigilantcitizen.com/moviesandtv/how-the-animated-series-g-i-joe-predicted-todays-illuminati-agenda (accessed June 20, 2013).

48. "G.I. Joe: Collapse of the Dollar and the New World Order Plot," www.youtube.com/watch?v=AnhKatKiBLg (accessed June 20, 2013).

49. "G.I. Joe: The Animated Movie 1987," http://en.wikipedia.org/wiki/G.I._Joe:_The_Movie (accessed June 20, 2013).

50. "Jim Morrison, 'Celebration of the Lizard,'" http://allpoetry.com/poem/8578969-The_Celebration_Of_The_Lizard-by-James_Douglas_Morrison (accessed June 20, 2013).

51. "Jim Morrison quotes," www.thinkexist.com/english/author/x/author_3276_1.htm (accessed June 20, 2013).

CHAPTER 7.
CLOSE ENCOUNTERS OF
THUTMOSE III

1. Carol Roach, "The Lady Pharaoh," Yahoo! Voices, June 20, 2009, http://voices.yahoo.com/the-lady-pharaoh-3629199.html?cat=37 (accessed June 20, 2013).

2. Robert Anton Wilson, *The Illuminati Papers* (Berkeley, Calif.: Ronin Publishing, 1997), 104.

3. Jacques Bergier, *Extraterrestrial Intervention: The Evidence* (New York: Signet, 1975), 50.

4. "Tulli Papyrus," http://en.wikipedia.org/wiki/Tulli_Papyrus (accessed June 25, 2013).

5. George Hunt Williamson, *Other Tongues—Other Flesh: History and Proof of UFOs* (Charleston, S.C.: Forgotten Books, 2008), 196.

6. Boris de Rachewiltz, *Doubt* magazine, No. 41, official magazine of the Fortean Society, 214–15, Arlington, 1953, http://img167.imageshack.us/img167/2922/doubt411953p214215bg2.jpg (accessed June 20, 2013).

7. R. Cedric Leonard, "Fire Circles," December 19, 2010, www.atlantisquest.com/Firecircle.html (accessed June 25, 2013).

8. Zecharia Sitchin, *Divine Encounters* (New York: Avon, 1996), 232–33.

9. Charles Thomas, "Ancient Writings Reveal Egyptian Pharaoh Flew in Alien Spaceship!" *Weekly World News* (October 25, 1994): 6.

10. Samuel Rosenberg, "Condon Report: UFOs in History," http://files.ncas.org/condon/text/s5chap01.htm#s5 (accessed June 25, 2013).

11. Margaret Bunson, *Encyclopedia of Ancient Egypt* (New York: Facts on File, 2002), 86.

CHAPTER 8.
AKHENATEN VERSUS
THE BROTHERHOOD OF THE SNAKE

1. Geraldine Harris and Delia Pemberton, *Illustrated Encyclopedia of Ancient Egypt* (New York: Peter Bedrick Books, 1999), 142–43.

2. Nicholas de Vere, *The Dragon Legacy: The Secret History of an Ancient Bloodline* (San Diego: Book Tree, 2004), 20.

3. "Pharmaceuticals: The Sorceries of Babylon," http://theopenscroll.com/pharmakeia.htm (accessed June 25, 2013).

4. "Freeman," http://thefreemanperspective.blogspot.com/ (accessed June 25, 2013).

5. "Akhenaten," http://euler.slu.edu/~bart/egyptianhtml/kings%20and%20Queens/Akhenatenweb.htm (accessed June 25, 2013).

6. "Amenhotep III," http://guardians.net/egypt/amenhtp3.htm (accessed June 25, 2013).

7. Nicholas Reeves, *Akhenaten: Egypt's False Prophet* (London: Thames and Hudson, 2005), 87.

8. "The Reformation: Europe's Search for Stability," http://history-world.org/reformation.htm (accessed June 25, 2013).

9. Arthur Weigall, *The Life and Times of Akhnaton* (Edinburgh and London: William Blackwood and Sons, 1910), 92.

10. Ralph Ellis, *Jesus: Last of the Pharaohs* (Kempton, Ill.: Adventures Unlimited Press, 2002), 116.

11. Kate Spence, "Akhenaten and Amarna," BBC, February 7, 2011, www.bbc .co.uk/history/ancient/egyptians/akhenaten_01.shtml (accessed June 20, 2013).

12. Lorraine Evans, *Kingdom of the Ark* (London: Pocket Books, 2001), 218.

13. "The Restoration Stela of Tutankhamen," www.reshafim.org.il/ad/egypt/ tutankamun_restoration.htm (accessed June 25, 2013).

14. E. A. Wallis Budge, *Tutankhamen: Amenism, Atenism and Egyptian Monotheism* (New York: Dover Publications, 1992), 5–8.

15. Ibid.

16. "The Question of Psalm 104," www.seanet.com/~realistic/psalm104.html (accessed June 25, 2013).

17. Christina A. Salowey, *Great Lives from History: The Ancient World, Prehistory–476 C.E. Nefertiti: Egyptian Queen* (Hackensack, N.J.: Salem Press, 2004); see "Great Lives from History: Nefertiti: Egyptian Queen," http:// salempress.com/store/samples/great_lives_from_history_ancient_world/great_ lives_from_history_ancient_world_nefertiti.htm (accessed June 20, 2013).

18. "Enter Sigmund Freud," www.clt.astate.edu/wnarey/Religious%20 Studies%20Program/Religion%20Studies%20Program/Religious%20 Studies%20Program%20Files/Enter_Sigmund_Freud.htm (accessed June 20, 2013).

19. Nicholas Reeves, *Akhenaten: Egypt's False Prophet* (London: Thames and Hudson, 2005), 294.

20. Arthur Weigall, *The Life and Times of Akhnaton* (Edinburgh and London: William Blackwood and Sons, 1910), 226.

21. Cyril Aldred, *Akhenaten, Pharaoh of Egypt: A New Study* (New York: McGraw-Hill, 1968), 67.

22. Sir William Flinders Petrie, *Tell el Amarna* (London: Methuen and Co., 1894), 41.

23. John Coleman, "21 Goals of the Illuminati and the Committee of 300," www.infowars.com/21-goals-of-the-illuminati-and-the-committee-of-300/ (accessed June 20, 2013).

24. Antoine Gigal, "Egypt before the Pharaohs," www.gigalresearch.com/uk/ publications-pharaohs.php (accessed June 20, 2013).

25. John Marshall, *Mohenjo-Daro and the Indus Civilization* (Bombay, India: Asian Educational Services, 1996), 638.

CHAPTER 9.
THE ENIGMA OF ELONGATED SKULLS

1. "Encyclopedia of Ancient Egypt," Mobilereference (2010), http://books .google.com/books?id=MwvM09Z-7DwC&pg=PT597&lpg=PT597&dq =meritaten+chief+wife&source=bl&ots=UiZWDxfrd5&sig=jFPTLQrs Bq8eDpgchayITzA7HEA&hl=en&sa=X&ei=eUUzT5CwB6eq2QWxg-SiAg&ved=0CD8Q6AEwBTgK#v=onepage&q=meritaten%20chief%20 wife&f=false (accessed June 20, 2013).

2. "Who's Your Daddy? King Tut's Father Identified," NBC News.com, www .nbcnews.com/id/28279258/ns/technology_and_science-science/t/whos-your -daddy-king-tuts-father-identified/#.UZ_QQ5UalY8 (accessed June 20, 2013).

3. Adriana Stuijt, "Bizarre, Elongated Skulls Found in Siberia," DigitalJournal .com, February 28, 2009, http://digitaljournal.com/article/268227 (accessed June 25, 2013).

4. Fatima Sajid, "Myths and Mysteries: The Starchild Skull," Dawn.com, September 24, 2011, http://beta.dawn.com/news/661341/myths-and -mysteries-the-starchild-skull (accessed June 25, 2013).

5. "Starchild Skull: The Shocking DNA Results Are In," www.youtube.com/ watch?v=lOSbRCg0B4g (accessed June 25, 2013).

6. Brandon Keim, "Humans and Aliens Might Share DNA Roots," Wired.com, April 7, 2009, www.wired.com/wiredscience/2009/04/thermodynamino (accessed June 25, 2013).

7. Jane McEntegart, "NASA Finds Alien DNA in California Lake," Tomsguide .com, December 2, 2010, www.tomsguide.com/us/alien-DNA-NASA-Mono -Lake-Bacteria,news-9183.html (accessed June 25, 2013).

8. "Starchild Skull DNA Analysis Report: 2011," www.starchildproject.com/ dna2011march.htm#10 (accessed June 25, 2013); "Lloyd Pye: Starchild Skull DNA, Disclosure & Directed Panspermia," http://thestarnations .wordpress.com/2011/05/08/lloyd-pye-starchild-skull-dna-disclosure-directed -panspermia (accessed June 25, 2013).

9. "The Neanderthal Genome Project," www.eva.mpg.de/neandertal (accessed June 25, 2013).

10. Carl Zimmer, "Siberian Fossils Were Neanderthals' Eastern Cousins, DNA Reveals," *New York Times,* December 22, 2010, www.nytimes .com/2010/12/23/science/23ancestor.html (accessed June 25, 2013).

11. Ibid.

12. *Pursuit* 6 (July 1973): 69–70; *Mysteries of the Unexplained* (Chappaqua, N.Y.: Reader's Digest, 1992), 39.

13. "A Grave Assertion That Byron Had Horns," *Michigan Argus* (January 7, 1870): 1.

14. Richard Carnac Temple, *Indian Antiquary,* vol. 24 (Bombay, India: Education Societies Press, 1895), 260.

15. Sir Thomas Browne, *Pseudodoxia Epidemica,* Books 4–7 (London: William Pickering, 1835), 116.

16. Frederick Thomas Elworthy, *Horns of Honour* (London: Murray, 1900), 22; Rosemary Guiley, *The Encyclopedia of Magic and Alchemy* (New York: Facts on File, 2006), 168.

17. John Noble Wilford, "Homo Floresiensis," *New York Times,* May 7, 2009, http://topics.nytimes.com/topics/news/science/topics/archaeology_and_ anthropology/homo_floresiensis/index.html (accessed June 25, 2013).

18. Renato Vesco and David Hatcher Childress, *Man-Made UFOs: WWII's Secret Legacy* (Kempton, Ill.: Adventures Unlimited, 2007), 172.

19. "StarChild Skull is that of a Grey Alien?" www.youtube.com/watch?v=7y2_ YavFjDA (accessed June 20, 2013).

20. Paul Milligan, "Is This an Alien Skull? Mystery of Giant-Headed Mummy Found in Peru," *Daily Mail,* November 24, 2011, www.dailymail.co.uk/ sciencetech/article-2063486/alien-skull-Peru-Mystery-giant-headed-mummy -city-Andahuaylillas.html (accessed June 20, 2013).

CHAPTER 10.
SLOW DISCLOSURE

1. "Giordano Bruno, 1548–1600," www.historyguide.org/intellect/bruno .html (accessed June 20, 2013).

2. Jeffrey Van Camp, "ALIEN INVASION Movies Are Taking Over Hollywood! 16 of Them!" Cinemasoldier.com, July 29, 2010, www .cinemasoldier.com/articles/2010/7/29/alien-invasion-movies-are-taking -over-hollywood-16-of-them-f.html (accessed June 20, 2013).

3. Michael Weiss, "The Assad Regime Now Reports That Extraterrestrials Are in Syria. No, Really," *The Telegraph*, January 6, 2012, http://blogs .telegraph.co.uk/news/michaelweiss/100127635/the-assad-regime-now -reports-that-extraterrestrials-are-in-syria-no-really/#.TwjfMlF1E8Q.facebook (accessed June 25, 2013).

4. Richard Dolan, *UFOs and the National Security State: An Unclassified History, Volume 1: 1941–1973* (Newburyport, Mass.: Hampton Roads Publishing, 2002), 15.

5. Twining Memo, "AMC Opinion Concerning Flying Discs," September 23, 1947, www.nicap.org/docs/1947docpage.htm (accessed June 25, 2013).

6. "Protection of Vital Installations," www.project1947.com/gfb/pvi-1.htm (accessed June 25, 2013).

7. Lee Spiegel, "30 Years Later, Tense UFO Encounter Leaves Military Officers Shaken," Aolnews.com, November 4, 2010, www.aolnews.com/ 2010/11/04/30-years-later-tense-ufo-encounter-leaves-military-officers-sha (accessed June 20, 2013).

8. Daniel Bates, "America's X Files: Top U.S. Airmen to Accuse Air Force of Cover-Up As They Claim UFOs Have Been Deactivating Nuclear Missiles Since 1948," *Daily Mail*, September 28, 2010, www.dailymail .co.uk/sciencetech/article-1315479/aliens-interfered-weapons-UFOs -deactivating-nuclear-missiles.html (accessed June 25, 2013); "Larry King: UFOs Shut Down Nuclear Weapons (Part 1)," www.youtube.com/ watch?v=aTrGF6tSwZM (accessed June 25, 2013).

9. "Aerial Encounter with Disc," The National Investigations Committee on Aerial Phenomena, July 9, 1951, www.nicap.org/510709d.htm (accessed June 20, 2013).

10. Brian Appleyard, *Aliens: Why They Are Here* (New York: Scribner, 2005), 24.

11. Dan Berliner and Whitley Strieber, *UFO Briefing Document: The Best Available Evidence* (New York: Dell, 2000), 99.

12. Michael C. Luckman, *Alien Rock: The Rock 'n' Roll Extraterrestrial Connection* (New York: Simon & Schuster, 2005), 100–101.

13. Rick Giombetti, "Pentagon Vs. Spiderman," OutlookIndia.com (May 21, 2002), www.outlookindia.com/article.aspx?215707 (accessed June 25, 2013).

14. "Disney's Alien Encounters. Disney UFO Video Raises Questions on

Aliens," Want to Know.net, July 29, 2011, www.wanttoknow.info/ufos/ufos_video_disney (accessed June 25, 2013).

15. "Alien Encounters from New Tomorrowland," www.youtube.com/watch?v=w8CRyJ4Vo0I (accessed June 20, 2013).

16. Ibid.

17. "NSA Releases 29 Messages from Space," *NSA Journal,* vol. XIV, no. 1 (FOIA Case #41472), http://reinep.wordpress.com/2011/04/29/breaking-news-nsa-releases-29-messages-from-space (accessed June 20, 2013).

18. "Cylon Raider or Algae? Swedish Booze Hunters May Have Made the UFO Find of the Century," *News Australia,* July, 21, 2011, www.news.com.au/technology/sci-tech/cylon-raider-or-algae-swedish-booze-hunters-may-have-made-the-ufo-find-of-the-century/story-fn5fsgyc-1226098833887 (accessed June 20, 2013).

19. Mary Elaine Ramos, "UFO Baltic Sea 2012 Update: UFO Baltic Sea Causes Electric Disrupment?" *International Business Times,* June 29, 2012, http://au.ibtimes.com/articles/357747/20120629/ufo-baltic-sea-2012.htm (accessed June 20, 2013).

20. "Richard Hoagland Talks about the Baltic Sea UFO," *Coast to Coast AM,* June 25, 2012, www.youtube.com/watch?v=YJ8AeT_AhBA (accessed June 20, 2013).

21. Natalie Wolchover, "Baltic Sea 'Sunken UFO' Begins to Smell Like an Elaborate Scam," Msnbc.com, June 29, 2012, www.msnbc.msn.com/id/48018365/ns/technology_and_science-science/#.T_iqeUZ40fQ (accessed June 20, 2013).

22. Lee Spiegel, "Former Canadian Defense Official Blasts US on UFO Cover-Up," AOL News, February 25, 2011, www.aolnews.com/2011/02/25/former-canadian-defense-official-blasts-us-on-ufo-cover-up/?a_dgi=aolshare_email (accessed June 20, 2013).

23. "Was JFK Killed Because of His Interest in Aliens? Secret Memo Shows President Demanded UFO Files 10 Days before Death," *Daily Mail,* April 19, 2011, www.dailymail.co.uk/news/article-1378284/Secret-memo-shows-JFK-demanded-UFO-files-10-days-assassination.html (accessed June 20, 2013).

24. "Skunkworks CEO Admits UFOs Are Real," Majorstar, September 3, 2011, UFOweek.com, http://ufoweek.com/tag/mufon-ufo-journal (accessed June 20, 2013).

25. Nick Cook, *The Hunt for Zero Point: Inside the Classified World of Antigravity Technology* (New York: Broadway Books, 2003), 117.

26. "Secret UFO Propulsion Systems, Boyd Bushman, Senior Research Scientist," www.youtube.com/watch?v=VzwOFCSFms4 (accessed June 20, 2013).

27. "Apollo 14 Astronaut Claims Aliens HAVE Made Contact—But It Has Been Covered Up for 60 Years," *Daily Mail,* July 24, 2008, www.dailymail .co.uk/sciencetech/article-1037471/Apollo-14-astronaut-claims-aliens -HAVE-contact--covered-60-years.html (accessed June 20, 2013).

28. "Ancient Aliens: The NASA Connection," www.youtube.com/ watch?v=ZNgPKzNhmr0 (accessed June 20, 2013).

29. Michael Hanlon, "Titan's Siren Call," *Daily Mail,* January 5, 2012, http:// hanlonblog.dailymail.co.uk/2012/01/titans-siren-call.html (accessed June 20, 2013).

30. "Titan Sensation: Saturn's Moon Has Watery Ocean under Thick Ice Crust," RT.com, June 29, 2012, www.rt.com/news/titan-moon-water -ocean-062 (accessed June 20, 2013).

31. Trent J. Perrotto, "Hubble Breaks New Ground with Discovery of Distant Exploding Star," Nasa.gov, January 11, 2012, www1.nasa.gov/mission_ pages/hubble/science/exploding-star_prt.htm (accessed June 20, 2013).

32. Lizzy Davies, "Higgs Boson Announcement Live: CERN Scientists Discover Subatomic Particle," *Guardian,* July 4, 2012, www.guardian.co.uk/science/ blog/2012/jul/04/higgs-boson-discovered-live-coverage-cern (accessed June 20, 2013).

33. Nick Collins, "Billions of Habitable Planets in Milky Way," *London Telegraph,* January 11, 2012, www.telegraph.co.uk/science/space/9008012/ Billions-of-habitable-planets-in-Milky-Way.html (accessed June 20, 2013).

34. Brian Vastag, "New 'Super-Earth' That Is 36 Light-Years Away Might Hold Water, Astronomers Say," *Washington Post,* December 9, 2011, www .washingtonpost.com/national/health-science/new-super-earth-is-36 -light-years-distant-might-hold-water-astronomers-say/2011/09/12/ gIQA4nN6MK_story.html (accessed June 20, 2013).

35. Rob Waugh, "'Star Wars' Planets with Two Suns Are Common, Says Nasa— and Could Be a Hunting Ground for Alien Life," *Daily Mail,* January 12, 2012, www.dailymail.co.uk/sciencetech/article-2085732/Star-Wars-planets -suns-common-says-Nasa--hunting-ground-alien-life.html (accessed June 20, 2013).

36. Robert T. Gonzalez, "Meet Iapetus, Saturn's Mysterious "Yin-Yang" Moon," io9, January 13, 2012, http://io9.com/5876050/meet-iapetus-saturns-mysterious -yin+yang-moon; www.redicecreations.com/winterwonderland/death-moonspheres.html (accessed June 20, 2013).

37. Charles Bergin, "SLS Capability Touted for Europa Lander Capability, Enceladus Sample Return," Nasaspaceflight.com, January 6, 2012, www .nasaspaceflight.com/2012/01/sls-capability-europa-lander-capability -enceladus-sample-return (accessed June 20, 2013).

38. Leslie Mullen, "New Missions Target Mars Moon Phobos," Space.com, April 30, 2009, www.space.com/6629-missions-target-mars-moon-phobos .html (accessed June 20, 2013).

39. James Nye, "NASA Discovers Portals in Space between the Earth and the Sun (But Don't Book Your Ticket Just Yet)," *Daily Mail,* July 4, 2012, www.dailymail.co.uk/news/article-2168938/NASA-discovers -portals-space-Earth-Sun-dont-book-ticket-just-yet.html (accessed June 20, 2013).

40. Vladimir Dzhunushaliev's Reports, http://scholar.google.com/citations?user =tdWjvXsAAAAJ&hl=en (accessed June 20, 2013).

41. Lisa Zyga, "Scientists Investigate the Possibility of Wormholes between Stars," Physorg.com, February 5, 2011, www.physorg.com/news/2011 -02-scientists-possibility-wormholes-stars.html (accessed June 20, 2013).

42. Eduardo Guendelman and Mahary Vasihoun, "Fully Explorable Horned Particles Hiding Charge," Cornell University Online archive, January 2, 2012, http://arxiv.org/abs/1201.0526 (accessed June 20, 2013).

43. Rebecca Boyle, "Researchers Achieve Quantum Teleportation Over 10 Miles of Empty Space," *Popular Science,* May 19, 2010, www.popsci.com/ science/article/2010-05/researchers-achieve-quantum-teleportation-over -10-miles (accessed June 20, 2013).

44. "New Type of Entanglement Allows 'Teleportation in Time,' Say Physicists," *MIT Technology Review,* January 11, 2011, www.technologyreview.com/ blog/arxiv/26270/?ref=rss; Original Report, http://arxiv.org/abs/1101.2565 (accessed June 20, 2013).

45. "Beam Me Up, BEAMS: Teleporting Breakthrough As Scientists Transport Light Particles," *Daily Mail,* April 15, 2011, www.dailymail.co.uk/ sciencetech/article-1377370/Teleporting-breakthrough-scientists-transport -light-particles.html#socialLinks (accessed June 20, 2013).

46. "Stealth Now Old Hat—USAF Looks into Teleportation," Technovelgy .com, November 1, 2004, www.technovelgy.com/ct/Science-Fiction-News .asp?NewsNum=249 (accessed June 20, 2013).

47. Paul Davies, "It Wouldn't Be Easy, But It Might Be Possible," *Scientific American*, September 2002, www.scientificamerican.com/article .cfm?id=how-to-build-a-time-machi-2002-09 (accessed June 20, 2013).

48. Carol Hughes, "Cosmic Thinker Paul Davies to Explore Time Travel in Lecture at ASU," Asunews.com, January 12, 2012, http://asunews.asu .edu/20120112_timetravel (accessed June 20, 2013).

49. Marvin J. Cetron, "Vision: Teleportation; Beam Me Up, DARPA," *The Futurist*, September 1, 2008, www.questia.com/library/1G1-183437134/ vision-teleportation-beam-me-up-darpa (accessed June 20, 2013).

50. "ARPA-DARPA: The History of the Name," About.com, http://inventors .about.com/library/inventors/blARPA-DARPA.htm (accessed June 20, 2013).

51. Michael Cooney, "DARPA Set to Develop Super-Secure 'Cognitive Fingerprint,'" Networkworld.com, January 17, 2012, www.networkworld .com/community/node/79581 (accessed June 20, 2013).

52. Duncan Graham-Rowe, "Fifty Years of DARPA: Hits, Misses and Ones to Watch," NewScientist.com, May 15, 2008, www.newscientist.com/article/ dn13907-fifty-years-of-darpa-hits-misses-and-ones-to-watch.html?page=1 (accessed June 20, 2013).

53. "DARPA 'Cheetah' Robot Can Run Faster Than You," Infowars.com, March 6, 2012, www.infowars.com/darpa-cheetah-robot-can-run-faster -than-you (accessed June 20, 2013).

54. Michael Belfiore, *The Department of Mad Scientists: How Darpa Is Remaking Our World* (New York: HarperCollins, 2009), xxi.

55. Ted Thornhill, "Did Life Once Thrive on Super-Earth 40 Light Years Away? It Has More Water Than Earth and Once Lingered in the 'Goldilocks Zone,' Say Scientists," *Daily Mail*, March 6, 2012, www.dailymail.co.uk/ sciencetech/article-2110936/Planet-GJ1214b-water-Earth-say-CfA-researchers .html (accessed June 20, 2013).

56. Mike Wall, "Ideas Wanted for 100-Year Starship Project by DARPA, NASA" Space.com, May 11, 2011, www.space.com/11639-darpa-100-year -starship-study-ideas.html (accessed June 20, 2013).

CHAPTER 11.
GET YOUR ASS TO MARS!

1. Alfred Lambremont Webre, "Secret DARPA Time Travel Program May Hold Key to Understanding The Deep Politics of 9/11," Examiner .com, March 16, 2010, www.examiner.com/exopolitics-in-seattle/ secret-darpa-time-travel-program-may-hold-key-to-understanding-the-deep -politics-of-9-11 (accessed June 20, 2013).

2. "Coast to Coast AM with Mars Visitor Andrew Basiago," www.youtube .com/watch?v=Ao2PHpHF9tI (accessed June 20, 2013).

3. Michael Rundle, "White House Denies President Obama Travelled to Mars Via Teleport at Age 19," Huffingtonpost.com, January 4, 2012, www .huffingtonpost.co.uk/2012/01/04/white-house-denies-president-obama -travelled-to-mars_n_1183069.html (accessed June 20, 2013).

4. "Ed Dames Calls Andrew Basiago Delusional," http://exopolitics.blogs .com/exopolitics/2011/11/video-111111-coast-to-coast-am-basiago-stillings -and-eisenhower-barack-obama-visited-mars.html (accessed June 20, 2013).

5. Alfred Lambremont Webre, "Whistleblower Laura Magdalene Eisenhower, Ike's Great-granddaughter, Outs Secret Mars Colony Project," Examiner .com, February 10, 2010, www.examiner.com/exopolitics-in-seattle/ whistleblower-laura-magdalene-eisenhower-ike-s-great-granddaughter-outs -secret-mars-colony-project (accessed June 20, 2013).

6. Anthony Bond, "President Eisenhower Had Three Secret Meetings with Aliens, Former Pentagon Consultant Claims," *Daily Mail,* February 15, 2012, www.dailymail.co.uk/news/article-2100947/Eisenhower-secret -meetings-aliens-pentagon-consultant-claims.html (accessed June 20, 2013).

7. "Laura Eisenhower: Mars Agenda, Illuminati Origins, Positive Timeline, Teleportation," www.youtube.com/watch?v=v0TkqrKtTLs (accessed June 20, 2013).

8. "The D & M Pyramid on Mars and Richard Hoagland's Theories about Cydonia," www.math.washington.edu/~greenber/DMPyramid.html (accessed June 20, 2013).

9. "Richard Hoagland, What Is REALLY on Mars," www.youtube.com/ watch?v=Iu--3ivhTGc (accessed June 20, 2013).

10. Jay Weidner, "How Stanley Kubrick Faked the Apollo Moon Landings," www.realitysandwich.com/kubrick_apollo (accessed June 20, 2013).

11. "Torsion Field Fraud: RAS Investigating Akimov and Shipov Claims,"

Russian Academy of Science, http://torsionfraud.narod.ru (accessed June 20, 2013).

12. "UVITOR: A New Paradigm in Transportation and Energy," www.shipov .com/history.html (accessed June 20, 2013).

13. Darold Treffert, "'Ancestral' or 'Genetic' Memory: Factory Installed Software," Wisconsin Medical Society, www.wisconsinmedicalsociety .org/professional/savant-syndrome/resources/articles/ancestral-or-genetic -memory-factory-installed-software/ (accessed June 20, 2013).

14. "Buzz Aldrin Reveals Existence of Monolith on Mars Moon Phobos," www .youtube.com/watch?v=bDIXvpjnRws (accessed June 25, 2013); "Buzz Aldrin Alien Creatures Built Phobos Monolith: Alex Jones Show," www .youtube.com/watch?v=LjcAwJRTQ8o (accessed June 20, 2013).

15. Stuart Clark, "Destination Phobos: Humanity's Next Giant Leap," NewScientist.com, January 27, 2010, www.newscientist.com/article/ mg20527451.100-destination-phobos-humanitys-next-giant-leap.html (accessed June 20, 2013).

16. Alissa De Carbonnel, "Europe and Russia to Launch Mars Mission," Chinadaily.com, March 16, 2013, www.chinadaily.com.cn/cndy/2013 -03/16/content_16312911.htm (accessed June 20, 2013).

17. Spencer Ackerman, "Pentagon Denies Downing Russian Mars Probe," Wired, January 24, 2012, www.wired.com/dangerroom/2012/01/ radar-russian-reagan-probe (accessed June 20, 2013).

18. "US Space Command," www.globalsecurity.org/space/agency/afspc.htm (accessed June 25, 2013); www.fas.org/spp/military/program/nssrm/ initiatives/usspace.htm (accessed June 25, 2013).

19. "The Deep Black Aurora Project: The TR3-Black Manta," www.disclose .tv/action/viewvideo/64567/The_Deep_Black_Aurora_Project__The_ TR3_Black_Manta (accessed June 20, 2013).

20. Nancy Atkinson, "White House: No E.T. Visits, No UFO Cover-Up," Msnbc, November 11, 2011, www.msnbc.msn.com/id/45176460/ns/ technology_and_science-space/t/white-house-theres-no-sign-et-or-ufo -cover-up (accessed June 20, 2013).

21. Phillip Gibbs, "Why Is the Sky Blue?" University of California–Riverside, http://math.ucr.edu/home/baez/physics/General/BlueSky/blue_sky.html (accessed June 20, 2013).

22. David R. Williams, "Hubble's Look at Mars Shows Canyon Dust Storm, Cloudy

Conditions for Pathfinder Landing," Nasa.gov, December 30, 2004, http://nssdc.gsfc.nasa.gov/planetary/marsdust_970701.html (accessed June 20, 2013).

23. Richard Hoagland, "Revealing the True Colors of NASA," Enterprise Mission, 2002, www.enterprisemission.com/colors.htm (accessed June 20, 2013).

24. Ted Twietmeyer, "Mars Blue Sky, Lightning & Self-Removing Dust," http://rense.com/general80/sunmr.htm (accessed June 20, 2013).

25. George A. Filer, "Blue River Canyons on Mars," www.rense.com/general48/filers2404.htm (accessed June 20, 2013).

26. "True Colors of Mars," http://xfacts.com/spirit2004 (accessed June 20, 2013).

27. "Scientists Seek Signs of Life in the Universe," www.youtube.com/watch?v=uYAjudD51EY (accessed June 20, 2013).

28. Barry E. DiGregorio, "Viking Data May Hide New Evidence for Life," Spacedaily.com, July 16, 2000, www.spacedaily.com/news/mars-life-00g.html (accessed June 20, 2013).

29. See www.gillevin.com/Mars/Mars_The_Living_Planet_-_II_2011.pdf (accessed June 20, 2013).

30. "NASA Images Suggest Water Still Flows in Brief Spurts on Mars," Nasa.gov, December 6, 2006, www.nasa.gov/mission_pages/mars/news/mgs-20061206.html (accessed June 20, 2013).

31. Rob Waugh, "Nasa Rover Finds 'Bulletproof' Evidence of Water on Mars," *Daily Mail,* December 10, 2011, www.dailymail.co.uk/sciencetech/article-2071988/Mars-water-Nasa-Rover-finds-bulletproof-evidence-water-Mars.html (accessed June 20, 2013).

32. "Ancient Water Found on Mars!!!," www.youtube.com/watch?v=-VrvwNLCs3Q (accessed June 25, 2013); "Mars Could Have Supported Life," Space.com, www.space.com/20193-mars-could-have-supported-life-nasa-finds-video.html (accessed June 25, 2013).

33. Denise Chow, "NASA Launches Most Sophisticated Rover Yet to Mars," Christian Science Monitor.com, November 28, 2011, www.csmonitor.com/Science/2011/1128/NASA-launches-most-sophisticated-rover-yet-to-Mars (accessed June 20, 2013).

34. "Methane Result of Life on Mars?" Australian Broadcasting Corporation, December 3, 2011, www.abc.net.au/radionational/programs/scienceshow/methane-clue-to-life-on-mars/3709874 (accessed June 20, 2013).

35. Barry Evans, "Curiosity en Route," Northcoastjournal.com, January

12, 2012, www.northcoastjournal.com/outdoors/2012/01/12/curiosity -en-route/ (accessed June 20, 2013).

36. "Large Parts of Mars 'Habitable,'" The Telegraph.com, December 12, 2011, www.telegraph.co.uk/science/space/8950104/Large-parts-of-Mars -habitable.html (accessed June 20, 2013).

37. "Worms, Glass Tunnels, and Domes on Mars," www.youtube.com/ watch?v=EaxVh5II3mY (accessed June 20, 2013).

38. Joseph P. Skipper, "The Real Mars Report #221," July 6, 2012, www .marsanomalyresearch.com/evidence-reports/2012/221/real-mars.htm (accessed June 20, 2013).

CHAPTER 12.
ETERNAL CLONES,
MUMMIES, AND HYBRIDS

1. Stephen S. Mehler, *From Light into Darkness: The Evolution of Religion in Ancient Egypt* (Kempton, Ill.: Adventures Unlimited Press, 2005), 172.

2. Joshua Mark, "Egyptian Afterlife and the Feather of Truth," Joshua-mark .suite101.com, December 3, 2008, http://joshua-mark.suite101.com/egyp tian-afterlife-and-the-feather-of-truth-a81966 (accessed June 20, 2013).

3. Heather Whipps, "How the Council of Nicea Changed the World," Livescience.com, March 30, 2008, www.livescience.com/2410-council -nicea-changed-world.html (accessed June 20, 2013).

4. "Kemetic/Egyptian Origin of Christianity: Gerald Massey's Comparative List of Kemetic/Egyptian (pre-Christian) Religious-Philosophical Data, Christianized in the Canonical Gospels and the Book of Revelation," http://kemetway.com/massey1.html (accessed June 20, 2013).

5. "The Nag Hammadi Library Codex Index," Gnostic Society Library, www .gnosis.org/naghamm/nhlcodex.html (accessed June 20, 2013).

6. W. Gunther Plaut, Bernard Jacob Bamberger, and William W. Hallo, *The Torah* (New York: Union of American Hebrew Congregations, 1981), 316.

7. "How Freezing Cells from the Umbilical Cord Can Save Your Baby's Life," The Independent.com, June 12, 2007, www.independent.co.uk/life-style/ health-and-families/features/how-freezing-cells-from-the-umbilical-cord -can-save-your-babys-life-452800.html (accessed June 20, 2013).

8. Razib Khan, "Out of Africa and Out of Siberia," Discovermagazine.com,

January 27, 2012, http://blogs.discovermagazine.com/gnxp/2012/01/out-of-africa-and-out-of-siberia (accessed June 20, 2013).

9. "The Mystery of King Tut's Spanish and European Ancestors," FOX News Latino, August 2, 2011, http://latino.foxnews.com/latino/lifestyle/2011/08/02/king-tut-ancestor-to-70-spaniards-europeans (accessed June 20, 2013).

10. Ker Than, "Scientists Create Butterfly Hybrid," Foxnews.com, June 16, 2006, www.foxnews.com/story/0,2933,199680,00.html (accessed June 20, 2013).

11. Erich von Däniken, *The Eyes of the Sphinx* (New York: Berkley, 1996), 31.

12. E. A. Wallis Budge, *The Egyptian Book of the Dead* (New York: Dover, 1967), 69.

13. Gaston Maspero, *The Dawn of Civilization: Egypt and Chaldea* (New York: D. Appleton and Company, 1894), 564.

14. Morris Jastrow, *The Civilization of Babylonia and Assyria: Its Remains, Language, History* (Philadelphia: J.B. Lippincott Company, 1915), 265.

15. Jon D. Mikalson, *Herodotus and Religion in the Persian Wars* (Chapel Hill: University of North Carolina Press, 2003), 180.

16. Matthew George Easton, *The Bible Dictionary: Your Biblical Reference Book* (Charleston, S.C.: Forgotten Books, 2007), 68.

17. "Yellow Biotechnology: Using Plants to Silence Insect Genes in a High-Throughput Manner," Max Planck Institute, February 2, 2012, www.ice.mpg.de/ext/881.html (accessed June 20, 2013).

18. Daniel Martin and Simon Caldwell, "150 Human Animal Hybrids Grown in UK Labs: Embryos Have Been Produced Secretively for the Past Three Years," www.dailymail.co.uk/sciencetech/article-2017818/Embryos-involving-genes-animals-mixed-humans-produced-secretively-past-years.html#ixzz1THWxR1lf (accessed June 20, 2013).

19. Megan Gannon, "De-Extinction of Woolly Mammoth & Other Ancient Animals Could Become Reality, Scientists Say," Huffingtonpost, March 25, 2013, www.huffingtonpost.com/2013/03/15/de-extinction-wooly-mammoth-poll_n_2888386.html (accessed June 20, 2013).

20. "Future of Zoos: Cloned Animals, Robots and Cageless Habitats under Consideration," Huffingtonpost.com, March 5, 2012, www.huffingtonpost.com/2012/03/05/future-of-zoos-conference_n_1321749.html (accessed June 20, 2013).

21. James Chapman, "Kidney Breakthrough 'Could End the Need for Donors,'"

Daily Mail, March 3, 2012, www.dailymail.co.uk/news/article-97207/Kidney-breakthrough-end-need-donors.html (accessed June 20, 2013).

22. Peter Korn, "OHSU [Oregon Health and Sciences University] Creates World's First 'Chimeric' Monkey Clones," Portland Tribune, January 11, 2012, http://portlandtribune.com/scs/83-news/18200-ohsu-creates-worlds-first-chimeric-monkey-clones (accessed June 20, 2013).

23. "300-Million-Year-Old Forest Discovered Preserved in Volanic [*sic*] Ash," ScienceDaily, February 20, 2012, www.sciencedaily.com/releases/2012/02/120220161307.htm (accessed June 20, 2013).

24. Robin Mckie, "Cloning Scientists Create Human Brain Cells," Guardian, January 28, 2012, www.guardian.co.uk/science/2012/jan/29/brain-cloning-breakthrough-mental-illness (accessed June 20, 2013).

25. Harold M. Schemck Jr., "Intact Genetic Material Extracted from an Ancient Egyptian Mummy," New York Times.com, April 16, 1985, www.nytimes.com/1985/04/16/science/intact-genetic-material-extracted-from-an-ancient-egyptian-mummy.html?pagewanted=all (accessed June 20, 2013).

26. "NASA Research Shows DNA Building Blocks Can Be Made in Space," Nasa.gov, August 8, 2011, www.nasa.gov/centers/ames/news/releases/2011/11-60AR.html (accessed June 20, 2013).

CHAPTER 13.
SECRET SPACE ODYSSEY

1. Richard Hoagland and Mike Bara, *Dark Mission: The Secret History of NASA* (Port Townsend, Wash.: Feral House, 2007).

2. "Apollo 11 Press Conference," www.youtube.com/watch?v=BI_ZehPOMwI (accessed June 20, 2013).

3. Andrew Letten, "'Lost' Apollo 11 Moonwalk Tapes Restored," CosmosMagazine.com, October 26, 2010, www.cosmosmagazine.com/news/3827/lost-apollo-tapes-restored-and-broadcast (accessed June 20, 2013).

4. Rob Waugh, "Inception Becomes Reality," Daily Mail, March 23, 2012, www.dailymail.co.uk/sciencetech/article-2077185/Inception-reality-People-teach-new-skills-dreams.html (accessed June 20, 2013).

5. "Astronauts Gone Wild: Investigation into the Authenticity of Moon Landings," www.youtube.com/watch?v=7bD47eteBII (accessed June 20, 2013).

6. Rob Waugh, "Red Gold Rush: Once-in-a-Lifetime Rain of Meteorites from

Mars Yields 15 Pounds of Rocks 10 Times as Valuable as Gold," Daily Mail, January 18, 2012, www.dailymail.co.uk/sciencetech/article-2087964/Mars -meteorite-shower-Morocco-yields-15-pounds-rocks-10-times-valuable-gold .html (accessed June 20, 2013).

7. Manny Fernandez, "NASA Searches for Lott That Traveled from Space to Another Void," New York Times.com, January 21, 2012, www.nytimes .com/2012/01/22/science/space/nasa-tackles-problem-of-missing-moon -rocks.html?pagewanted=all (accessed June 20, 2013); "Moon Rocks Revisited," www.youtube.com/watch?v=0eDaQo29E-w (accessed June 20, 2013).

8. "Moon Rock Is Really Just Petrified Wood," NPR, August 28, 2009, www .npr.org/templates/story/story.php?storyId=112324216 (accessed June 20, 2013).

9. "Caught on Tape: JFK Had Doubts about Moon Landing," Msnbc, May 25, 2011, http://video.msnbc.msn.com/nightly-news/43174749 (accessed June 20, 2013).

10. R. Prasad, "Moon to Have No-Fly Zones by Month End," The Hindu.com, September 7, 2011, www.thehindu.com/sci-tech/science/article2432999.ece (accessed June 20, 2013).

11. Helen Pidd, "India's First Lunar Mission Finds Water on Moon," The Guardian, September 3, 2009, www.guardian.co.uk/world/2009/sep/24/ water-moon-space-exploration-india (accessed June 20, 2013).

12. "Giant Underground Chamber Found on Moon by India's Chandrayaan-1 Spacecraft," Dailygalaxy.com, March 2, 2011, www.dailygalaxy.com/my_ weblog/2011/03/giant-underground-chamber-found-on-moon-by-indias- chandrayaan-1-spacecraft.html (accessed June 20, 2013).

13. "Corey Hart: Water from the Moon," www.youtube.com/watch?v=p -vXHtMyuy0 (accessed June 20, 2013).

14. "NASA 'Bombs' the Moon," www.youtube.com/watch?v=lXKZr0OlM3c (accessed June 20, 2013).

15. J. D. Velasco, "Schiff Questions NASA Chief over Cuts to Mars Exploration," Pasadena Star News, March 23, 2011, www.pasadenastarnews .com/news/ci_20240527/schiff-questions-nasa-chief-over-cuts-mars -exploration (accessed June 20, 2013).

16. Coast to Coast AM, August 1, 2008, http://archive.coasttocoastam.com/ shows/2008/08/01.html (accessed June 20, 2013).

17. "UFO TV: What Is NASA Hiding? Secret Space, UFOs and NASA," www .youtube.com/watch?v=PqN-KLOCS5k (accessed June 20, 2013).

18. Timothy Good, *Need to Know: UFOs, the Military, and Intelligence* (London: Pegasus, 2007), 419.

19. "Electro Gravitics & UFO Propulsion," www.youtube.com/watch ?v= eBhsz3iXgGk (accessed June 20, 2013).

20. Aaron Dykes, "Obama's Signing Statement on NDAA: I Have the Power to Detain Americans . . . But I Won't," Infowars.com, January 1, 2012, www .infowars.com/president-obamas-ndaa-signing-statement-i-have-the-power -to-detain-americans-but-i-wont (accessed June 20, 2013).

21. Nigel Watson, "'UFO Hacker' Tells What He Found," Wired.com, June 21, 2006, www.wired.com/techbiz/it/news/2006/06/71182?currentPage= all (accessed June 20, 2013).

22. "Out of the Black: The Declassification of the NRO," George Washington University, September 18, 2008, www.gwu.edu/~nsarchiv/NSAEBB/ NSAEBB257/index.htm (accessed June 20, 2013).

23. "Top 10 Most Sinister PSYOPS Mission Patches," Vigilantcitizen.com, June 10, 2011, http://vigilantcitizen.com/vigilantreport/top-10-most-sinister -psyops-mission-patches/ (accessed June 20, 2013).

24. "What's That on Your Arm?" Newsweek, May 1, 2008, www.thedailybeast .com/newsweek/2008/03/01/what-s-that-on-your-arm.html (accessed June 20, 2013).

25. "Dr. Bob Bowman & Alex Jones Discuss: DARPA's Secret Little Air Force in Space," Infowars.com, August 19, 2011, www.infowars.com/dr-bob -bowman-alex-jones-darpas-secret-little-air-force-in-space/ (accessed June 21, 2013).

26. "US 'Planned to Blow Up a Nuclear Bomb on the Moon,'" www.telegraph .co.uk/science/space/9707686/US-planned-to-blow-up-a-nuclear-bomb-on -the-Moon.html (accessed June 26, 2013).

27. Ted Twietmeyer, "Color Artifacts on Mars," Rense.com, August 25, 2007, http://rense.com/general78/color.htm (accessed June 21, 2013).

28. Ted Twietmeyer, "What Nasa Isn't Telling You . . . about Mars," www .scribd.com/doc/78131804/What-NASA-Isn-t-Telling-You-About-Mars -Ted-Twietmeyer (accessed June 21, 2013).

CHAPTER 14.
POLYMER SCIENCE, THE GIZA PLATEAU,
AND THE BUILDING BLOCKS FROM MARS

1. Philip Coppens, "The Pyramid Heretic," www.philipcoppens.com/davidovits .html (accessed June 21, 2013).

2. Joseph Davidovits, "#A: X-Ray Analysis of Pyramids' Casing Stones and Their Limestone Quarries," Geopolymer Institute, April 4, 2006, www.geopolymer .org/library/archaeological-papers/a-x-ray-analysis-pyramids-casing-stones-and -their-limestone-quarries (accessed June 21, 2013).

3. Colin Nickerson, "Did the Great Pyramids' Builders Use Concrete?" New York Times, April 23, 2008, www.nytimes.com/2008/04/23/world/africa/23iht -pyramid.1.12259608.html?pagewanted=all (accessed June 21, 2013).

4. "Mars Pathfinder Science Results," NASA, http://mars.jpl.nasa.gov/MPF/ science/mineralogy.html (accessed June 21, 2013); "Finally, Scientific Proof of the Connection between Ancient Egypt and Mars," www.youtube.com/ watch?v=kj6gpEhBHVU (accessed June 21, 2013).

5. Flavius Josephus, *The Works of Flavius Josephus: The Learned and Authentic Jewish Historian* (Cincinnati: E. Morgan and Co., 1841), 27.

6. "Egyptian Pyramids: A Mars-Earth Connection," www.youtube.com/ watch?v=mzsyYLmZkRc (accessed June 21, 2013).

7. Andrew Petersen, "Cairo (Arabic: al-Qahira)," Islamic-arts.org, September 13, 2011, http://islamic-arts.org/2011/cairo-arabic-al-qahira (accessed June 21, 2013).

8. "Ares Myths," www.theoi.com/Olympios/AresMyths.html (accessed June 21, 2013).

9. "Das Geheimnis des Gruselfingers aus Ägypten [The Mystery of the Creepy Giant Mummified Finger]," Bild.de, March 9, 2012, www.bild.de/news/ mystery-themen/mystery/in-aegypten-gefunden-23053704.bild.html (accessed June 21, 2013).

10. "Giant Footprint in South Africa 200 Hundred Million Years Old," www .youtube.com/watch?v=dRuxw-nZoJw (accessed June 21, 2013).

11. "Göbekli Tepe 12,000 Years Old Rewrites History," www.youtube.com/ watch?v=OWeCI_1jnzU (accessed June 21, 2013); "John Anthony West & Laird Scranton—Göbekli Tepe, Egypt & the Dogon," Red Ice Radio, www .redicecreations.com/radio/2010/10oct/RIR-101012-SUB.html (accessed June 21, 2013).

12. "Göbekli Tepe Deciphered: Ancient Alien Star Map Human Origins Deciphered—Bull Göbekli Tepe," www.youtube.com/watch?v=IdoUnTm 2E28 (accessed June 21, 2013).

13. "Mysterious Pipes Left by 'ET' Reported from Qinghai," People's Daily Online .com, http://english.peopledaily.com.cn/200206/25/eng20020625_98530 .shtml (accessed June 21, 2013).

14. "William Henry Back from Egypt. They Are Digging Near the Osirion," www.unknowncountry.com/revelations/william-henry-back-egypt-they-are -digging-near-osirion (accessed June 21, 2013).

RECOMMENDED READING

Baikie, James. *Amarna Age: A Study of the Crisis of the Ancient World.* New York: Macmillan, 1926.

Benson, Margaret. *The Temple of Mut in Asher.* London: J. Murray, 1899.

Budge, E. A. Wallis. *Egyptian Literature.* New York: Dover, 1997.

Caulfeild, G. *The Temple of the Kings at Abydos.* London: Bernard Quaritch, 1902.

Davis, Theodore. *The Funeral Papyrus of Iouiya.* London: Archibald Constable and Co., 1908.

Drake, Walter Raymond. *Gods and Spacemen in the Ancient East.* New York: Sphere, 1973.

Mariette, Augustus. *Outlines of Ancient Egyptian History.* New York: Charles Scribner's Sons, 1892.

Maspero, Gaston. *The Dawn of Civilization: Egypt and Chaldae.* New York: D. Appleton & Co., 1897.

Murray, Margaret. *The Osireion at Abydos.* London: Bernard Quaritch, 1904.

Perrot, Georges. *A History of Art in Ancient Egypt.* Seattle: Amazon Digital Services, Inc., 2012.

Petrie, W. M. Flinders. *Ancient Egypt and the East.* London: Macmillan and Co., 1914.

Randall-MacIver, David. *El Amrah and Abydos, 1899–1901.* Charleston, S.C.: Nabu Press, 2010.

Seiss, Joseph. *A Miracle in Stone.* Santa Cruz, Calif.: Evinity Publishing, 2009.

Smyth, Charles Piazzi. *Life and Work at the Great Pyramid.* Charleston, S.C.: Nabu Press, 2010.

Weigall, Arthur. *Akhnaton.* London: T. Butterworth, 1922.

ACKNOWLEDGMENTS

This book would not have been possible without the love and support of my parents, Gary and Theresa Schroeder. A warm intergalactic hug eternally goes to Estrella Eguino, my "estrellita," for being the best editor, ghostwriter, psychic, partner, and soul mate a pharaoh of Mars could ever dream of. A special thanks goes to Jon Graham and the whole staff at Inner Traditions • Bear & Company. Thanks for believing in me! And to all the fearless researchers, philosophers, artists, and intellectuals who have paved the way before me, I can only hope this book follows their example.

INDEX

Pages with **bold** numbers contain illustrations.